Wage-led Growth

Advances in Labour Studies

Advances in Labour Studies is a wide-ranging series of research titles from the International Labour Office (ILO), offering in-depth analysis of labour issues from a global perspective. The series has an interdisciplinary flavour that reflects the unique nature of labour studies, where economics, law, social policy and labour relations combine. Bringing together work from researchers from around the world, the series contributes new and challenging research and ideas that aim both to stimulate debate and inform policy.

Published in the series

THE LABOUR MARKETS OF EMERGING ECONOMIES: HAS GROWTH TRANSLATED INTO MORE AND BETTER JOBS?
(*by Sandrine Cazes and Sher Verick*)

BEYOND MACROECONOMIC STABILITY: STRUCTURAL TRANSFORMATION AND INCLUSIVE DEVELOPMENT
(*edited by Iyanatul Islam and David Kucera*)

REGULATING FOR DECENT WORK: NEW DIRECTIONS IN LABOUR MARKET REGULATION
(*Edited by Sangheon Lee and Deirdre McCann*)

WAGE-LED GROWTH: AN EQUITABLE STRATEGY FOR ECONOMIC RECOVERY
(*edited by Marc Lavoie and Engelbert Stockhammer*)

SHAPING GLOBAL INDUSTRIAL RELATIONS: THE IMPACT OF INTERNATIONAL FRAMEWORK AGREEMENTS
(*edited by Konstantinos Papadakis*)

Forthcoming in the series

CREATIVE LABOUR REGULATION: INDETERMINACY AND PROTECTION IN AN UNCERTAIN WORLD
(*edited by Deirdre McCann, Sangheon Lee, Patrick Belser, Colin Fenwick, John Howe and Malte Luebker*)

TOWARDS BETTER WORK: UNDERSTANDING LABOUR IN APPAREL GLOBAL VALUE CHAINS
(*edited by Arianna Rossi, Amy Luinstra and John Pickles*)

Wage-led Growth

An Equitable Strategy for Economic Recovery

Edited by

Marc Lavoie

and

Engelbert Stockhammer

First published 2013 by
PALGRAVE MACMILLAN
and the INTERNATIONAL LABOUR OFFICE

Palgrave Macmillan in the UK is an imprint of Macmillan Publishers Limited, registered in England, company number 785998, of Houndmills, Basingstoke, Hampshire RG21 6XS.

Palgrave Macmillan in the US is a division of St Martin's Press LLC, 175 Fifth Avenue, New York, NY 10010.

Palgrave Macmillan is the global academic imprint of the above companies and has companies and representatives throughout the world.

Palgrave® and Macmillan® are registered trademarks in the United States, the United Kingdom, Europe and other countries.

ISBN: 978–1–137–35792–2

ILO ISBN: 978–92–2–127487–2

This book is printed on paper suitable for recycling and made from fully managed and sustained forest sources. Logging, pulping and manufacturing processes are expected to conform to the environmental regulations of the country of origin.

A catalogue record for this book is available from the British Library.

A catalog record for this book is available from the Library of Congress.

Contents

List of Tables and Figures

Tables

Figures

Foreword

The current global crisis, known as the Great Recession, is challenging much of the 'conventional wisdom' which has dominated economic thinking and policies. In particular, it has raised strong concerns about the widespread view that 'growth should be in the driver's seat and distribution in the backseat'. One important corollary of such trickle-down economics is that wage moderation can boost economic growth and hence reduce poverty. It has sometimes been twisted to suggest that low wages are a necessary condition for economic growth, especially in the early stages of development. This conventional view is now being questioned, as it seems clear that the Great Recession has had much to do with widening income inequality, in terms of both personal and functional income distribution. Yet, not much is known about why income inequality widened, how it impacted the crisis, and what lessons can be drawn from the observed changes.

This volume makes a very important contribution to our understanding of the causes and consequences of inequality, by mainly investigating a critical aspect of income distribution, functional income distribution, that is, the division of national income between capital (the profit share) and labour (the labour income share or wage share). Empirical studies have shown that the share of income going to labour has significantly declined in advanced economies, thus challenging the stylized fact that the division of income between labour and capital is roughly constant.

The contributions to this volume are impressively comprehensive, ranging from theory, to empirical evidence and to policy advice. First, the volume offers a new theoretical framework that can better explain the secular changes in the labour income share and expands empirical knowledge on the subject by exploring these changes in major developing countries, including Brazil, China and South Africa. Second, the authors examine the significance of the various factors underlying the declining labour income share and show the critical importance of financialization, globalization and labour market and social security policies. Third, the volume goes one step further and explores the economic consequences of the shift in functional income distribution. This highly original and extensive research argues that the distributional shifts in favour of capital and the rise in income inequality have reduced economic growth and increased economic instability. In doing so, it shows that the risk of wage moderation is real and that the debt-led and export-led strategies pursued in many countries are related to these economic problems. Finally, the book outlines a wide range of policy implications, pointing to the need to "rebalance" functional income distribution. This "rebalancing" act in favour of wages will be an essential element of equitable and sustainable growth and requires strong policy coordination at the global level.

The findings of this volume are reflected in the *Global Wage Report 2012/13: Wages and Equitable Growth* published by the International Labour Office (ILO). As emphasized in the report, it is high time for the global community to revisit its past policies and make coordinated efforts and actions in search of balanced and equitable growth that benefits all.

Sangheon Lee
Research and Policy Coordinator,
Conditions of Work and Equality Department,
International Labour Office

Preface

The main goal of this book is to go beyond the microeconomic view of wages as a cost having negative consequences on the economy and to consider the positive macroeconomic dynamics associated with wages as a major component of aggregate demand. Wage growth can generate demand growth and productivity growth. Insufficient wage growth, or more broadly the polarization of income distribution have contributed to the economic crisis.

The book is the final product of a joint ILO research project that involves six themes or modules all tied to the potential of a wage-led growth strategy. It examines the causes and the consequences associated with the falling wage share and the rising inequality in income distribution, both on aggregate demand and labour productivity. It revisits existing theories, in particular those that claim that a higher wage share could alleviate the global balance problems that have been associated with new mercantilist policies designed to grow by restraining wage costs relative to those of competitor countries as well as the global financial problems that have been associated with rising household debt needed to sustain consumption. It provides new empirical and econometric evidence regarding the economic cause and potential impact of changing income distribution. It also provides policy strategies and the policy implications of a wage-led recovery. In particular, the book provides an overarching framework used by all the authors of the chapters which, it is hoped, will be useful to both future researchers and policy-makers.

Notes on Contributors

Giorgos Galanis is a doctoral candidate in Economics at the University of Warwick and a Research Economist at the New Economics Foundation. He already holds a PhD in Mathematical Methods and Systems from City University, London, where he is also a Visiting Research Fellow. Since November 2009, he has been a member of the editorial board of *Historical Materialism: Research in Critical Marxist Theory*. His research interests include growth, distribution and financial instability; complexity economics; agent-based models and Marxian and post-Keynesian economic theory.

Eckhard Hein is Professor of Economics at the Berlin School of Economics and Law. He is a member of the coordination committee of the Research Network Macroeconomics and Macroeconomic Policies (FMM) and a managing co-editor of the *European Journal of Economics and Economic Policies: Intervention (EJEEP)*. He has published in the *Cambridge Journal of Economics, European Journal of the History of Economic Thought, International Review of Applied Economics, Journal of Post Keynesian Economics, Metroeconomica, Structural Change and Economic Dynamics*, and *Review of Political Economy*, among others. His most recent books are *The Macroeconomics of Finance-dominated Capitalism – and its Crisis* (2012) and *A Modern Guide to Keynesian Macroeconomics and Economic Policies* (co-editor, 2011).

Marc Lavoie is Professor in the Department of Economics at the University of Ottawa and an IMK Research Fellow. He is a managing co-editor of the *European Journal of Economics and Economic Policy: Intervention*. He is the author of *Foundations of Post-Keynesian Economic Analysis* (1992), *Introduction to Post-Keynesian Economics* (2006), and *Monetary Economics: An Integrated Approach to Money, Income, Production and Wealth* (2007) with Wynne Godley. With Mario Seccareccia, he has written the Canadian edition of the Baumol and Blinder first-year textbook (2009). He has edited *Alfred Eichner and Post-Keynesian Economics* (with Seccareccia and L.P. Rochon, 2010), *Selected Writings of Wynne Godley* (with Gennaro Zezza, 2012), and *In Defense of Post-Keynesian and Heterodox Economics* (with Frederic Lee, 2013).

Matthias Mundt obtained an MA in International Economics from the Berlin School of Economics and Law in 2013. He completed several internships: at the Institute for Ecological Economy Research, the Confederation of German Trade Unions and the Federal Ministry of Economics and Technology. His research on Cape Verde is reflected in *Effects of European Fisheries Partnership Agreements on Fish Stocks and Fishermen: The Case of Cape Verde* (Institute for International Political Economy Berlin Working Paper).

C.W.M. (Ro) Naastepad is Assistant Professor at Delft University of Technology, the Netherlands. She has worked on real-financial computable general equilibrium (CGE) models in the past. Subsequent work on economic policies conducive to technological progress has been published in, for instance, the *Cambridge Journal of Economics*, *Industrial Relations*, and in her book, *Macroeconomics Beyond the NAIRU* (2012, co-authored with Servaas Storm). Her current research concerns the philosophy, methodology and implementation of a capital theory that recognises a dual role of capital as both the financier of production for material livelihood and the enabler of human capacities (which cannot unfold unless they are financed).

Özlem Onaran is Professor of Workforce and Economic Development Policy at the University of Greenwich. She is a member of the Coordinating Committee of the Research Network Macroeconomics and Macroeconomic Policies, a research associate at the Political Economy Research Institute of the University of Massachusetts, Amherst, and a fellow of the Global Labour University. Her research areas include globalization, crisis, distribution, employment, investment, development, and gender. She has articles in books and journals such as the *Cambridge Journal of Economics*, *World Development*, *Environment and Planning A*, *Public Choice*, *Economic Inquiry*, *European Journal of Industrial Relations*, *International Review of Applied Economics*, *Structural Change and Economic Dynamics*, *Eastern European Economics*, *Capital and Class* and *Review of Political Economy*.

Engelbert Stockhammer is Professor of Economics at Kingston University. His research areas include macroeconomics, financial systems and political economy. He is Research Associate at the Political Economy Research Institute at the University of Massachusetts at Amherst, and a member of the coordination committee of the 'Research Network Macroeconomics and Macroeconomic Policies' (FMM) and of the Committee of the Post Keynesian Economics Study Group (PKSG).

He has published widely in academic journals on the determinants of unemployment, on distribution-led demand regimes, and on financialization. He is the author of *The Rise of Unemployment in Europe* (2004), and co-editor of *Macroeconomic Policies on Shaky Foundations – Whither Mainstream Economics?* (2009), *Heterodoxe Ökonomie* (2009) and *A Modern Guide to Keynesian Macroeconomics and Economic Policies* (2012).

Servaas Storm is Assistant Professor at Delft University of Technology, the Netherlands. He works on macroeconomics, financial institutions, economic development and climate change. He has published papers on these subjects in the *Cambridge Journal of Economics, Industrial Relations, Journal of Post Keynesian Economics, Development and Change* and *Journal of Development Economics*. His most recent book (co-authored with C.W.M. Naastepad) is *Macroeconomics Beyond the NAIRU* (2012). He is one of the editors of *Development and Change*.

Simon Sturn is a graduate student at the University of Massachusetts at Amherst. From 2008 to 2011 he worked at the Macroeconomic Policy Institute (IMK) in Düsseldorf. He studied economics in Vienna. He has published in *Applied Economics* and the *International Labour Review*.

Till van Treeck is a Senior Economist at the Macroeconomic Policy Institute (IMK) at Hans Boeckler Foundation in Duesseldorf and is currently a visiting professor at the University of Duisburg-Essen. He is a member of the organizing committee of the Research Network Macroeconomics and Macroeconomic Policies (FMM) and a managing co-editor of the *European Journal of Economics and Economic Policies: Intervention* (EJEEP). His research interests include German and European economic policy, macroeconomic theory and income distribution.

Introduction

Marc Lavoie and Engelbert Stockhammer

The financial crisis that began in the summer of 2007 turned into the worst economic crisis since the Great Depression of the 1930s. The crisis began in the financial sector, but has since spread throughout the economy. National income levels are well below trend and unemployment rates are double their pre-crisis level. In many countries households and governments remain burdened by high debt levels, which prolong subdued demand. In the euro area the crisis morphed into a sovereign debt crisis, laying bare the dysfunctional nature of the European economic policy regime.

The crisis has led to an intensified debate over the role of the state. The orthodox austerity policies claim to be aimed at reducing government debt; but as they are unable to revitalize demand growth, they often result in rising debt, as is illustrated by the recent UK experience. Austerity policy usually attempts to change not only the size, but also the *nature* of government interventions by reducing welfare expenditures (including pensions) and by privatizing public services. The academic debate is mirrored by increasingly bitter political struggles. Government intervention, almost by necessity, has distributional effects. A strong welfare state usually strengthens labour and the poor as they benefit most from welfare expenditures and public infrastructure. The question of how to engineer a recovery is thus closely tied to the question of who pays for the crisis. The political confrontations have gained in intensity as the effects of the crisis have been felt more widely in the form of rising unemployment, wage cuts, and rising levels of homelessness; they follow three decades of a rapid and historically unprecedented increase in inequality, in which the very top of the income distribution, and, in particular, top earners in the financial sector have gained at the expense of wage earners.

1

The main goal of the book is to go beyond the microeconomic view of wages as a cost that has negative consequences on the economy and to consider the positive macroeconomic dynamics associated with wages as a major component of aggregate demand. Wage growth can generate both demand growth and productivity growth. Insufficient wage growth and, more broadly, the polarization of income distribution have contributed to the economic crisis, and thus this process has to be reversed. What we need is a new growth strategy, which the ILO (2012), in its latest global wage report, has called 'equitable growth'. This will involve increased domestic consumption, supported by rising wages.

The book is the final product of a research project sponsored by the ILO, which involves six themes or modules all tied to the potential of a wage-led growth strategy. The book examines the causes and the consequences associated with the falling wage share and the rising inequality in income distribution, on both aggregate demand and labour productivity. It revisits existing theories, in particular those which claim that a higher wage share could alleviate the global imbalances problem that have been associated with new mercantilist policies designed to grow by restraining wage costs relative to those of competitor countries as well as the global financial problems that have been associated with rising household debt needed to sustain consumption. The book provides new empirical and econometric evidence regarding the economic causes and potential impact of changing income distribution. It also provides policy strategies and the policy implications of a wage-led recovery. In particular, the book provides an overarching framework, inspired by post-Keynesian economics, that takes into account the impact of changes in income distribution on various aspects of economic activity and aggregate demand in particular (to be explained in the next section). This framework was used by all the authors of the chapters, and it will be useful to both future researchers and policy-makers.

Three views of the crisis

Several arguments have been offered to explain the development of the subprime financial crisis and its devastating consequences. Broadly speaking, we may say that there are three explanations. The first one, closest to the neo-Austrian school, the Chicago school à la Milton Friedman and the so-called 'fresh-water' economists, is that the market system works fairly well as long as market forces are left unhindered.

Thus for these economists, the financial crisis occurred in the United States because of a series of government interferences, such as the overly low US short-term interest rates or the inducements for banks to provide loans to poorer communities, or, looking further, the crisis was triggered by the Chinese government, who rigged exchange rates, thus flooding long-term US bond markets. It is also argued by these economists that the stimulus packages put in place to respond to the crisis only made matters worse and amplified the crisis.

The second point of view, which is best associated with the so-called 'salt-water' economists and New Keynesians, sees the financial crisis as an extreme example of market failure and poor information. Financial innovations, such as securitization, also called the new 'originate and distribute' banking model, which replaced the former 'originate and hold' model, turned out to have unwanted consequences as lenders managed to get rid of bad loans by transforming them into securities. These failures were due in part to inappropriate pay structures in the banking and financial industry, while fraud or quasi-fraud was made possible by the gradual relaxation of financial regulation and the lack of appropriate supervision.

The third explanation, while it recognizes the validity of the microeconomic elements highlighted by the second group of economists, relies in addition on deeper structural causes tied to the evolution of macroeconomic variables, most importantly income distribution. This explanation is usually associated with non-mainstream economists. The economists who rely on the third explanation emphasize the fact that since the 1980s there has been a switch in economic policies, which have moved from policies aiming to promote full employment to policies targeting low inflation. They also emphasize the general transformation of society towards the acceptance of neoliberal precepts, in particular the increasing importance of finance and that of shareholders, a phenomenon which has been called financialization and which is associated with a 'downsize and distribute' model, where firms make profits by reducing the size of their workforce instead of increasing their investment levels. Both of these changes have weakened the bargaining power of labour, leading in most countries to a substantial decrease in the share of wages in national income, as well as to a noticeable increase in wage and income inequality, as described in Tables I.1 and I.2.

These phenomena have led to a change in the way accumulation proceeds. Whereas growth had previously been supported by wage-led consumption, with wages rising broadly in line with labour productivity, growth over the past two decades has been based either on household

Table I.1   Labour income share as percentage of GDP at current factor costs or wage share in GDP, in percentage, G20 countries, average values over the trade cycle, early 1980s–2008

	1. Early 1980s–early 1990s	2. Early 1990s–early 2000s	3. Early 2000s–2008	Change (3 – 2), percentage points
Argentina[a,b]	...	38.42	32.79[c]	–5.63
Australia	66.70	65.76	62.57	–3.19
Brazil[a,b]	...	43.33	39.64[c]	–3.69
Canada	66.89	67.79	63.75	–4.05
China[a,b]	15.58	13.11	10.82	–2.28
France	71.44	66.88	65.87	–1.01
Germany	67.11	66.04	63.37	–2.67
India[a,b]	34.03	32.25	32.18[c]	–0.07
Indonesia[a]	...	...	...	...
Italy	68.70	63.25	62.37	–0.88
Japan[a]	72.38	70.47	65.75	–4.73
Korea, Rep. of [a]	81.62	80.53	76.97	–3.56
Mexico[a]	...	46.35	46.16	–0.19
Russian Federation[a,b]	...	45.87	45.56[c]	–0.31
Saudi Arabia[a]	...	...	...	...
South Africa[a,b]	56.65	54.87	50.18[c]	–4.69
Turkey[a]	48.07	54.12	50.34	–3.78
United Kingdom	72.98	71.99	70.73	–1.26
United States	68.20	67.12	65.87	–1.25

Notes: The labour income share is given by the compensation per employee divided by GDP at factor costs per person employed. The beginning of a trade cycle is given by a local minimum of annual real GDP growth in the respective country.
[a] adjusted to fit in 3 cycle pattern, [b] wage share in GDP or in gross value added, [c] incomplete trade cycle

Source: E. Hein and M. Mundt, 'Financialisation and the requirements and potentials for wage-led recovery – a review focussing on the G20', Conditions of Work and Employment Series No. 37, (Geneva: ILO), http://www.ilo.org/wcmsp5/groups/public/---ed_protect/---protrav/---travail/documents/publication/wcms_191782.pdf.

debt (*'debt-led growth'*) or on low wages so as to help generate exports to foreign countries (*'export-led growth'*). These regimes of accumulation eventually proved to be unsustainable. This book offers an analysis

Table I.2   The share of top 1 per cent earners' income in total income, mid-1970s to mid-2000s

Country	Mid-1970s	Mid-2000s	Change, percentage points
G20-countries			
Argentina[e]	9.9	16.8	+6.9
Australia[d]	5.0	9.7	+4.7
Canada[d]	8.2	12.8	+4.6
China[a,e]	2.6	5.9	+3.3
France[d]	8.2	8.7	+0.5
Germany[e]	10.4	12.1	+1.7
India[b,e]	7.0	9.5	+2.5
Indonesia[c,e]	7.2	9.1	+1.9
Italy[d]	7.0	9.2	+2.2
Japan[d]	6.9	9.0	+2.1
United Kingdom[e]	6.1	14.3	+8.2
United States[d]	7.9	18.0	+10.1

Notes: [a] First data point is from the mid-1980s; [b] second data point is from the end of the 1990s; [c] first data point is from the early 1980s.

Source: [d] *2012 OECD Employment Outlook*, supporting material for chapter 3, Table 3.A2.1; [e] http://g-mond.parisschoolofeconomics.eu/topincomes/#Database.

of demand formation and productivity growth as dependent on wage growth and thus sheds light on the central role of functional income distribution in determining growth performance.

The book thus forms part of a renewed interest in the question of whether or not rising inequality is one of the causes of the global financial crisis. Several authors have recently highlighted that inequality may have contributed to the crisis. Raghuram Rajan (2010) was one of the first to highlight the ties between income distribution and the crisis, but his findings were based on what we defined as the first explanation of the crisis. Rajan contends that the observed rising income inequality induced governments to look for new ways to raise aggregate demand. The US administration fostered a new 'ownership society' by encouraging credit growth and, ultimately, the subprime boom. According to this argument, it is not the rise in inequality itself per se that caused the crisis, but rather the government's reaction to rising inequality. Joseph Stiglitz (2012) sees this transformation as an ideological battle between the Right and the Left, with the upper economic class having taken control of the reins of government and having succeeded in achieving regulation capture, on top of having convinced voters that trickle-down economics was a fact rather than simply a theory. This has allowed the upper classes to pursue and achieve rent-seeking. For Stiglitz the negative effects of rising inequality are mostly to be found on the supply side. Thomas Palley (2012) argues that economists and economic theory are very much to blame for the global financial crisis, because of their focus on supply-side economics and the optimal properties of unfettered markets, while ignoring the demand-generating process. What he calls 'emergency Keynesianism' – expansionary monetary and fiscal policies in crisis periods – is unlikely to succeed, because it ignores the underlying problem, that of the structural lack of aggregate demand, caused by excessively low wages and overly large income dispersion. However, he does not provide systematic evidence for this claim. James Galbraith (2012) presents a novel measure of economic inequality and argues that it reflects a concentration of wealth at the very top of the distribution. It has been brought about by financial rather than real forces. Interest rates, stock market booms and international payments, but not technology or education are responsible. While Galbraith repeatedly stresses inequality as a cause of the crisis, he is rather vague about the exact mechanisms and criticizes the Bush administration and its drive for an ownership society for a deterioration of lending standards.

All of these contributions share a focus on the experience of the United States. Our approach differs, firstly, in systematically highlighting the link between income distribution and demand formation, in particular the effect of wage growth on consumption growth. This link is substantiated empirically. Second, we take an internationally comparative approach, highlighting that different countries have adopted different strategies in dealing with the rise in equality. The US debt-led growth model is only one variant among many. Other countries have pursued export-led growth strategies. Both strategies do rely on rising imbalances (the former on rising debt ratios, the latter on rising trade imbalances). A wage-led growth strategy offers a sounder macroeconomic alternative.

Presentation of the six chapters

The objective of the first chapter, by Marc Lavoie and Engelbert Stockhammer, is to present the common framework of the book and to clarify the concept of a wage-led growth strategy, which combines pro-labour distributional policies with structural policies that strengthen a wage-led economic regime. One of the main findings of the research project, based on data from the last thirty years or so, is that aggregate demand and productivity in most G20 countries would respond favourably to an increase in the wage share. Looking at aggregate demand specifically, we thus can say that most countries are in a wage-led regime. This, however, must not be confused with the fact that most countries over the last three decades have pursued pro-capital distributional policies that have led to a decrease in the share of labour and/or to an increase in income inequality, as exemplified by Tables I.1 and I.2. These two concepts, a wage-led demand regime and pro-labour distributional policies, must thus be distinguished, although we could say that pursuing pro-labour distributional policies in an economy whose structure is such that this economy is in a wage-led regime would constitute an appropriate wage-led growth strategy. The argument of Lavoie and Stockhammer is that neoliberalism as it has occurred in practice has meant that most countries have instead pursued pro-capital distributional policies that have generated stagnant or unstable growth processes because these countries are mostly in a wage-led economic regime, thus necessitating external drivers such as household debt or export-led growth to maintain GDP growth. Lavoie and Stockhammer also explain that while a number of countries may be in a profit-led *total* demand regime when taking into account all elements of aggregate demand, including net exports, nearly all of them are in a wage-led *domestic* demand regime when only domestic demand is taken into account. Thus while pro-capital distributional policies may be demand-enhancing when a country is taken in isolation, this will not generally be the case when all countries are considered as a whole.

But why is it that the wage share has fallen in most countries, both industrialized and developing ones, since the 1980s? This is the question that Engelbert Stockhammer endeavours to answer in Chapter 2. He recalls that from the mainstream standpoint, income distribution is determined primarily by technological developments, along the lines of the marginal productivity theory, the argument being that technical progress has been capital-augmenting, thus leading to an increase in the share of capital income. An alternative view, which is common to all the authors of the book, is that income distribution is mainly a matter of bargaining power. Thus globalization, financialization and the abandonment of full-employment policies (welfare state retrenchment) would all lead to a reduction in the bargaining power of labour and, consequently, generate a reduction in the wage share. Stockhammer thus provides an econometric analysis that intends to measure the impact of these various factors, for both industrialized and developing countries, by estimating a wage share equation that includes proxies of these factors. In the case of advanced economies, high unemployment rates and high GDP growth rates have a clear negative impact on the wage share. In addition, union density and the share of government consumption in GDP have a substantial positive effect on the wage share, whereas the ratio of foreign assets and liabilities to GDP (financialization) and the ratio of exports and imports to GDP (globalization) both have a substantial negative effect on the wage share. By contrast, the technological proxies – the capital to labour ratio and the share of information and communication technologies – once all these other effects are taken into consideration, have a minor negative impact on the wage share. When advanced and developing countries are combined, using a slightly different set of variables for 71 countries, similar results are obtained, with financialization having the largest negative effect on the wage share, while globalization and welfare state retrenchment also have a negative effect. Ironically, technological change, here also including changes in the sectoral composition of manufacturing and agriculture, has a positive effect on the wage share. Stockhammer thus concludes that the main cause of the decrease in the share of wages in national income has been the drop in the bargaining power of labour over time, and not technological change, which implies that the increase in the profit share and in income inequality can be reversed by appropriate policies.

But is there any evidence that an increase in the wage share could have positive effects on aggregate demand? Özlem Onaran and Giorgos Galanis endeavour to examine this question through a vast econometric study that deals with 16 of the G20 countries. This sample covers approximately 80 per cent of the world GDP. Onaran and Galanis estimate three equations that measure the impact of a change in the profit share on three of the four components of aggregate demand: consumption, investment and net exports. The impact of an increase in the wage share on consumption is usually positive because wage recipients have a higher propensity to consume than do the recipients of profit. By contrast, an increase in the wage share normally has a negative impact on investment, as lower profit margins are likely to decrease the incentive to invest. Finally, an increase in the wage share will also have a negative impact on net exports, as such increases are usually associated with higher unit costs, which reduce competitiveness. Whether the first effect is larger than the second one, or larger than the sum of the last two, is an empirical question. The authors find that all 16 countries of the G20 sample, as well as the whole of the euro area, are in a domestic demand-led regime. Of these, only Australia, Canada, Mexico, Argentina, China, India and South Africa exhibit a profit-led total demand regime. However, Onaran and Galanis demonstrate that if all countries were to simultaneously decrease their wage share by one percentage point, only Australia, China and South Africa would benefit from an expansion of aggregate demand, while the world GDP would decrease by 0.36 percentage points. This shows clearly that the world economy is in a wage-led demand regime. The authors also point out that it is possible to find a scenario whereby all countries would benefit from an increase in their wage share even if this increase is smaller for countries that are in a profit-led total demand regime. They thus conclude that a global wage-led recovery is one way out of the current recession.

The chapter by Servaas Storm and C.W.M. Naastepad investigates the supply-side effects of higher wage growth, in particular the effect of productivity growth. Whereas Stockhammer as well as Onaran and Galanis focus on the wage share, Storm and Naastepad start their analysis by considering the growth rate of wages. Storm and Naastepad rely on the Dutch experience since the early 1980s as a case study of the economic impact brought about by the interrelationship between the growth rate of wages and the growth rate of productivity. They point out that real wages have two effects on productivity growth: first, a direct effect, which is usually positive, as higher real wages will induce firms to introduce more productive methods of production so as to safeguard their profits; secondly, an indirect impact, which arises because higher real wages will have an impact on aggregate demand, as pointed out empirically in the previous chapter, and the change in the rate of growth of aggregate demand will feed a change, of the same sign, in the growth rate of productivity, with this last relationship being called the Kaldor–Verdoorn effect. Storm and Naastepad explain that in the case of the Netherlands there was an overly slow increase in real wages and a fall in the wage share for over twenty years. Because the Netherlands are in a wage-led demand regime, this led to a slowdown in the growth rate of aggregate demand, which itself induced very slow productivity growth. It was this slow or nearly zero-productivity growth that explained the Dutch employment miracle of the 1980s and 1990s, when unemployment rates fell both in absolute and relative terms, because the low growth rate of demand surpassed the even lower growth rate of labour productivity, thus generating a fair growth rate of employment. Based on consensual estimates of the Kaldor–Verdoorn effects and of the relatively weak impact of wage growth on demand growth in the euro zone and in the United States, Storm and Naastepad deduce that most countries that are in a wage-led demand regime are likely to be in a profit-led employment regime. This means that faster increases in real wages are likely to generate slower increases in employment. As a result of their findings Storm and Naastepad conclude that whereas pro-labour policies are favourable to productivity growth and to aggregate demand (as shown in the previous chapter), they are likely to be unfavourable to job creation. This implies that, to avoid this contradiction, pro-labour policies, in most wage-led regimes, must be accompanied by supportive fiscal and monetary policies. Some could infer from the above that wage-restraining policies should be pursued; but such policies, although they are likely to reduce unemployment by creating low-wage jobs, will keep aggregate demand and productivity stagnant. This is an option that Storm and Naastepad reject, and which they encourage trade unions to reject as well, because it leads to stagnant living standards and also removes the possibility of rising living standards accompanied by a reduced number of working hours.

We have so far focused our attention on the distribution of functional income, that is, the wage and profit shares in national income. However, as we saw in Table I.2, personal income, including wage income, has also been subjected to large changes over time. The income share of recipients of the top decile and, most particularly, the top 1 per cent or even 0.1 per cent has increased considerably in a large number of countries. Until now, we have argued that the greater inequality in income distribution is likely to have slowed down aggregate demand, as high-income earners have a higher propensity to save than do low-income earners. And indeed, there is a great deal of literature that argues that income inequality is inimical to fast growth, in contrast to the past mainstream view that argued that income inequality was a necessary side effect of growth and efficiency. But can we draw any other consequence from this change in the distribution of personal income? This is the task that Simon Sturn and Till van Treeck have assigned to themselves. To do so, they examine the case of three quite different countries: the United States, China and Germany. Van Treeck and Sturn first argue that the rising income inequality in the United States has led to a change in the consumption and borrowing behaviour of American households. After having increased working hours, and having easy access to credit, for the purposes of both consumption and housing, middle-income Americans have reacted to the growing gap between their revenues and those of their better-to-do neighbours by increasing the extent of their borrowing and thus reducing their saving rates. This has led to structural changes – a debt-led consumption boom as well as a real estate boom – and not merely to temporary changes in debt so as to absorb transitory changes in income as argued by the mainstream. Another consequence of this structural change has been the large US current account deficits, which have arisen from this fall in aggregate household saving and the expenditures of rich income recipients on luxury goods coming from abroad. By contrast, China and Germany have both suffered from a lack of domestic aggregate demand, thus experiencing large current account surpluses, because, besides the standard effect of differential household saving rates by deciles, rising income inequality and greater job insecurity have induced households to save more. In China, the rise in household income inequality in the context of an underdeveloped financial system and a weak social and health safety net can be identified as one of the main causes of this rise in the propensity to save, while in Germany stagnant incomes as well as labour market deregulation and welfare state reforms have induced households to raise their precautionary savings.

The final chapter, written by Eckhard Hein and Matthias Mundt, looks at the role of financialization as a cause of the crisis and and explicitly discusses a broader economic policy package, highlighting that the wage-led growth strategy should be part of, what they call, a Global Keynesian New Deal to achieve a long-run stable recovery. Hein and Mundt first assess the three main causes of the deep recession that arose as a consequence of the subprime financial crisis: inefficient regulation of the financial markets; increased inequality in income distribution; and large global imbalances. They focus in particular on the effects of the process of financialization that we have already mentioned. In a number of countries, notably the United States, the United Kingdom and Australia, this has generated a 'debt-led consumption boom' regime. The main features of this regime are weak investment in capital stock, because of the shareholder value orientation of management, short-termism regarding high target rates of return on equity, large distributions of dividends and substantial capital gains. The latter have supported an expansion of consumption expenditures, this expansion being itself encouraged by easier access to credit and the concomitant increase in financial and real estate wealth. These higher consumption expenditures have vindicated high profit margins despite relatively low investment expenditures. But because these debt-led countries tend to generate current account deficits, other countries – such as China, Indonesia, Japan, the Republic of Korea and Germany – have chosen 'strongly export-led mercantilist' policies, generating growth through their exports to these debt-led consumption boom countries. As the financial crisis and the Great Recession have shown, the imbalances generated by such strategies are unsustainable in the long run. Hein and Mundt thus recommend a wage-led recovery strategy embedded into their Global Keynesian New Deal. The wage-led growth strategy requires enhanced trade union bargaining power, a reduction of managerial overheads and the profit claims of financial wealth holders, and the downsizing of the profit-intensive financial sector. More generally, the New Deal requires first, the re-regulation of the financial sector in order to prevent future financial excesses and financial crises; second, the reorientation of macroeconomic policies towards stimulating and stabilizing domestic demand, in particular in the current account surplus countries; and third the reconstruction of international macroeconomic policy co-ordination and a new world financial order along the lines of Keynes's international clearing union, so as to discourage countries from adopting export-led mercantilist policies based on low wages or low wage growth. The chapter by Hein and Mundt thus concludes this book on wage-led growth strategies with a broad vision of the economic policies that are needed for a sustainable economic recovery.

Acknowledgements

Finally, we wish to take this opportunity to thank our colleagues who accepted the invitation to be part of this endeavour, as well as Lance Taylor who agreed to chair a session at which all of the chapters were presented. We also wish to thank all those at the ILO who have given technical, financial and intellectual support to the project that has culminated in the present book, namely Manuela Tomei, Frank Hoffer, Patrick Belser, Matthieu Charpe, and especially Sangheon Lee, who showed great determination in getting the project going.

References

Galbraith, J.K. 2012. *Inequality and Instability: A Study of the World Economy Just Before the Great Crisis* (New York: Oxford University Press).
International Labour Office (ILO). 2012. *Global Wage Report 2012–13: Wages and Equitable Growth* (Geneva: ILO).
Palley, T.I. 2012. *From Financial Crisis to Stagnation: The Destruction of Shared Prosperity and the Role of Economics* (Cambridge: Cambridge University Press).
Rajan, R.G. 2010. *Fault Lines: How Hidden Fractures Still Threaten the World Economy* (Princeton, NJ: Princeton University Press).
Stiglitz, J.E. 2012. *The Price of Inequality: How Today's Divided Society Endangers Our Future* (New York: W.W. Norton).

1
Wage-led Growth: Concept, Theories and Policies[1]

Marc Lavoie and Engelbert Stockhammer

1.1 Introduction

The subprime financial crisis that started in 2007 and which became the global financial crisis challenges economists and policy-makers to reconsider the theories and policies that had gradually been accepted as conventional wisdom over the last thirty years. It is widely recognized that the global financial crisis has called into question the efficiency and stability of unregulated financial markets. This chapter argues that it has also demonstrated the limitations and even falsehood of the claim that wage moderation, accompanied by more flexible labour markets as well as labour institutions and laws more favourable to employers, will ultimately make for a more stable economy and a more productive and dynamic economic system.

The introductory chapter has recalled that in a large number of countries the past decades have witnessed falling wage shares and a polarization of personal income distribution. As will be argued in the next chapter, we believe that these phenomena are, at most, only partially associated with technical change and changes in the composition of output, and that the essential cause of the long-run evolution of income distribution and its rising dispersion is the change in economic policies and in the institutional and legal environment that has been more favourable to capital and its high-end supervisory employees over the last thirty years or so.

It is time to reconsider the validity of these pro-capital distributional policies, and to examine the possibility of an alternative path, one based on pro-labour distributional policies, accompanied by legislative changes and structural policies that will make a wage-led growth regime more likely, that is, pursue what we call a *wage-led growth strategy*, which, in our view, will generate a much more stable growth regime for the future. This issue is particularly important in view of the fact that the financial crisis has plunged many economies in recession, thus further weakening the ability of workers to resist attempts to lower wages or real wages, and hence with the consequence, at the macroeconomic level, of further reducing the wage share in national income.

The advocacy of a wage-led economic strategy has a long history. It has been articulated in reformist visions within the labour movement and in nineteenth-century economics the phenomenon was discussed under the heading of 'underconsumption'.[2] Within the Marxist tradition, underconsumption theories have been discussed as problems in the realization of profit.[3] These ideas received a further boost from their endorsement by Keynes, when he proposed his theory of effective demand, arguing that excessive saving rates, relative to deficient investment rates, were at the core of depressed economies. In the more recent academic debate, post-Keynesian economists have done the most to analytically clarify the relation between income distribution and effective demand.[4] More recently, the policy-oriented concept of a wage-led growth strategy was prominently used by UNCTAD (2010, 2011).

A standard objection to the consideration of the underconsumption thesis, or the consideration of problems related to the lack of effective demand, is that long-run growth – the trend rate of growth, also called the potential growth or the natural rate of growth – is ultimately determined by supply-side factors, such as the growth rate of the labour force and the growth rate of labour productivity. While adepts of the so-called 'endogenous growth theory' will recognize that investment in human capital or research and development may end up modifying the potential growth rate, they usually set aside the idea that actual growth rates could have an influence on potential growth rates. Yet, since the advent of the global financial crisis, government agencies and central banks in many industrialized countries have lowered their forecasts of long-run real growth, thus demonstrating clearly that weak aggregate demand does have an impact on potential growth. As Dray and Thirlwall (2011, p. 466) recall, 'it makes little economic sense to think of growth as supply constrained if, within limits, demand can create its own supply'. This explains why we shall focus on the income distribution determinants of aggregate demand, paying less attention to the supply-side factors.

The main objective of the present chapter is to provide an accessible introduction to the topic of a wage-led growth strategy for policymakers. Another important objective is to present the overarching framework underlying the efforts of the authors of the other chapters of the book, thus also providing an introduction to the notions of *wage-led* and *profit-led* economic *regimes*, in the hope that other researchers will adopt these distinctions and embark on the kind of empirical research required to assess whether various other individual countries or regions are in a wage-led or a profit-led regime.

In the next section, section 1.2, we provide a policy-oriented framework for the analysis of the interaction between distribution and growth. We will need to make a distinction between distributional policies and a macroeconomic regime. It is important to make these conceptual definitions and distinctions because they are not always obvious to non-economists. On the one hand governments can pursue pro-labour or pro-capital distributional policies, which aim respectively to increase or decrease the share of wages in national income; while on the other hand we have wage-led and profit-led economic regimes, which are associated with the structural macroeconomic features of the country under investigation. More technically, distributional policies are about the *determinants* of income distribution, the economic regime is about the *effects* of changes in income distribution on the economy. We will also see how policies and regimes can interact to create either stable and high growth processes or whether some combination can lead instead to slow or unstable growth processes.

In section 1.3, we shall examine why an economy would exhibit a wage-led economic regime, looking both at supply-side effects, that is the relationship between the share of wages and labour productivity growth, and also demand-side effects, which is our main concern in this section and in this chapter. Section 1.4 provides a summary of the key empirical findings regarding demand and productivity regimes. Finally, section 1.5 argues that since the world economy as a whole is likely to be in a wage-led regime, an economically sustainable process of growth requires the adoption of a wage-led strategy, with pro-labour distributional and structural policies. This will generate a wage-led growth process, which will ultimately be favourable to all concerned, including employers.

1.2 Distribution and growth: A conceptual framework

The relation between distribution and growth had been at the centre of macroeconomic analysis in classical economics, but with the dominance of neoclassical economics in the twentieth century, issues of distribution have been neglected, since income distribution was assumed to be regulated by marginal productivity relations within a perfect competition model, with wages for various occupations being determined by the pure market forces of supply and demand. But such a mechanical model of wage determination and income distribution does not hold up in a world where monopsonist features, imperfect competition and economic and social power come into play.[5] In such a world, in contrast to the ideal world of market fundamentalism, market forces do not produce optimum results and there is room for modifying income distribution. In the following we offer a policy-oriented framework to analyse the relation between distribution and growth. We start by contrasting pro-labour and pro-capital distributional policies.

1.2.1   Pro-capital versus pro-labour distributional policies

Income distribution is the outcome of complex social and economic processes, but governments directly influence it by means of tax policy, social policy and labour market policy. As shown in Table 1.1, we define as pro-capital distributional policies those policies that lead to a long-run decline in the wage share in national income, while pro-labour distributional policies are policies that result in an increase in the wage share. Pro-capital distributional policies usually claim to promote 'labour market flexibility' or wage flexibility, rather than increasing capital income. They include measures that weaken collective bargaining institutions (by granting exceptions to bargaining coverage), labour unions (for example, by changing strike laws) and employment protection legislation, as well as measures (or lack of measures) that lead to lower minimum wages. There are also measures that alter the secondary income distribution in favour of profits and the rich, such as exempting capital gains from income taxation, or reducing the corporate income tax. Ultimately, pro-capital policies impose wage moderation.

Pro-labour policies, in contrast, are often referred to as policies that strengthen the welfare state, labour market institutions, labour unions, and the ability to engage in collective bargaining (for example, by extending the reach of bargaining agreements to non-unionized firms). Pro-labour policies are also associated with increased unemployment benefits, higher minimum wages and a higher minimum wage relative to the median wage, as well as reductions in wage and salary dispersion. All else being equal, with a pro-labour distributional policy, the wage share will remain constant or will increase over the long run, as real wages grow in line with labour productivity or exceed productivity. By contrast, in the case of a pro-capital distributional policy, real wages will not grow as fast as labour productivity.

Of course, there are also other factors influencing income distribution, such as technological changes, trade policy, globalization, financialization and financial deregulation. These factors have recently played an important role (Stockhammer 2013), but we will not elaborate on them here, as we wish to focus on the interaction of distributional policies and economic regime.

1.2.2 Profit-led versus wage-led economic regimes

So far we have considered the economic policies pursued by a government, which could alter income distribution in favour of profits or of wages or the median wage. Next we consider the following question: knowing that income distribution is shifting in favour of profits or wages, what is the effect of such a shift on economic performance? For instance, if income distribution in a country is shifting in favour of profit recipients, does this by itself have favourable consequences on aggregate demand in the short run, on the growth rate of aggregate demand in the long run, or on the growth rate of labour productivity? If indeed this shift towards profits has favourable repercussions on the economy, as we have just defined them, then we shall say that this economy is in a *profit-led economic regime*. If not, if the shift towards profits has a negative impact on the economy, then the economy is in a *wage-led economic regime*. By symmetry, we can argue that economies that, all else being equal, experience rising wage shares that induce a favourable outcome are part of a wage-led regime, while rising wage

Seem to lead to ↓ MRVP

Table 1.1 Pro-labour and pro-capital distributional policies

	Distributional policies		
	Pro-capital	**Pro-labour**	**Other factors**
Policies	'Labour market flexibility' Abolish minimum wages Weaken collective bargaining Impose wage moderation	'Welfare state' Increase minimum wages Strengthen collective bargaining	Changes in technology Globalization Financialization
Results	Weak wage growth Wage share ↓ Increased wage dispersion	Rising real wages Stable (or ↑) wage share Decreased wage dispersion	

enduring Productivity returns (MRVP) → competitiveness implic's shares that generate an unfavourable outcome indicate the presence of a profit-led regime. This is all summed up in Table 1.2. At this stage, we do not attempt to distinguish between demand and productivity effects, but only discuss the economic regime, assuming for the moment that demand and productivity react in a similar direction to distributional changes. We shall tackle this issue in more detail in the next section.

Whether an economy is under a profit-led or a wage-led regime is affected by the structure of the economy. It will depend in part on the existing income distribution in the country, but also on various behavioural components, such as the propensity to consume of wage earners and recipients of profit incomes, on the sensitivity of entrepreneurs to changes in sales or in profit margins, and on the sensitivity of exporters and importers to changes in costs, foreign exchange values, and changes in foreign demand, as well as the size of the various components of aggregate demand – consumption, investment, government expenditures and net exports. While an economic regime also depends on the various economic structures and institutions, as well as various forms of government policy, it should be clear that the nature of the economic regime as defined in Table 1.2 is not a choice variable for economic policy in any straightforward sense. It should not be understood as designed by economic policy, but rather as determined by the institutional structure of the economy.

We can now bring together the analyses of distributional policies and of economic regimes, as shown in Table 1.3. Between the two sets of distributional policies and the two economic regimes, four different combinations are possible with quite different properties. If pro-capital distributional policies are pursued in a profit-led economy, this will result in a profit-led growth process. Inversely, if pro-labour policies are pursued in a wage-led economy, this will result in a wage-led growth process. These are the two cells in the main diagonal in

Table 1.2 Definition of profit-led and wage-led regimes

		Overall impact on the economy	
		Expansionary	**Contractionary**
Income distribution change imposed on society	**An increase in the profit share**	Profit-led regime	Wage-led regime
	An increase in the wage share	Wage-led regime	Profit-led regime

Table 1.3. In both cases distributional policies and economic structures are consistent with each other. However, if pro-capital policies
are pursued in a wage-led economy or if pro-labour policies are pursued in a profit-led economy, this will result in stagnation. In practice, inconsistent distributional policies and regimes are also likely to
evolve towards unstable growth patterns as growth will have to rely
on external stimulation.

Table 1.3 is useful in classifying different political ideologies as the
four different combinations allow us to classify many important arguments. Take the first cell (pro-capital policies in a profit-led economy).
This scenario, as shown in Table 1.4, corresponds to liberal ideology and
what is often called trickle-down economics. Policies more favourable
to profit recipients and to employers and their high-ranking employees
are said to lead to improved macroeconomic performance. Under such
a scenario, the average worker will eventually benefit from wage cuts
and harsher working conditions as higher profit margins will induce
entrepreneurs and executive officers to work harder and invest in more
numerous machines and more productive capacity, so that rewards
will eventually trickle down to workers as well, in the form of higher
employment rates and higher purchasing power. This scenario could be
called 'neoliberalism in theory'. It rests on the idea of a trickle-down
process whereby increasing profits lead to virtuous cycle of higher
growth that ultimately also benefits labour and the poor.

The cell that mixes pro-labour policies in a wage-led regime summarizes what many economists (for example, Marglin and Schor 1990)
regard as a key characteristic of the post-war era. The expansion of the
welfare state (in advanced economies) led to a golden age of growth
which was favourable to both workers and entrepreneurs, as rising real
wages generated large increases in labour productivity and profits until
the 1970s.

Table 1.3 Viability of growth regimes

		Distributional policies	
		Pro-capital	Pro-labour
Economic regime	**Profit-led**	Profit-led growth process	Stagnation or unstable growth
	Wage-led	Stagnation or unstable growth	Wage-led growth process

Table 1.4   Actual growth strategies in the economic regime/distributional
policies framework

		Distributional policies and strategies	
		Pro-capital	**Pro-labour**
Economic regime	**Profit-led**	'Neoliberalism in theory' Trickle-down capitalism	'Doomed social reforms' (TINA)
	Wage-led	'Neoliberalism in practice' – Unstable, has to rely on exogenous growth drivers (debt-led growth or export-led growth)	Social Keynesianism Post-war Golden Age

[handwritten annotations across the table]

The next cell (pro-labour policies in a profit-led economy) could be
termed 'doomed social reforms'. It is the scenario that neoliberals claim
would happen if progressive social reforms were implemented. Margaret
Thatcher's famous dictum, later repeated by several think-tanks and even
left-wing politicians, that 'there is no alternative' (TINA), makes sense in
this cell. Some Marxists use a similar scenario to illustrate the futility of
attempts to restore a more humane economy within the capitalist mode
of production. Within this cell, attempts to raise workers' compensation or the wage share inevitably lead to a slowdown of the economy, as
such changes in income distribution are inconsistent with the profit-led
regime of the economy, usually leading to their quick abandonment.

Finally there is the fourth cell, which combines pro-capital distributional policies with a wage-led regime. We will argue that this
describes 'neoliberalism in practice' in several countries, since two or
more decades of pro-capital redistribution policies have resulted in a
general increase in economic inequalities and in a mediocre economic
performance relative to the performance achieved in the Golden Age.[6]
Furthermore, this neoliberalism in practice, has been accompanied by
a heavy reliance on a bloated financial sector or on external demand,
which has generated economic and financial instability. The reliance
on these external drivers – export-led growth and debt-led growth –
constitutes an attempt to circumvent the slow growth inherent to the
contradiction between the pro-capital distribution policies being pursued by society and the intrinsic properties of an area under a wage-led
economic regime, as explained in detail by Hein and Mundt (2013) in
the final chapter of the book.

Thus far, we can conclude that if several countries, or if some regions, are under a wage-led regime, then pro-capital policies that pertain to boost the confidence of employers will fail. These policies will not generate favourable effects on aggregate demand and productivity. In a wage-led regime, what we need instead are pro-labour policies, which will help to generate sustainable growth. In other words, in a wage-led regime, what we need is a wage-led growth strategy. What we now have to examine are the factors that determine whether an economy is in a wage-led or a profit-led regime. And we shall see later still the results of a set of empirical studies on this specific question.

1.3 Profit-led or wage-led economic regimes?

In this section, we wish to present the tools that will help us distinguish between wage-led and profit-led economic regimes. Following conventional practice among researchers in the field established since Boyer (1988), we will distinguish between demand regimes and productivity regimes, although, as we shall see, the overall effects on aggregate demand and productivity growth are interdependent. We first deal with the demand side, emphasized by Keynesian economists.

1.3.1 Demand regimes

To assess whether an economy is in a *wage-led demand regime* or in a *profit-led demand regime*, we need to consider the four components of gross domestic product (GDP), that is, the four components of aggregate demand, which are private consumption (C), private investment (I), government expenditure (G), and net exports (NX, exports minus imports), which we can write as:

$$AD = C + I + G + NX$$

Broadly speaking, we will say that an economy is in a wage-led demand regime when an increase in the wage share (or a decrease in the profit share) leads to an increase in the sum of the components of aggregate demand; and we will say that an economy is in a profit-led demand regime when an increase in the profit share (or a decrease in the wage share) leads to an increase in the sum of the components of aggregate demand.

It is customary to consider that the first three components of aggregate demand – consumption, investment and government expenditure – are the *domestic* components of aggregate demand. This will thus allow us to make the distinction between the *domestic demand* regime and the *total demand* regime. Since it is difficult to treat government expenditures as anything but exogenous, to assess the domestic demand regime we only need to consider the impact of a change in income distribution on consumption and investment.

Let us start with the effect of an (exogenous) increase in the wage share (or in real wages at constant labour productivity) on private consumption. If the propensities to consume out of profits and out of wages are the same, then the change in real wages will have no impact whatsoever on consumption, which is the standard assumption in mainstream models, where income distribution plays no role. However, if the propensity to consume out of wages is higher than the propensity to consume out of profits, then a shift in income distribution towards wages will induce an increase in consumption demand. This occurs because the redistribution of income towards a higher wage share generates an increase in consumption expenditures, since wage earners spend a greater portion of their income than profit recipients. A decrease in wage dispersion, providing a greater share of income to the lower quintiles, would lead to a similar result. These effects are at the core of the arguments of the underconsumptionist economists who highlight the detrimental impact of rising or high profit shares, as can be found in the modern and canonical Kaleckian models of Rowthorn (1981), Taylor (1983) and Dutt (1987).

These consequences are well supported by empirical evidence, which shows that the propensities to save out of profits are much higher than those to save out of wages (in part because firms, by definition, save all of their retained earnings) and which also shows that the propensities to save of the richest quintiles are higher, as one would expect, than those of the poorest quintiles.[7] These effects reinforce each other since wage earners generally are poorer than most profit recipients. Capital gains on real estate and the stock market may reduce somewhat the differential between the propensities to consume of wage earners and profit recipients, and this differential will also be affected by the existing social security system.

The favourable effects of higher wage shares on consumption and aggregate demand may, however, be overturned by the detrimental effects of a higher wage share on private investment expenditures. Most Kaleckian economists argue that expected profitability depends on past realized profitability, and hence on sales, relying on the strength of the accelerator effect, and thus believing that investment should not be negatively affected by an increase in the wage share.[8] By contrast, Marxists and several other economists tend to claim instead that expected profitability depends on the share of profits in national income, that is, on the profit margin of firms, or, more precisely, on the profit rate that firms expect to achieve on their capital when capacity is utilized at its normal rate (see Lavoie 1995, pp. 795–800). As higher real wages, all else constant, imply lower profit margins and lower profitability at the normal rate of capacity utilization, it implies a downward shift of the investment function. These profitability effects have been formalized by Bhaduri and Marglin (1990), the article of which is famous for having defined the dichotomy between wage-led and profit-led demand regimes. Similar formalizations of the investment function were also adopted by Kurz (1990), Taylor (1991) and Blecker (2002), as well as by many authors wishing to assess the presence of these regimes in empirical studies. This variant of the canonical Kaleckian model is often referred to as the post-Kaleckian model of growth and distribution. It is worth quoting Bhaduri and Marglin in full here:

Any increase in real wage rate, depressing profit margin and profit share ..., must decrease savings and increase consumption to validate the under-consumptionist thesis... Nevertheless, aggregate demand (*C* + *I*) may still rise or fall depending on what impact that lower profit margin/share has on investment. Since it is plausible to argue that, other things being equal, a lower profit margin/share would weaken the incentive to invest, the contradictory effects of any exogenous variation in the real wage on the level of aggregate demand become apparent. A higher real wage increases consumption but reduces investment, in so far as investment depends on the profit margin. (Bhaduri and Marglin 1990, p. 378)

Table 1.5 summarizes the various factors that will determine whether the structure of an economy is such that it is in a wage-led or a profit-led demand regime. Of course, there are many more factors other than income distribution that determine aggregate demand: monetary policy, fiscal policy, various shocks such as oil price shocks, the bursting of stock market bubbles, changes in real exchange rates, changes in the growth rate of foreign GDP, and so on. Indeed, for most year-to-year changes, income distribution will only be a minor influence on the determination of aggregate demand, with other developments playing a more prominent role. However, if there are long-lasting deep changes in income distribution as have occurred in the last quarter century, they will end up having a substantial role.

Table 1.5 Economic structure: wage-led and profit-led demand regimes

	Demand regime	
	Profit-led	**Wage-led**
Economic structure	Small differentials in propensities to consume	Propensity to consume out of wages is much higher than the propensity to consume out of profits
	Investment is highly sensitive to profitability and accelerator parameter is low	Investment is not sensitive to profitability and accelerator parameter is high
	Very open economy with high net export price elasticity and high import income elasticity	Relatively closed economy with low net export price elasticity and low import income elasticity
Other factors	Other sources of demand: Government fiscal and monetary policies Financial factors: financial asset and real estate price bubbles Exchange rate evolution and changes in world demand Changes in world commodity prices...	

1.3.2   Demand regimes with net exports

So far, we have not taken into account net exports, having only discussed the domestic components of aggregate demand. It is usually argued that an increase in real wages or the wage share will have a negative impact on the trade balance. It is further argued that the negative effects on net exports of a higher wage share are more likely to be significant in small open economies with high net export price elasticity. Finding out whether an economy is in a wage-led or profit-led demand regime, *in total*, one must thus consider the net effect of an increase in the wage share on the three private components of aggregate demand – consumption, investment and net exports – and hence the net effect is not clear a priori and will depend on the relative size of the effects on the three components.

Blecker (1989, 2011) as well as Bhaduri and Marglin (1990) have examined the possible effects of changes in income distribution on net exports. If wages are pumped up, without a rise in export prices, this will lead to a reduction in profit margins and may render some exports unprofitable; if prices are pushed up, some export products will no longer be competitive. As Blecker (1989, p. 404) said, 'this is essentially the case of a 'profit squeeze', in which profit margins are compressed between domestic costs on the one side and foreign competition on the other'.[9] Hence an economy which is in a profit-led domestic demand regime will normally necessarily be in a profit-led total demand regime as well. Table 1.6 shows this and summarizes the various possibilities when distinguishing between the effects of an increase in the wage share on domestic aggregate demand and the effects on total aggregate demand, also taking into account the foreign sector.

To take into account international trade and net exports when assessing the impact of changes in income distribution certainly adds a degree of complexity. First, the favourable domestic impact of an increase in the wage share may get reversed once we consider the effects on net exports, as shown in Table 1.6. As long as the negative impact of a higher wage share on profitability is not too large, we may be easily persuaded that 'there is no necessary antagonism between capitalists and workers in a mature capitalist economy characterized by excess capacity: it is possible to increase both real wages and employment on the one hand, and realised profits and growth on the other hand. This comforting conclusion must be drastically revised in the light of the model of an open economy... The possibility of a conflict between a redistribution towards wages and maintaining international competitiveness greatly reduces the prospects for a happy coincidence of worker's and capitalists' interests' (Blecker 1989, pp. 406–7).[10]

But there is a second delicate point in the case of an open economy – the possibility of an error of composition – especially when an economy

Table 1.6 Effects of an increase in the wage share and domestic and total demand regimes

		Effect on total aggregate demand, including net exports	
		Positive	Negative
Effect on domestic aggregate demand (investment and consumption)	**Positive**	Wage-led domestic demand regime and wage-led total demand regime	Wage-led domestic demand regime and profit-led total demand regime
	Negative		Profit-led domestic demand regime and profit-led total demand regime

is in a domestic wage-led demand regime. It is worth quoting Blecker's views on this in full:

> A situation in which competitive wage cuts (or 'wage restraints') are pursued in all countries will potentially harm the interests of workers everywhere: real wages will be sacrificed, as long as mark-ups are flexible; but employment will not increase, as long as the competitive gains cancel each other out. In this case, the regressive effect of multilateral wage cuts on income distribution could well lead to a world-wide depression of demand and employment. On the one hand, if workers in all countries increase their money wages, and if the international competitive effects roughly cancel out, then the world economy as a whole can potentially enjoy wage-led growth – provided that firms still feel sufficient competitive pressures to compel them to cut their mark-ups in response to the wage increases. (Blecker 1989, p. 407)

Knowing whether the economy is within a *domestic* wage-led or profit-led regime is important in itself. Since one country's exports are some other country's imports, this raises the possibility of a fallacy of composition: while each individual country can increase its demand by exporting more, not all countries can do so simultaneously. The world economy overall is a closed economy. It is thus essential to look at the domestic effect and the total effects (that is, including net exports) separately. The domestic effects *of the world economy* only include the effects on consumption and investment and should be interpreted as a scenario where the change in the wage share affects all trading partners simultaneously. It can be thought of as the result of a change in the world wage share. Thus, while a country may be under a profit-led demand regime when considering the total effect of an increase in the wage share, a simultaneous increase in the wage share of all countries may still have a positive effect on the aggregate demand of a profit-led country if its domestic demand is wage-led. We will see that this is indeed the case when we go over the most recent empirical results related to demand regimes.

1.3.3   Productivity regimes

So far we have dealt with aggregate demand. What about supply effects? From our standpoint, the key summary variable for the supply side is labour productivity. Thus this section will focus on the productivity regime.

Productivity will be profit-led if an increase in wages discourages productivity-enhancing capital investment and, as a consequence, the growth of labour productivity slows down (as most forms of techno-logical progress require capital investment, this is called embodied technological progress). Increases in wage growth may have a posi-tive effect on productivity growth, if either firms react by increasing productivity-enhancing investments in order to maintain competitive-ness or if workers' contribution to the production process improves. This may be the case either because of enhanced workers' motivation or, in developing countries, if their health and nutritional situation improves. This case is often referred to as the efficiency wage hypoth-esis in the mainstream literature.[11] But we may as well call it the Webb effect, since a positive causal relationship going from higher real wages to higher productivity was already proposed a long time ago by Sidney Webb (1912), one of the founders of the London School of Economics. The main features of the two productivity regimes are presented in Table 1.7.

Defined as we just did, even mainstream economists might recognize that all economies are in a wage-led productivity regime, since main-stream economists would argue that rising real wages induce firms to invest in more capital-intensive methods, which, under the standard assumptions of neoclassical production functions, would lead to higher labour productivity.[12] We may, however, also take into account indirect effects, based on another branch of post-Keynesian economics – the Kaldorian branch – as do Boyer (1988), Setterfield and Cornwall (2002) as well as Naastepad and Storm (2010), to assess whether a productivity regime is wage-led or profit-led.

Table 1.7 Economic structure: wage-led and profit-led productivity regimes

		Productivity regime
Economic structure	**Profit-led**	Wage restraint leads to productivity-enhancing investment
		Higher real wage growth or a higher wage share leads to slower productivity growth
	Wage-led	Wage growth has strong positive effects on labour effort and productivity-enhancing investments
		Higher real wage growth or a higher wage share leads to faster productivity growth

In this case, we must also incorporate the demand effects. Kaldorians have for a long time argued that supply-side growth is endogenous, thus predating the mainstream theories of endogenous growth. This is the so-called Kaldor–Verdoorn law, for which there is a substantial amount of empirical evidence (McCombie and Thirlwall 1994; McCombie 2002) and the formal origins of which can be traced back to Kaldor's (1957) technical progress function. The Kaldor–Verdoorn law claims that there is a positive relation between the growth rates of GDP and the growth rate of labour productivity. In other words, demand-led growth will have an impact on the supply components of growth (Léon-Ledesma and Thirlwall 2002; Dray and Thirlwall 2011). More simply, it is claimed that there is a positive causal relationship going from the growth rate of the economy to the growth rate of labour productivity (and even the growth rate of the labour force).[13]

What does the Kaldor–Verdoorn relation imply for the assessment of the productivity regime? Suppose there is an increase in the wage share or in growth rate of real wages. As argued before, the partial effect on productivity growth is likely to be positive. In the case of a wage-led demand regime the indirect Kaldor–Verdoorn effect will reinforce the direct productivity effect. Hence in this case, the total productivity effect will always be positive and we will always have a wage-led total productivity regime. Take now the case of a profit-led demand regime. An increase in the wage share or in the growth rate of real wages will generate a decrease in the growth rate of the economy. The Kaldor–Verdoorn effect will translate this decrease into a decrease in the growth rate of labour productivity. However, this indirect negative effect of increasing the growth rate of real wages may be partially or entirely wiped out by the direct positive productivity effect, assuming once more a wage-led partial productivity regime, as empirically verified for Organisation for Economic Co-operation and Development (OECD) countries by Storm and Naastepad (2008, p. 535) and Hein and Tarassow (2010, pp. 747–9). Thus, although the economy is in a profit-led demand regime, the effect on labour productivity growth of an increase in the wage share may be positive overall, since the direct positive productivity effect of the increase in the wage share or in the growth rate of real wages may still overwhelm the negative indirect productivity effect arising from the decrease in economic activity generated by wage expansion in this regime. Table 1.8 summarizes the possible combined results of the productivity and demand regimes when the partial productivity regime is wage led, which is the most likely case, and the wage share or the growth rate in real wages is increased.

Table 1.8   Total productivity effect of an increase in the wage share, when the partial productivity regime is wage-led

Demand regime	Partial productivity effect	Indirect productivity effect (Kaldor–Verdoorn effect)	Total productivity effect (sum of partial and indirect effects)
Profit-led	Positive	Negative	Positive or negative
Wage-led	Positive	Positive	Positive

Confuses 2 theoretical views w. 2 real regimes?

So far we have assumed that economic activity or economic growth has an effect on the growth in labour productivity. But we have not yet taken into account the possibility that productivity growth could have a feedback effect on economic growth and economic activity. Thus what happens on the productivity front as result of changes in income distribution could have an additional indirect effect on the demand regime. Since the various possible cases of this interdependence between the demand and the productivity regimes are discussed extensively by Storm and Naastepad (2013), here we simply mention the fact that the feedback effects of productivity growth on output growth may transform an apparent profit-led demand regime into a wage-led one (whereas the opposite is impossible). This will happen when the total productivity effects of an increase in the wage share are positive and large, and when the positive effects of productivity growth on aggregate demand overwhelm the presumably weak negative effects of a higher wage share on aggregate demand (Hein and Tarassow 2010, pp. 737–9).

1.4   Summary of empirical estimates

The previous section has developed a conceptual framework to define wage-led and profit-led economic regimes. The key components of this framework have been investigated empirically by various authors, including those who participate in the current book. Here we report their main results.

as real.

1.4.1   Demand effects

The Bhaduri and Marglin (1990) post-Kaleckian model has recently inspired a rich empirical literature that attempts to identify demand regimes by econometric means. Hein and Vogel (2008), Stockhammer and Stehrer (2011) and Onaran and Galanis (2013) offer extensive discussions of the literature, so here we only present a quick assessment. Although they use different methods and rely on different sources of data and time periods, a vast majority of the studies agree that the few OECD countries that have been studied turn out to be running under wage-led domestic demand regimes. The results are less homogeneous when it comes to the total demand regimes, with different authors often coming to different conclusions regarding the same country.

Onaran and Galanis (2013) in the present book provide new consistent estimates for most G20 countries, which are summarized in Table 1.9. This presents the effects of a reduction in the (adjusted) wage share. More precisely, it details the effects of a one percentage point increase in the profit share of an individual country on the components of demand of that country (columns A, B and C), on private excess demand (the sum of those three components, column D) and on aggregate demand (taking multiplier effects into account, column E). Comparing the estimates of columns A and B, it can be verified that their sum is always negative and hence that all the countries of the sample are in a wage-led domestic demand regime, thus retrieving the consensus result that was achieved in previous studies. The impact of the increase in the profit share on private excess demand (column D) is negative in a majority of countries, thus meaning that these countries are in a wage-led total demand regime, but there are still a number of countries that have a profit-led total demand.

However, as countries trade with each other, the effects of changes in income distribution in individual countries are not the same as the effects that would arise as a result of a worldwide change in income distribution. Thus the table also reports the results of simulating the complex interactions of the international demand components. Column G gives the results for a simultaneous ('worldwide') decrease in the wage share in all G20 countries by one percentage point. This effect is negative in the vast majority of the countries. Several countries that were in a profit-led total demand regime, when assessed individually, nonetheless do suffer reductions in demand if their trade partners also experience a decline in the wage share. Indeed, total G20 GDP declines by 0.36 per cent in reaction to a worldwide one percentage point decline in the wage share, thus helping to explain why even countries that are in a profit-led total demand regime might suffer nevertheless from a worldwide reduction in the wage share.

These results have important policy implications. They indicate that, at least with regard to aggregate demand, an internationally coordinated wage-led growth strategy seems viable. Aggregate demand in the world economy is clearly wage led. While there are some countries

Table 1.9 Summary of the results of Onaran and Galanis (2013): effects of a national and global one percentage point increase in the profit share

	Effects of national increase in profit share on:					Effect of worldwide increase in profit share on aggregate demand
	C/Y	I/Y	NX/Y	private excess demand/Y	aggregate demand	
	A	B	C	D (A+B+C)	E	G
Euro area-12	−0.439	0.299	0.057	−0.084	−0.133	−0.245
Germany	−0.501	0.376	0.096	−0.029	−0.031	−
France	−0.305	0.088	0.198	−0.020	−0.027	−
Italy	−0.356	0.130	0.126	−0.100	−0.173	−
United Kingdom	−0.303	0.120	0.158	−0.025	−0.030	−0.214
United States	−0.426	0.000	0.037	−0.388	−0.808	−0.921
Japan	−0.353	0.284	0.055	−0.014	−0.034	−0.179
Canada	−0.326	0.182	0.266	0.122	0.148	−0.269
Australia	−0.256	0.174	0.272	0.190	0.268	0.172
Turkey	−0.491	0.000	0.283	−0.208	−0.459	−0.717
Mexico	−0.438	0.153	0.381	0.096	0.106	−0.111
Korea, Rep. of	−0.422	0.000	0.359	−0.063	−0.115	−0.864
Argentina	−0.153	0.015	0.192	0.054	0.075	−0.103
China	−0.412	0.000	1.986	1.574	1.932	1.115
India	−0.291	0.000	0.310	0.018	0.040	−0.027
South Africa	−0.145	0.129	0.506	0.490	0.729	0.390

Note: The global simulation excludes Germany, France and Italy since they are part of the euro zone.

Source: Onaran and Galanis (2013, Table 2).

'Effect of worldwide change in profit share on aggregate demand': effect of a simultaneous change in the profit share in all countries, including domestic multiplier effects and international trade effects

that are individually profit led, the positive effect of the profit share on demand relies on net exports. Effectively this means that some individual countries can successfully pursue 'beggar-thy-neighbour' policies via wage moderation, but this does not constitute a viable strategy for

demand on a global scale. If all countries pursue wage moderation policies, a much smaller subset of the countries in a profit-led total demand
regime will still benefit from their pro-capital distributional policies.
This highlights the need for policy-makers to realize the role of wages
as a source of demand. On a more technical level, it highlights the need
for international coordination when dealing with wage and social policies, so as to prevent a race to the bottom in wages.

1.4.2   Productivity effects

On the supply side, the key question is how changes in the wage share
or in real wages affect productivity growth (or, more broadly speaking, technological progress). Mainstream economists typically argue
that competitive markets are most conducive to growth and, in the
next step, argue for labour market (and product market) deregulation.
Critical economists highlight that not only can labour market institutions have positive social effects as they help to overcome market
failures, but they also may have positive effects on economic growth
because good labour relations will improve the propensity of workers to
contribute to the production process.

Recently, this has inspired several empirical studies, which are sur-
veyed by Storm and Naastepad (2013). Naastepad (2006) found that a
one percentage point increase in real wages would lead to a 0.52 percentage point increase in labour productivity for the Netherlands.
Storm and Naastepad (2009) investigate labour market institutions in
twenty OECD countries from 1984 to 2004. They find that relatively
regulated and coordinated ('rigid') institutions lead to higher productivity growth. Vergeer and Kleinknecht (2010–11) perform a panel analysis for OECD countries from 1960 to 2004 and also find that stronger
labour market institutions lead to faster long-run growth. Both studies
also look at the impact of real wage growth on productivity growth.
Both Storm and Naastepad (2009) and Vergeer and Kleinknecht (2010–
11) find that faster real wage growth leads to faster productivity growth,
the former with an elasticity ranging from 0.50 to 0.55 while the latter
gets numbers ranging from 0.31 to 0.39 for a longer time period. Hein
and Tarassow (2010) analyse the link between income distribution and
productivity growth for six OECD economies by means of time series
analysis over the 1960–2007 period. They also report that faster real
wage growth leads to faster productivity growth, the elasticity running
around 0.30 except for Austria where it reaches 0.67.

All of these studies face challenges in identifying the direction of
causality and the distinction between short-run and long-run effects,

and more research is certainly needed. Indeed, simple national growth accounting makes it clear that faster productivity growth should be associated with faster real wage growth, thus bringing about the problem of reverse causality. However, Marquetti (2004) has found that while real wages appear to Granger-cause productivity, the reverse is not true – there is unidirectional causality. This would thus justify studies that pertain to study the impact of real wage growth on productivity growth.

Storm and Naastepad (2013) summarize these findings by positing that, as a reasonable order of magnitude (for advanced economies), one can assume that a one percentage point increase in real wage growth leads to a 0.38 percentage point increase in labour productivity growth. This illustrates that higher real wages induce firms to increase labour productivity in order to protect their profitability. Hence, despite the small number of studies, it seems fair to conclude that the available evidence suggests that real wage growth has a positive long-run effect on labour productivity growth. This is important for economic policy as it suggests that excessive wage constraint is likely to lead to weak productivity performance, while a wage-led growth strategy is consistent with positive developments on the supply side.

[handwritten margin note: a symmetric? untested]

Indeed, Storm and Naastepad (2013) suggest that countries, such as the Netherlands, which seem recently to have been successful in achieving full employment with pro-capital income distribution policies, obtain such results because slow growth in real wages has also generated slow growth in labour productivity, thus so avoiding the advent of technological unemployment, but at the cost of slow improvements in living standards.

[handwritten margin note: assn = calibrated model really]

[handwritten note: Ignores how PT work can avoid waste & idle time → hourly producty ↑.]

1.5   Conclusion: Wage-led growth – a viable economic strategy

Wages have a dual function in capitalist economies. They are a cost of production as well as a source of demand. An increase in the wage share has several effects on demand and whether actual demand regimes are wage led or profit led is subject to an ongoing academic debate. Our understanding of the available evidence is that domestic demand regimes are likely to be wage led in most economies. In open economies the net export effects may overpower the domestic effects and total demand in many individual countries may well be profit led. However larger geographical (or economic) areas are likely to be wage led. The most recent empirical studies show that the world economy overall is in a wage-led demand regime and if all countries pursue pro-labour distributional policies simultaneously, even countries that are profit-led will experience increases in aggregate demand, their economic activity being driven up by faster growth abroad. This can be contrasted to a situation where all countries are pursuing an export-led strategy: it is clear that only half of them will be successful, as all countries cannot be simultaneously net exporters.

There is comparatively less research on the supply-side effects of an increase in the wage share. However, there are several studies that find positive effects of wage increases on productivity growth, suggesting that the long-term effects of wage expansion are likely to be favourable to the economy.

There is an alternative to neoliberalism. A wage-led growth strategy is a viable option and the most likely strategy to succeed if coordinated internationally.[14] A wage-led growth strategy would combine pro-labour distributional social and labour market policies, along with a proper regulation of the financial sector.

Distributional policies that are likely to increase the wage share and reduce wage dispersion include increasing or establishing minimum wages, strengthening social security systems, improving union legislation and increasing the reach of collective bargaining agreements.[15] All of these policies go against orthodox economic wisdom and, under the perceived pressure to reduce public budget deficits, current economic policy seems to be moving in the opposite direction, with calls for government austerity policies, which are most likely to affect the middle class and the poor, and calls for structural reforms – a euphemism for more flexible labour markets and reduced wage rates. However, in times of crisis and with a lack of effective demand, what economies need is more state involvement, not less. A successful policy package to economic recovery needs to have sustained wage growth as one of its core building blocks. Only when wages grow with productivity growth will consumption expenditures grow without rising debt levels.

To be successful a modern version of a wage-led growth strategy will require a restructuring of the financial sector. The deregulated financial sector has fuelled speculative growth and resulted in the worst recession since the 1930s. If a repeat of the crisis is to be prevented, this will require managing international capital flows, a refocussing of the financial sector on narrow banking, the elimination of destabilizing financial innovations, and a higher fiscal contribution of the financial sector (for example, in the form of a financial transactions tax). Briefly put, as suggested by Hein and Mundt (2013), what is needed is a 'Global Keynesian New Deal'.

Notes

1. The paper was presented at a session of the Regulating for Decent Work (RDW) conference, held at the ILO, Geneva, 6–8 July 2011. We wish to thank participants for their remarks and questions – in particular, Pierre Laliberté, Eckhard Hein and Simon Sturn.
2. See Bleaney (1976) for a historical account of underconsumptionist theories.
3. For example, Baran and Sweezy (1966).
4. Based on the analysis of Kalecki (1971), Steindl (1952) and Bhaduri (1986), the benefits of a wage-led growth strategy has been resurrected and formalized by several Kaleckian or post-Keynesian authors, starting with Rowthorn (1981), Taylor (1983), Dutt (1987) and Lavoie (1995). Taylor (1988) showed early on that when emerging countries had enough capacity to adjust, a wage-led growth strategy made sense.
5. It has sometimes been argued that because several empirical studies of aggregate production functions have yielded estimates of the output elasticities of factors that were consistent with the predictions of marginal productivity theory under conditions of perfect competition (because these elasticities equated pretty closely the shares of wages and profits), it was possible to conclude that markets behaved as if they were fully competitive. But it has since been shown that this success was achieved because what the regressions of aggregate production functions are really measuring are the wage and profit shares, not the output elasticities, as the regressions are in fact estimating national accounting identities. See Lavoie (2007) and Felipe and McCombie (2013) for a review of this critical literature.
6. Although some researchers would argue instead that reliance on free market mechanisms and more flexible labour markets have generated large increases in world real income over the last three decades (Balcerowicz and Fisher, 2006). But these authors forget to compare the last decades to the evolution of the 1950s and 1960s. Harvey (2003) and Glyn (2006) offer insightful discussions of neoliberalism in practice.
7. Both Marglin and Bhaduri (1990) and Bowles and Boyer (1995) found that this differential in propensities to save out of profits and out of wages was around 0.40 on average over several countries. This is in line with the estimates of Onaran and Galanis (2013).
8. Kalecki's equation, in its simplified version where wages are all consumed and profits are all saved, says that realized profits are equal to the value of investment expenditures. If investment depends on realized profits, the equation would imply that higher real wages that induce higher investment expenditures would always lead to higher profits, and hence taking profitability into account would never allow us to modify our previous conclusions. This has been called the paradox of costs by Rowthorn (1981): higher wage costs reduce profits for a single firm, but with the accelerator they increase overall profits if all firms face similar cost increases.
9. An increase in real wages may not have a negative effect on net exports if it arises as a result of a spontaneous change in the pricing strategy of firms, with producers and exporters deciding to reduce their profit margins.
10. Blecker refers to a mature economy, but it should be pointed out that Taylor (1983) figured that less developed countries also operate with excess capacity, and hence that the Kaleckian model also applies to emerging countries.

11. A meta-analysis – a regression on regressions – here based at the firm and industry level and conducted by Krassoi Peach and Stanley (2009), has shown that the best statistical studies find a strong and robust evidence of this efficiency wage effect, thus showing that higher real wages lead to higher productivity. This positive link is even reinforced when controlled for simultaneity.

12. Indeed, this is tied to the standard assumption of a downward-sloping labour demand curve. One could also define an employment regime, which would depend on an interaction of the demand regime and the productivity regime, as defined in the rest of this subsection (see Storm and Naastepad 2012). Keynes doubted that a wage cut would stimulate employment and thought that, at least in some circumstances, it might decrease employment (Keynes 1936, chapter 19). This latter case is akin to a wage-led employment regime. For modern post-Keynesian discussions of employment and wages, see Lavoie (2003) and Stockhammer (2011).

13. McCombie (2002, p. 106) says that the Verdoorn coefficient is in the 0.3 to 0.6 range, meaning that a one percentage point addition to the growth rate of output will generate a 0.3 to 0.6 percentage point increase in the growth rate of labour productivity, a number which is also consistent with the one obtained recently by Storm and Naastepad (2008). Hein and Tarassow (2010), looking at 1960–2007 data, find a similar range for European countries, but a lower range for the United Kingdom and the United States, between 0.1 and 0.25.

14. It is sometimes argued by Marxist authors that wage-led demand regimes are unstable, meaning that high output and employment growth rates achieved with high wage shares will generate further increases in the wage share because of the stronger bargaining power of workers. Thus the feedback effects of aggregate demand and employment on income distribution, effects that we have not considered in this paper since we assumed the wage share to be an exogenous element, can make the wage-led demand regime unstable in that growing wage shares and higher growth may create a reinforcing cycle (Stockhammer 2004). This argument however omits the feedback effects driven by the productivity regime. Fast output growth may not entail fast employment growth, because of the rise in productivity growth generated by the Kaldor–Verdoorn effect, as explained in detail in Storm and Naastepad (2013).

15. Meta-analysis has shown that raising minimum wages do not lead to reduced employment, in contrast to what is asserted by mainstream authors on the basis of a partial equilibrium analysis. Doucouliagos and Stanley (2009) demonstrate that the minimum wage literature is contaminated by publication bias, and that the best studies support the claim that there is no negative relationship between minimum wages and employment.

References

Balcerowicz, L. and Fisher, S. (eds). 2006. *Living Standards and the Wealth of Nations: Successes and Failures in Real Convergence* (Cambridge, MA and London: MIT Press).

Baran, P. and Sweezy, P. 1966. *Monopoly Capital* (New York: Monthly Review Press).

Bhaduri, A. 1986. *Macroeconomics: The Dynamics of Commodity Production* (Armonk, NY: M.E. Sharpe).

Bhaduri, A. and Marglin, S., 1990. 'Unemployment and the real wage: the economic basis for contesting political ideologies', *Cambridge Journal of Economics*, vol. 14(4), pp. 375–93.

Bleaney, M. 1976. *Underconsumption Theories: A History and Critical Analysis* (New York: International Publishers).

Blecker, R., 1989. 'International competition, income distribution and economic growth', *Cambridge Journal of Economics*, vol. 13(3), pp. 395–412.

Blecker, R. 2002. 'Distribution, demand and growth in neo-Kaleckian macro-models', in M. Setterfield (ed.), *The Economics of Demand-led Growth: Challenging the Supply-side Vision of the Long Run* (Cheltenham: Edward Elgar), pp. 129–52.

Blecker, R. 2011. 'Open economy models of distribution and growth', in E. Hein and E. Stockhammer (eds), *A Modern Guide to Keynesian Macroeconomics and Economic Policies* (Cheltenham: Edward Elgar), pp. 215–39.

Bowles, S. and Boyer, R. 1995. 'Wages, aggregate demand, and employment in an open economy: an empirical investigation', in G. Epstein and H. Gintis (eds), *Macroeconomic Policy after the Conservative Era: Studies in Investment, Saving and Finance* (Cambridge: Cambridge University Press), pp. 143–71.

Boyer, R. 1988. 'Formalizing growth regimes', in G. Dosi, C. Freeman, R. Nelson, G. Silverberg and L. Soete (eds), *Technical Change and Economic Theory* (London and New York: Pinter Publishers), pp. 608–30.

Doucouliagos, H. and Stanley, T.D. 2009. 'Publication selection bias in minimum-wage research? A meta-regression analysis', *British Journal of Industrial Relations*, vol. 47(2), pp. 406–28.

Dray, M. and Thirlwall, A.P. 2011. 'The endogeneity of the natural rate of growth for a selection of Asian countries', *Journal of Post Keynesian Economics*, vol. 33(3), 451–68.

Dutt, A.K. 1987. 'Alternative closures again: a comment on "Growth, distribution and inflation"', *Cambridge Journal of Economics*, vol. 11(1), pp. 75–82.

Glyn, A. 2006. *Capitalism Unleashed: Finance, Globalization and Welfare* (Oxford: Oxford University Press).

Harvey, D. 2003. *A Short History of Neoliberalism* (Oxford: Oxford University Press).

Hein, E. and Mundt, M. 2013. 'Financialization, the financial and economic crisis, and the requirements and potentials for wage-led recovery' (chapter 6 in this volume), M. Lavoie and E. Stockhammer (eds), *Wage-Led Growth: An Equitable Strategy for Economic Recovery* (Basingstoke and Geneva: Palgrave Macmillan and ILO).

Hein, E. and Tarassow, A. 2010. 'Distribution, aggregate demand and productivity growth: theory and empirical results for six OECD countries based on a post-Kaleckian model', *Cambridge Journal of Economics*, vol. 34(4), pp. 727–54.

Hein, E. and Vogel, L. 2008. 'Distribution and growth reconsidered – empirical results for Austria, France, Germany, the Netherlands, the UK and the USA', *Cambridge Journal of Economics*, vol. 32(3), pp. 479–511.

Kaldor, N. 1957. 'A model of economic growth', *Economic Journal*, vol. 67(December), pp. 591–624.

Kalecki, M. 1971. *Selected Essays in the Dynamics of the Capitalist Economy* (Cambridge: Cambridge University Press).

Keynes, J.M. 1936. *The General Theory of Employment, Interest and Money* (London: Macmillan).

Krassoi Peach, E. and Stanley, T.D. 2009. 'Efficiency wages, productivity and simultaneity: A meta-regression analysis', *Journal of Labor Research*, vol. 30(3), pp. 262–8.

Kurz, H. 1990. 'Technical change, growth and distribution: A steady-state approach to unsteady growth', in H. Kurz (ed.), *Capital, Distribution and Effective Demand: Studies in the Classical Approach to Economic Theory* (Cambridge: Polity Press), pp. 210–39.

Lavoie, M. 1995. 'The Kaleckian model of growth and distribution and its neo-Ricardian and neo-Marxian critiques', *Cambridge Journal of Economics*, vol. 19(6), pp. 789–818.

Lavoie, M. 2003. 'Real wages and unemployment with effective and notional demand for labor', *Review of Radical Political Economics*, vol. 35(2), pp. 166–82.

Lavoie, M. 2007. 'Neoclassical empirical evidence on employment and production laws as artefact', *Rivista Economía Informa*, vol. 351(March–April), pp. 9–36.

Léon-Ledesma, M. and Thirwall, A.P. 2002. 'The endogeneity of the natural rate of growth', *Cambridge Journal of Economics*, vol. 26(4), pp. 533–52.

Marquetti, A. 2004. 'Do rising real wages increase the rate of labour-saving technical change? Some econometric evidence', *Metroeconomica*, vol. 55(4), pp. 432–41.

Marglin, S. and Bhaduri, A. 1990. 'Profit squeeze and Keynesian theory', in Marglin and Schor (1990), pp. 153–86.

Marglin, S. and Schor, J. (eds). 1990. *The Golden Age of Capitalism: Reinterpreting the Postwar Experience* (Oxford: Clarendon Press).

McCombie, J. 2002. 'Increasing returns and the Verdoorn law from a Kaldorian perspective', in J. McCombie, M. Pugno and B. Soro (eds), *Productivity Growth and Economic Performance: Essays on Verdoorn's Law* (Basingstoke: Palgrave Macmillan), pp. 64–114.

McCombie, J. and Thirwall, A.P. 1994. *Economic Growth and the Balance-of-Payments Constraint* (London: Macmillan).

Naastepad, C.W.M. 2006. 'Technology, demand and distribution: A cumulative growth model with an application to the Dutch productivity growth slowdown', *Cambridge Journal of Economics*, vol. 30(3), pp. 403–34.

Naastepad, C.W.M. and Storm, S. 2006–07. 'OECD demand regimes (1960–2000)', *Journal of Post Keynesian Economics*, vol. 29(2), pp. 213–48.

Naastepad, C.W.M. and Storm, S. 2010. 'Feasible egalitarianism: demand-led growth, labour and technology', in M. Setterfield (ed.), *Handbook of Alternative Theories of Economic Growth* (Cheltenham: Edward Elgar), pp. 311–30.

Onaran, Ö. and Galanis, G. 2013. 'Is aggregate demand wage-led or profit-led? A global model' (chapter 3 in current volume), M. Lavoie and E. Stockhammer (eds), *Wage-led Growth: An Equitable Strategy for Economic Recovery* (Basingstoke and Geneva: Palgrave Macmillan and ILO).

Rowthorn, R. 1981. 'Demand, real wages and economic growth', *Thames Papers in Political Economy*, Autumn, 1–39.

Setterfield, M. and Cornwall, J. 2002. 'A neo-Kaldorian perspective on the rise and decline of the Golden Age', in M. Setterfield (ed.), *The Economics of Demand-led Growth: Challenging the Supply-side Vision of the Long Run* (Cheltenham: Edward Elgar), pp. 67–86.

Steindl, J. 1952. *Maturity and Stagnation in American Capitalism* (Oxford: Basil Blackwell).

Stockhammer, E. 2004. 'Is there an equilibrium rate of unemployment in the long run?', *Review of Political Economy*, vol. 16(1), pp. 59–77.

Stockhammer, E. 2011. 'Wage norms, capital accumulation, and unemployment: a post-Keynesian view', *Oxford Review of Economic Policy*, vol. 27(2), pp. 295–311.

Stockhammer, E. 2013. 'Why have wage shares fallen? An analysis of the determinants of functional income distribution' (chapter 2 in this volume), M. Lavoie and E. Stockhammer (eds), *Wage-Led Growth: An Equitable Strategy for Economic Recovery* (Basingstoke and Geneva: Palgrave Macmillan and ILO).

Stockhammer, E. and Stehrer, R. 2011. 'Goodwin or Kalecki in demand? Functional income distribution and aggregate demand in the short run', *Review of Radical Political Economics*, vol. 43(4), pp. 506–22.

Storm, S. and Naastepad, C.W.M. 2008. 'The NAIRU reconsidered: why labour market deregulation may raise unemployment', *International Review of Applied Economics*, vol. 22(5), pp. 527–44.

Storm, S. and Naastepad, C.W.M. 2009. 'Labor market regulation and productivity growth: evidence for twenty OECD countries (1984–2004)', *Industrial Relations*, vol. 48(4), pp. 629–54.

Storm, S. and Naastepad, C.W.M. 2013. 'Wage-led or profit-led supply: wages, productivity and investment' (chapter 4 in this volume), M. Lavoie and E. Stockhammer (eds), *Wage-led Growth: An Equitable Strategy for Economic Recovery* (Basingstoke and Geneva: Palgrave Macmillan and ILO).

Taylor, L. 1983. *Structuralist Macroeconomics: Applicable Models for the Third World* (New York: Basic Books).

Taylor, L. 1988. *Varieties of Stabilization Experience* (Oxford: Clarendon Press).

Taylor, L. 1991. *Income Distribution, Inflation and Growth: Lectures on Structuralist Macroeconomic Theory* (Cambridge, MA: MIT Press).

United Nations Conference on Trade and Development (UNCTAD). 2010. *Trade and Development Report 2010: Employment, Globalization and Development* (Geneva: UNCTAD).

United Nations Conference on Trade and Development (UNCTAD). 2011. *Trade and Development Report 2011: Post-Crisis Policy Challenges in the World Economy* (Geneva: UNCTAD).

Vergeer, R. and Kleinknecht, A. 2010–11. 'The impact of labor market deregulation on productivity: a panel data analysis of 19 OECD countries (1960–2004)'. *Journal of Post Keynesian Economics* 33(2), 371–408.

Webb, S. 1912. 'The economic theory of a legal minimum wage'. *Journal of Political Economy* 20(December), 973–98.

2
Why Have Wage Shares Fallen? An Analysis of the Determinants of Functional Income Distribution*

Engelbert Stockhammer

2.1 Introduction

In the last quarter century dramatic changes in income distribution have taken place. This refers to the personal distribution of income as well as to the functional distribution of income. Distribution has become more polarized in most OECD countries (OECD 2008, 2011), with the very top income groups increasing their income shares substantially in the Anglo-Saxon countries, in particular in the United States (Atkinson et al. 2011). Wage shares have fallen in virtually all OECD countries, with decreases typically being more pronounced in continental European countries (and Japan) than in the Anglo-Saxon countries. In the advanced economies[1] the (adjusted) wage share has, on average, fallen from 73.4 in 1980 to 64.0 per cent in 2007 (Figure 2.1). The data for Germany are very similar (72.2 to 61.8); the decline is somewhat stronger in Japan (77.2 to 62.2) and a little weaker in the United States (70.0 to 64.9). Overall, real wage growth has clearly lagged behind productivity growth since around 1980. This constitutes a major historical change as wage shares had been stable or increasing in the post-war era.

* The author is grateful to Hubert Kohler for excellent research assistance and to Matthieu Charpe, Vince Daly, Marc Lavoie, Özlem Onaran, Simon Mohun and Antonella Stirati for helpful comments and suggestions. Earlier versions of this paper were presented at the Regulating for Decent Work conference, ILO, Geneva and at Kingston University. All mistakes are, however, the author's.

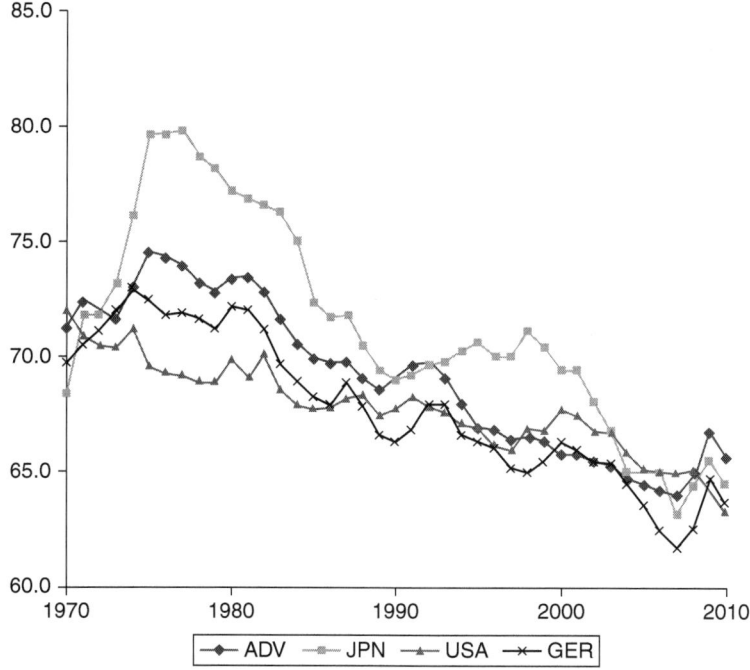

Figure 2.1   Adjusted wage shares in advanced countries, Germany, Japan and the United States, 1970–2010

Note: ADV stands for unweighted average of high income OECD countries (without the Republic of Korea).

Source: AMECO.

This shift in income distribution has taken somewhat different forms in different countries. In the Anglo-Saxon countries a sharp polarization of personal income distribution has occurred, combined with a modest decline in the wage share. In particular, top incomes (usually measured as the income share of the top 10 per cent, 5 per cent or 1 per cent of the income distribution) have increased their income share dramatically (Piketty and Saez 2003; OECD 2008; Atkinson et al. 2011). In the United States, for example, the top 1 per cent of the income distribution increased their share of national income by more than 10 percentage points. In continental European countries functional rather than personal income distribution has shifted dramatically. In the euro area, wage shares have decreased by around 10 percentage points of GDP (Stockhammer 2009), but personal income distribution has remained comparably stable and often has not changed in the same way as in the United States (OECD 2008, 2011). While these developments appear rather different at first sight, they share the common trend that the share of non-managerial wage earners in national income has decreased sharply. The increase in inequality in the United States is, to a significant extent, driven by changes in the remuneration of top managers, whose salaries and bonuses are counted as labour compensation, that is, wages, in the National Accounts.[2] If they were counted as part of profits, trends in the United States and in continental Europe would look rather similar.

Data on the functional income distribution are not readily available for developing economies[3] and, where available, they are typically less reliable. Figure 2.2 gives summary measures of the adjusted wage share for the groups of developing countries where comparatively long series are

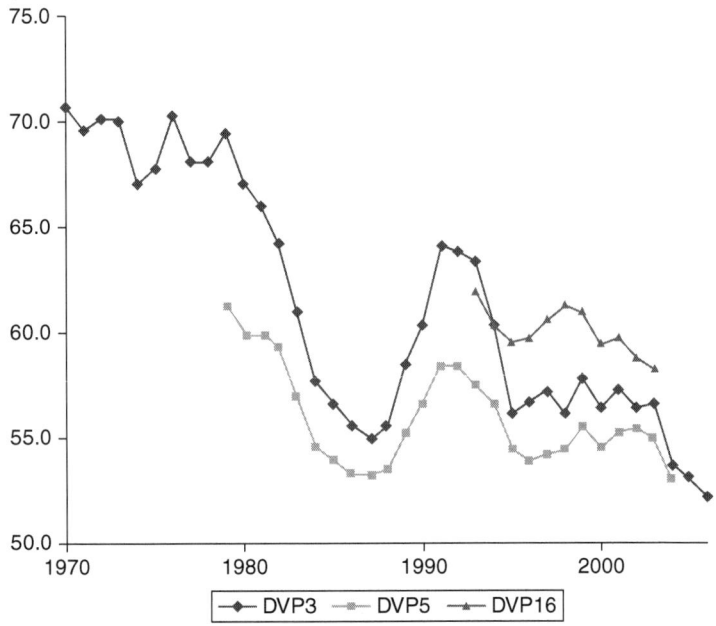

Figure 2.2   Adjusted wage share in developing countries

Note: DVP3: unweighted average of Mexico, the Republic of Korea and Turkey; DVP5: unweighted average of China, Kenya, the Republic of Korea, Mexico and Turkey; DVP16: unweighted average of Argentina, Brazil, Chile, China, Costa Rica, Kenya, the Republic of Korea, Mexico, Namibia, Oman, Panama, Peru, Russian Federation, South Africa, Thailand and Turkey.

Source: Data sources are discussed in section 2.4 and Table A.1.

available. DVP3 summarizes the data for three countries where data are available since 1970; DVP5 for five countries where data are available from 1979; and DVP16 for a group of 16 developing countries, where data are available from 1993. They all show a pronounced decline in (adjusted) wage shares since 1990. While there is more variation in terms of the development of the wage share in developing economies than in advanced economies,[4] it is clear that, on average, there has been a pronounced decline in the wage share in developing and emerging economies, at least since 1990.

For developing countries as well, this decline in the wage share is part of a broader trend in income distribution where social inequalities have increased. Goldberg and Pavcnik (2007) conclude a comprehensive survey of inequality in developing countries: 'In summary, the evolution of various measures of inequality suggests that most of the developing countries experienced an increase in inequality during the past two decades' (Goldberg and Pavcnik 2007, 54: see also OECD 2011, chapter 2).

This has led, in the past few years, to a renewed interest in the determinants of the distribution of income, with main international institutions such as the OECD, the International Monetary Fund (IMF) and the ILO publishing studies on these issues. Most work has been on changes in income distribution in advanced economies. OECD (2008) documents changes in personal income distribution. IMF (2007a) and the European Commission (EC) (2007) deal with changes in functional income distribution. The main findings of IMF (2007a) and EC (2007) are that technological change has been the main cause of changes in functional income distribution, that globalization (of trade and production) has also played an important role and, finally, that changes in labour market institutions have played a minor role. There is comparatively less research on developing and emerging economies. Jayadev (2007) and ILO (2011) investigate the determinants of functional income distribution in advanced as well as developing economies.

This study will investigate the determinants of functional income distribution in a broad sample of countries that includes both advanced and developing economies, based on an ILO/International Institute of Labour Studies (IILS) dataset. We will seek to identify the contribution of technological change, globalization, financial globalization and welfare state retrenchment. This is done with an (unbalanced) panel analysis covering up to 71 countries (28 advanced and 43 developing and emerging economies) from 1970 to 2007.

The chapter is structured as follows. Section 2.2 presents the key arguments that have been identified in the literature as potential determinants of functional income distribution. Section 2.3 offers a review of the recent empirical literature on the issue (using panel analysis). Section 2.4 discusses data issues. Section 2.5 presents the empirical results for the full group of countries. Section 2.6 presents results for OECD economies using a richer set of variables. Section 2.7 concludes.

2.2   Determinants of functional income distribution: key arguments in the recent debate

In recent years the issue of increasing inequality has received a lot of attention, albeit unevenly. The larger part of the literature has been concerned with changes in *personal* income distribution. There have been debates on the development of earnings inequality and, in particular, of the skill premium and of top incomes. *Functional* income distribution has received comparably less attention. However, very recently there have been several attempts to study the determinants of functional income distribution for advanced economies, but there are only a few studies on functional income distribution in developing economies. The studies that investigate functional income distribution, taking into account variations across countries and over time, will be subject of the next section. This section will, more broadly, provide the theoretical background for the empirical analysis by summarizing the key arguments in the debate on income distribution, highlighting skill-biased technological change, globalization, financialization and welfare state retrenchment.

2.2.1   Technological change

In a world of complete markets, perfect competition, full employment and well-behaved aggregate production functions, income shares are determined by technology. This is the core of the neoclassical theory of income distribution. However, none of these assumptions is likely to hold in the real world. Nonetheless, the basic neoclassical argument still carries a lot of weight in the present debate and many economists think of income distribution to be determined primarily by changes in technology. The presently popular incarnation of this argument is that since the early 1980s technological change has been skill biased. New capital goods, in particular those related to information and communication technology (ICT), are complementary to skilled labour and substitute unskilled labour. Thus, there has been a shift in income distribution towards skilled labour. This hypothesis has motivated a substantial number of empirical studies, in particular for the United States, where it was used to explain the sharp increase in personal income inequality (Autor et al. 1999; Card and Di Nardo 2002).

Technological change is also used to explain changes in functional income distribution. According to this theory, technological change has become capital augmenting rather than labour augmenting (which it used to be in the post-war era). Consequently, there has been a fall in wage shares (IMF 2007a; EC 2007). As the use of ICT capital increased, the demand for high-skilled labour increased and that of low-skilled labour decreased, which came with rising wages for high-skilled workers and falling wages for low-skilled workers. It so happens that the overall wage share is falling.

The literature often reports strong effects of technological change on income distribution in advanced economies. For example, IMF (2007a) finds that technological change has been the most important cause for the decline in wage shares. EC (2007) concludes that 'for the period for which the data is available (i.e. from the mid-1980s to early 2000s), the estimation results clearly indicate that technological progress made the largest contribution to the fall in the aggregate labour income share' (EC 2007, 260).

2.2.2. Globalization

The role of globalization features prominently in political debates as well as in economic analysis. There are two approaches in the literature, both of which come with many variations. Classical trade theory is built on the Stolper and Samuelson (1941) theorem, which states that the abundant factor will gain from international trade. For advanced countries this is capital whereas labour is abundant in developing countries. Globalization is thus supposed to benefit capital in the advanced and labour in the developing economies. In contrast to the Stolper–Samuelson theorem, the Political Economy approach to international trade highlights the changes in the bargaining position of labour and capital due to their relative mobility. According to this approach, labour can lose in the North as well as in the South.

The Stolper–Samuelson theorem assumes full employment and that neither capital nor labour is mobile. However, the recent period of globalization has been marked by an increase in capital mobility. But 'if capital can travel across borders, the implications of the theorem weaken substantially' (EC 2007, 45). It is therefore unclear whether the Stolper–Samuleson approach is a good guide to the present experience of globalization. Moreover, there are well-known problems of classical trade theory. On the theoretical level it does not allow for unemployment, which is at odds with popular perceptions of jobs being exported abroad. On the empirical level, the theory is unable to explain the actual pattern of international trade, which takes place mostly among developed countries rather than between rich and poor countries (as the theory would predict).

Despite these limitations the Stolper–Samuelson theorem has a firm place in the mainstream economics canon and it is widely used to argue that globalization will hurt workers in the developed economies and benefit workers in developing economies. While this may have become folk wisdom among economists, there is scant evidence to support it. While workers in the North have been hurt, it is doubtful whether workers in the South have benefited. There is limited research on the effect of globalization on functional income distribution in the South, but there is a substantial body of evidence that inequality has increased in developing economies as a result of globalization. 'Distributional changes went in the opposite direction from the one suggested by conventional wisdom: while globalization was expected to help the less skilled who are presumed to be the locally relatively abundant factor in developing countries, there is overwhelming evidence that these are generally not better off, at least not relative to workers with higher skill or education levels' (Goldberg and Pavcnik 2007, 54).

An important area of research has been to introduce heterogenous labour into trade models. These models use labour with different skill levels and allow for intermediate goods. While unskilled labour (in the North) may lose from globalization, skilled labour may indeed gain. The jobs relocated from advanced to developing countries via outsourcing and imports of intermediate goods will typically have a negative effect on unskilled labour in advanced economies. However, given the lower general education in developing economies, the relocated jobs may have positive effects on skilled labour in the developing country (Feenstra and Hanson 1997, 1999). These types of models are designed to analyse the effect of outsourcing on different groups of labour, but the effect on the total wage share is less clear.

The Political Economy of Trade approach argues that the main effect of trade on income distribution is not via relative prices, but through h its effect on the bargaining position of labour and capital (Rodrik 1997; Onaran 2011). In contrast to classical trade theory, even trade among similar countries may affect income distribution. Rodrik (1997) argues that trade liberalization benefits the more mobile factor, which will typically be capital. Unlike the Stolper–Samuelson approach, Rodrik's argument is set in a bargaining framework. The change in distribution takes place because of a redistribution of rents, not because of the equalization of factor costs. Moreover, in the Stolper–Samuelson theorem one would expect distribution to change *after* production has been relocated. Epstein and Burke (2001), based on a bargaining model, argue that due to threat effects redistribution can take place without changes in production locations.

Basically, all studies find substantial effects of globalization on functional income distribution in developed economies. For example, the IMF (2007a) concludes 'globalization is one of several factors that have acted to reduce the share of income accruing to labor in advanced economies' (IMF 2007a, 161). For a pool of developed and developing economies, Harrison (2002), Rodrik (1998) and Jayadev (2007) find that increased trade has a negative effect on the wage share.

2.2.3 Financialization

An increased role of financial activity and the rising prominence of financial institutions have been hallmarks of the transformations of economy and society since the mid-1970s. These changes are often referred to as financialization and include the rising indebtedness of households, more volatile exchange rates and asset prices, short-termism of financial institutions, and shareholder value orientation of non-financial businesses (Erturk et al. 2008; Stockhammer 2010). Financialization has had two important effects on the bargaining position of labour.[5] First, firms have gained more options for investing: they can invest in financial assets as well as in real assets and they can invest at home as well as abroad. They have gained mobility in terms of the geographical location as well as in terms of the content of investment. Second, it has empowered shareholders relative to workers by putting additional constraints on firms and the development of a market for corporate control has aligned management's interest to that of shareholders (Lazonick and O'Sullivan 2000; Stockhammer 2004). Rossmann (2009) illustrates this with reference to private equity funds, which buy firms by way of debt that is transferred to the firm. The surplus is syphoned off to the private equity fund through dividend payments or fees. The restructured firms then are heavily burdened with servicing their debt and have little alternative to pursuing an aggressive cost-cutting strategy.

The rise of financial incomes is well documented in the literature, despite the uneven availability of data. Dividend payouts and interest payments by non-financial firms has increased sharply (Duménil and Lévy 2001, 2004; Hein and Schoder 2011; Onaran et al. 2011). In addition, capital gains have, for some periods, increased dramatically (Power et al. 2003). The ILO (2008, 39) thus argues that 'financial globalization has led to a depression of the share of wages in GDP'. But so far econometric evidence of the effects of financialization on wage shares is mostly limited to country studies and some dimensions of financialization. For example Hein and Schoder (2011) present evidence of Germany and the United States; Argitis and Pitelis (2001) for the United Kingdom and the United States.

Econometric studies on changes in functional income distribution in OECD countries have not included financialization variables. Studies on both developed as well as developing countries have included variables of financial globalization. Rodrik (1998) and Harrison (2002) have included measures of capital controls and capital mobility. Onaran (2009) has included FDI inflows in a time series analysis on three emerging economies and found negative effects in several specifications. Jayadev (2007) and the ILO (2011) include dummy variables for exchange rate crises.

2.2.4 Welfare state retrenchment and the bargaining power of labour

Once one abandons the assumption of perfect competition income distribution becomes the outcome of a bargaining process between firms and labour, typically represented by labour unions. A higher bargaining power of workers will lead to an increase in wages and, if labour demand is inelastic, to an increase in the wage share. The bargaining power of workers and firms, however, is difficult to measure. The bargaining power of labour is usually conceived as determined by the generosity of the welfare state and the organizational strength of labour unions. Indeed much of the literature, which is inspired by neoclassical theory, equates welfare state generosity with the bargaining power of labour. From a political economy point of view that is too narrow, as financialization and globalization also affect the bargaining power of capital and labour. However, this is a disagreement in conceptualization, but there is agreement that the size, structure and generosity of welfare states affect the bargaining power of labour. While there is some debate in political science about the extent of welfare state retrenchment (Pierson 1994; Korpi and Palme 2003), there can be little doubt that a reduction in welfare state generosity has occurred since 1980.

For OECD countries recent empirical research tends to identify the bargaining power with labour market institutions (LMI). The background for these variables is a long debate about the determinants of unemployment that has led to the development of databases for LMI that have then also been used in the analysis of income distribution. Conceptually, these variables are designed to measure labour market inflexibility rather than genuine bargaining power. The IMF (2007a) and the European Commission (2007) include union density, employment protection legislation, unemployment benefit generosity and the tax wedge as wage-push variables that may also affect income distribution. Bentolila and Saint-Paul (2003) include (only) a variable measuring strike activity. The

European Commission (2007) and IMF (2007a) find surprisingly small, if any, effects of union density. The IMF (2007a) includes union density and the tax wedge after having found no effect of other LMI variables.[6] For developing economies, little comparative work exists on welfare state structures. Harrison (2002) and Jayadev (2007) include the government share in GDP.

2.2.5 A missing factor: bargaining power and market power of firms

The bargaining power, or, more narrowly, the market power of firms is a curiously underresearched topic. Globalization ought to have decreased the market power by means of the entrance of new competitors. At the same time it has increased the bargaining power of firms vis-à-vis labour (as discussed above). Things are further complicated by the fact that globalization is not a change that comes exogenously upon firms, but transnational corporations have been a driving force of globalization by establishing international production networks (or value chains). However important the issue may be, there exist practically no data that would allow the integration of firms' bargaining power in a panel setting. This is a serious omission in the literature (and in the present study).

Two studies have tried to analyse some of the dimensions of the power of firms. In a sectoral analysis Azmat, Manning and van Reenen (2007) analyse the bargaining power of firms in network industries. Hutchinson and Persyn (2009) use a Lerner index to measure concentration of firms on a sectoral basis and find that the concentration has an effect on income distribution.

2.2.6 Conclusion: a simple distribution equation

We estimate a *wage share equation* that includes variables for technological change (*tech*), globalization (*glob*), financialization (*fin*) and welfare state retrenchment (*wfst*):

$$WS = f(tech, glob, fin, wfst) \qquad (1.1)$$

Figure 2.3 illustrates the structure of the argument. The circles for technological change, globalization and financialization overlap. This reflects the difficulties in making an empirical distinction between these phenomena. These problems are in part for conceptual reasons; in part they are due to the empirical proxies, but in many cases the distinction is difficult even at the theoretical level. For example without the development of modern communication technologies international production networks would not be feasible. Merger and acquisition activities by foreign firms illustrate the problems of delineating globalization in production and financial globalization.

Figure 2.3 also highlights that the notion of the bargaining power of labour cuts across several of our categories. Changes related to financialization and to globalization are usually interpreted (by economists in the neoclassical tradition) as changes in relative price, but can also be interpreted as affecting the bargaining position between capital and labour. While it will be useful to keep these problems of identification in mind when interpreting empirical results, the exact delineation of what affects the bargaining power of labour is not important for our results as we will group variables into the categories technological change, financialization, globalization and welfare state retrenchment.

It is difficult to fill these conceptual categories with empirical data. In doing so one has to tread a fine balance between using the best

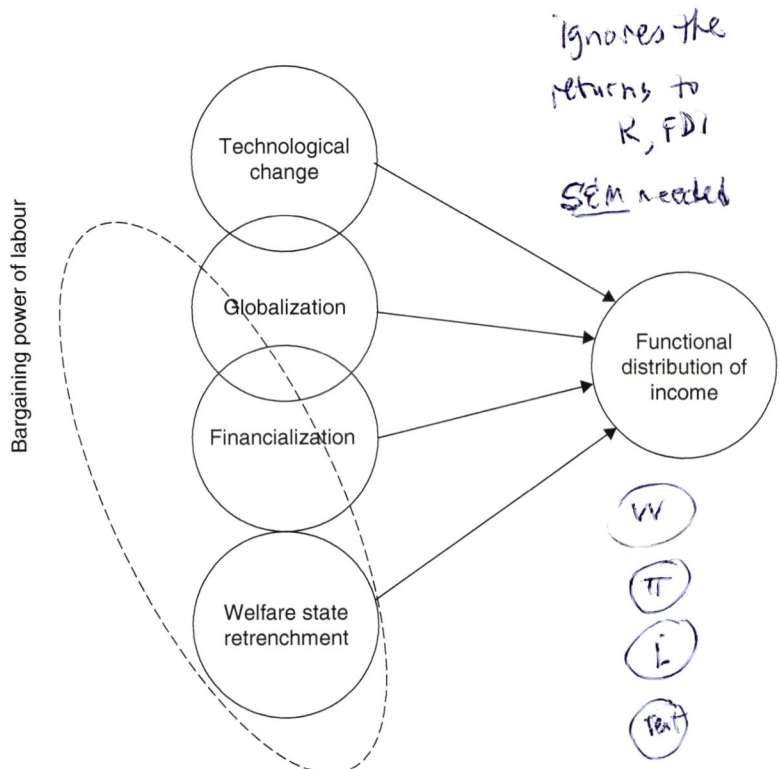

Figure 2.3   Key determinants of functional income distribution

variables available and keeping sample size as large as possible. Table 2.1 summarizes the variables that we will use as proxies for technological change, financialization, globalization and welfare state retrenchment in the baseline specification. Technological change will be proxied by GDP per worker in the pool of developing and advanced economies. For advanced economies we use the capital–labour ratio and ICT services. For the sample of developing and advanced economies we will additionally use the agricultural share and the industrial share as proxies for structural change and subsume that under technological change.

Table 2.1 Results for the baseline specification and variations

	1	2	4	5
GROWTH	–11.936	–11.97	–11.193	–11.603
t–value	–4.167***	–4.172***	–3.774***	–3.872***
LOG(FINGLOB)	–3.659	–3.677	–3.046	–3.556
t–value	–6.997***	–6.932***	–5.141***	–7.017***
OPEN	–3.811	–4.02	–6.225	–3.561
t–value	–3.211***	–2.540**	–4.436***	–2.869***
LOG(GDPPW)	–0.658	–0.667	–2.364	–4.098
t–value	–0.321	–0.325	–1.138	–1.786*
CG	0.801	0.801	0.392	0.954
t–value	3.975***	3.972***	2.052**	4.210***
AG	–0.235	–0.236	–0.139	–0.342
t–value	–2.719***	–2.721***	–1.338	–3.700***
IND	–0.159	–0.158	–0.261	–0.183
t–value	–2.457**	–2.457**	–3.697***	–2.731***
open*d_highin		0.513		
t–value		0.248		
tot			–4.22	
t–value			–3.253***	
unempl				–0.315
t–value				–4.743***
obs	1450	1450	1310	1302
adj r2	0.981	0.981	0.982	0.975
dw	1.719	1.719	1.675	1.741

Note: ***, **, and * denote statistical significance at the 1%, 5% and 10% level respectively.

As proxies for globalization we use trade openness and, in the sample for advanced economies, additionally the terms of trade. For financialization we will use financial globalization. As proxies for the welfare state we use the government consumption and, in the sample for advanced economies, additionally union density. The government consumption share, of course, is not a perfect proxy. There may be government consumption expenditures that are unrelated to the welfare state, but we hypothesize that, in general, there will be positive correlation between the size and generosity of the welfare state and government consumption. We regard the existence of trade unions (and collective bargaining arrangements) as part of the welfare state.

2.3   The recent empirical (panel) literature on the determinants of functional income distribution

There is a sizable, but uneven empirical literature on the determinants of change in functional income distribution. While income distribution has been a rather neglected research area by mainstream economic policy institutions, from 2007 onwards several high-profile studies have appeared, for example IMF (2007a, 2007b) in the *World Economic Outlook*, EC (2007) in *Employment in Europe* and in ILO's (2011) *World of Work Report*; the OECD has published related studies on the effects of globalization (OECD 2007) and on personal income distribution (OECD 2008, 2011). There is a natural grouping into studies that investigate advanced economies only and those that investigate panel with developing as well as advanced economies as the data availability differs. Several important variables are not available for developing economies. Among the larger number of studies that investigate advanced economies IMF (2007a) and EC (2007) are the most prominent representations of the mainstream view. They both perform a panel analysis for OECD countries and explain the wage share in a framework that allows to distinguish between effects from technological change, globalization and labour market institutions/bargaining power. IMF (2007a) finds that 'globalization is one of several factors that have acted to reduce the share of income accruing to labour in advanced economies, although rapid technological change has had a bigger impact' (IMF 2007a, 161). The findings of EC (2007) are similar. Curiously, EC (2007) finds that ICT services, the preferred variable of technological change in IMF (2007a), has no statistically significant effect. In addition, both report that the technology variables are not robust to the inclusion of time effects. Financialization is not considered as a possible explanatory factor in these studies. Stockhammer (2009) tries to replicate IMF (2007a) and EC (2007) and finds that their results, in particular regarding the role of technology are not robust. Globalization (in production), however, has a robust effect. He also reports strong distributional effects of financial globalization and of union density.

Harrison (2002), Jayadev (2007) and the ILO (2011) analyse the determinants of functional income distribution on developed as well as developing countries. The studies on panels with developing as well as advanced economies differ not only due to reasons of data availability, but also with respect to their theoretical approach. They tend to employ a Political Economy approach that highlights bargaining effects of globalization and financialization. Jayadev (2007) analyses the effect of financial openness and trade openness on the wage share in an econometric analysis covering up to 80 countries for the period 1970–2001. They do find negative effects of openness (even for developing economies) and of financialization. ILO (2011) takes a similar approach and highlights that financialization and trade openness has reduced the bargaining power of labour and that collective bargaining arrangements and well-designed minimum wages could have positive effects on the wage share.

There are two interesting studies that demonstrate a link between personal and functional income distribution. Daudey and Garcia-Peñalosa (2007) show that there is a correlation between changes in personal and functional income distribution. They estimate the Gini coefficient of a large group of countries as a function of the wage share and of various other control variables. Wolff and Zacharias (2007) use data on distribution of income and wealth across US households. They decompose the change in the Gini coefficient (of household income distribution) according to class, education and ethnicity and find that 'the entire increase in inequality between 1989 and 2000 is attributable to the increase in inter-class inequality' (Wolff and Zacharias 2007, 24).

There is a potential confusion around the Stolper–Samuelson theorem. Economists, being trained in deductive reasoning, have strong theoretical beliefs and most of them are only working on advanced economies. The finding that for advanced economies there is a negative effect of globalization on the wage share is then easily read as support for the Stolper–Samuelson theorem. On the other hand, the panel analyses including developing and advanced countries almost unanimously find that globalization has reduced wage shares in the developing as well as in advanced economies. This is supported by a broader literature on personal income distribution in developing economies that concludes that globalization has hurt workers. As the Stolper–Samuelson theorem predicts that globalization benefits workers in developing (labour-abundant) countries and hurts workers in advanced (capital-abundant) countries, we conclude that the available evidence rejects the empirical relevance of the theorem.

2.4   Variable definitions, data sources and econometric methodology

This section first gives variable definitions and data sources. Second, it indicates the development of key variables. Third, it discusses times series properties and clarifies the econometric methods employed.

Our dependent variable is the private, adjusted wage share (WSAP). The wage share is the share of wages in national income. Two adjustments are made to the wage share. First, there is an adjustment that imputes wage payments for self-employed workers. This is particularly important for developing countries where a large part of the population is self-employed. The adjusted wage share imputes wage payments for the self-employed to avoid counting all their income as profit income (Krueger 1999; Gollin 2002). This adjustment is standard in the literature and we directly use adjusted data from ILO/IILS and other sources.

The second adjustment transforms the wage share for the total economy into the private wage share. This is because our measure for the welfare state will be the size of government consumption. However, the wage share in government consumption is 100 per cent as the public sector does not generate profits. Government consumption is thus by definition related to the wage share and would lead to endogeneity problems in the regression analysis.

The wage share of the total economy is the sum of the private wage share (WSP) and the government wage share (WSG) weighted by their respective sizes. We use government consumption (CG) as a percentage of GDP as a measure for the size of the government sector:

$$WS = (1 - CG)*WS^P + CG*WS^G$$

As the wage share in the government sector is equal to 1, we can reconstruct the private wage share as

$$WS^P = (WS - CG)/(1 - CG)$$

We employ several sources for the adjusted wage share (WSA). Our primary source is the ILO/IILS database (compiled by Matthieu Charpe). As the

AMECO database, the OECD, and some national statistics provide longer series for certain countries we complement the ILO/IILS series with data from these alternative sources. For the EU-15 member states and Australia, Canada, Japan and the United States we use series from the AMECO database. For the Republic of Korea, Mexico and Turkey we employ data from the OECD. For China we use a national series.

The following variables are used in the baseline specification for developing and advanced economies: Growth (GROWTH) is real GDP growth (in national currency) taken from the World Bank World Development Indicators (WDI). Financial globalization (FINGLOB) is the logarithm of external assets plus external liabilities divided by GDP, taken from Lane and Milesi-Ferretti (2007). Trade openness (OPEN) is measured as exports plus imports divided by GDP, taken from the World Bank WDI. Government consumption as a percentage of GDP (CG) is taken from the Penn World Tables. The logarithm of the purchasing power parity (PPP) converted GDP per worker at constant prices (GDPPW), taken from the Penn World Tables, is used as a measure of technological change. Structural change in developing countries is operationalized with the variables for agricultural share (AG), that is the value added by forestry, hunting, fishing, the cultivation of crops, and livestock production as a percentage of GDP, and industry share (IND), which stands for value added in mining, manufacturing, construction, electricity, water and gas as a percentage of GDP. AG and IND are taken from the World Bank WDI dataset.

For the baseline variables we get an unbalanced panel that includes up to 71 countries for a maximum period of 1970 to 2007. However, for most developing countries the series are much shorter than that.

For advanced economies data are more reliable and in some areas more data are available: The impact of technological change on the wage share in advanced economies is measured by the capital–labour ratio (KL_KLEMS), which is the logarithm of capital services divided by the number of persons engaged, and ICT services (ICT_KLEMS), which is the logarithm of ICT capital services divided by gross value added. Both variables are from the EU KLEMS dataset. Union density (UNION) is from Bassanini and Duval (2006) and has been chained with data from the BGHS dataset prior to 1982. The sample covers 16 countries with data usually available for the period from 1970 to 2003.

Figure 2.4 gives an overview of the development of the key explanatory variables for developing countries. The figures report averages of an unbalanced panel. The development of any variable depicted is thus not only influenced by the development within a group of countries, but also by data availability. The broad trends are clear enough.

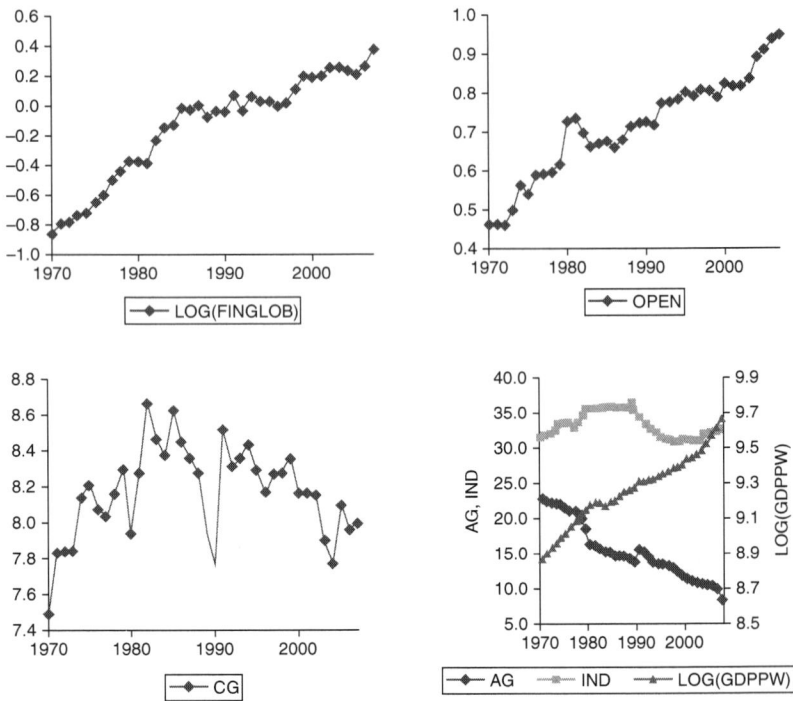

Figure 2.4　Baseline explanatory variables for developing countries
Source: See text and Table A.1.

Financialization has a clear and strong upward trend, as does globalization. Our variable for welfare state retrenchment suggests a hump-shaped development over time: government expenditures as a percentage of GDP peaked in the early 1980s and have had a declining trend thereafter. Among the variables of technological and structural change GDP per worker shows a clear upward trend and the agricultural share shows a downward trend. The industrial share has a modest upward trend until the late 1980s and declines thereafter, but seems to stabilize in the mid-1990s.

Figure 2.5 summarizes the development of key explanatory variables for advanced economies. Financialization has a steady upward trend. Financialization seems to have been substantially stronger in advanced than in developing economies. Among the globalization variables trade openness has a stable upward trend, whereas the terms of trade declined from the early 1970s to the mid-1980s and stabilize thereafter.

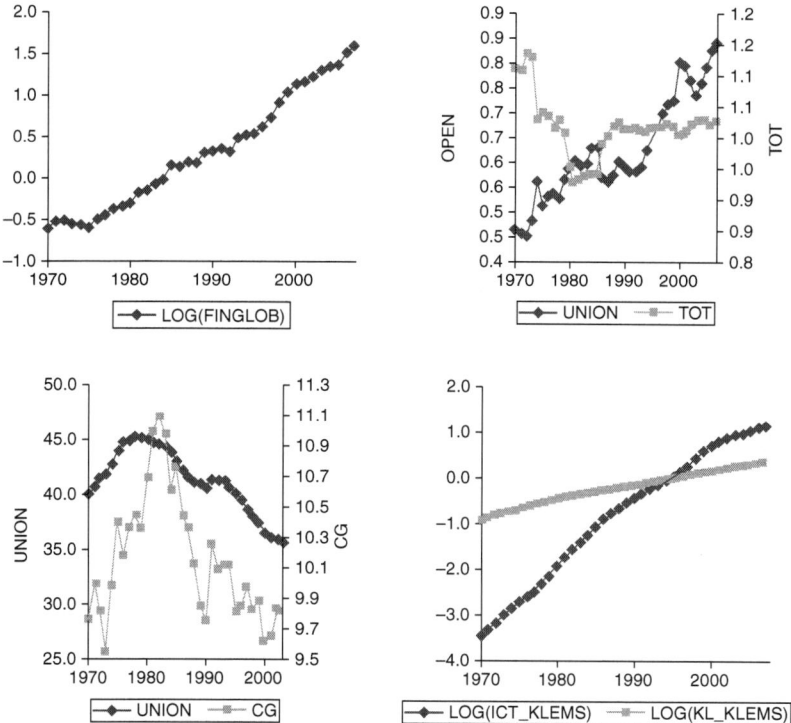

Figure 2.5 Baseline explanatory variables for advanced countries
Source: See text and Table A.1.

The welfare state variables show a structurally similar picture. Both are hump-shaped, indicating an increase until the late 1970s/early 1980s and a decline thereafter. Union density reaches its peak in the mid-1970s and declines below the initial levels; government consumption reaches its peak in the early 1980s. Both measures of technological change show a steady upward trend with ICT services experiencing a steeper rise than the capital–labour ratio.

Given the number of variables that we wish to investigate and the fact that for many developing economies we have short samples, panel analysis is used in the econometric analysis. The coefficient estimates have to be interpreted as average effects across a group of possibly heterogeneous countries as the pooling restriction (that is, the assumption of identical coefficients across countries) is likely to hold only as an approximation in our sample. We use cross-section fixed effects, and autocorrelation correction and heteroscedasticity-consistent standard errors. This is also called the Parks estimator (Beck and Katz 1995; Wooldridge 2002). Stockhammer (2013) also reports results for other estimation techniques.

2.5   Results for developing and advanced countries

This section reports results for a broad sample of advanced and developing economies (we will refer to this sample as 'all countries'). The sample contains an unbalanced panel with up to 71 countries, of which 28 are OECD high-income economies. We first present the baseline specification and then calculate the contributions of financialization, globalization, welfare state retrenchment and technological change to changes in the wage share. Stockhammer (2013) presents further econometric results.

The baseline specification for the sample with all countries is:

WSAP = f(GROWTH, FINGLOB, OPEN, CG, Gdppw, AG, IND)

Where WSAP is the adjusted private wage share, GROWTH the real GDP growth, FINGLOB (the logarithm of) financial globalization, OPEN trade openness, CG government consumption, GDPpw (the logarithm of) GDP per worker, AG the agricultural share, IND the industrial share.

For the calculation of medium-run contributions to changes in income distribution this set of variables will be grouped as follows: FINGLOB will measure the effect of financialization, OPEN will measure the effect of globalization, CG will measure the effect of welfare state retrenchment, GDPpw, AG and IND will measure technological and structural change.

This baseline specification is the result of pre-testing and includes variables that have proven robust. In choosing this set of variables we have tried to maintain a balance between a large sample and including robust variables. Including additional variables typically implies losing some observations due to missing data.

Table 2.2 presents our baseline specification and some extensions. Specification 1 is the baseline specification. For our baseline variables the results are very similar in the different specifications. FINGLOB consistently has a statistically significant negative effect (at the 1 per cent level) in all specifications (except specification 9). OPEN has a statistically significant negative effect in all specifications (at the 1 per cent or the 5 per cent level). CG has a positive effect (at the 5 per cent level) in all specifications except for specifications 6 and 7. GDPpw only has a statistically significant negative effect (at the 10 per cent level) in specification 5. AG has a statistically significant negative effect (at the 1 per cent level) in all specifications except specification 4. IND has a statistically significant negative effect (at the 1 per cent or 5 per cent level) in all specifications. This is probably due to the fact that manufacturing sectors have a high capital intensity and thus require higher profit shares to maintain their capital stock.

Table 2.2 Results for the baseline specification – advanced countries

	1	2
GROWTH	−16.434	−16.27
t-value	−5.212***	−5.371***
LOG(FINGLOB)	−2.418	−2.14
t-value	−3.370***	−3.077***
OPEN	−5.888	−6.566
t-value	−3.206***	−3.569***
tot	−4.546	−4.662
t-value	−2.570**	−2.687***
CG	0.929	1.255
t-value	3.836***	5.241***
UNION	0.099	0.135
t-value	1.782*	2.502**
LOG(KL_KLEMS)	−7.034	−0.162
t-value	−1.821*	−0.039
LOG(ICT_KLEMS)	1.436	0.141
t-value	1.635	0.151
unempl		−0.322
t-value		−4.282***
obs	470	470
adj r2	0.94	0.944
dw	1.814	1.884

Note: ***, **, and * denote statistical significance at the 1%, 5% and 10% level respectively.

GROWTH has a statistically significant negative effect in all specifications. This is the case in practically all specifications to be presented later. Presumably, this reflects the fact that, in the short run, prices are more flexible than wages. GROWTH is included in all specifications as a short-run variable. As the study is interested in medium-term developments and for our time period growth performance has been rather stable, we will not discuss this variable further.

Specification 2 interacts the OPEN with a dummy variable for high-income countries. This is to test whether globalization has a different effect in advanced and in developing economies as the Stolper–Samuelson theorem would imply. We find no statistically significant effect. Stockhammer (2013) reports extensive robustness tests.

To illustrate the relative size of effects implied in our estimation results, Figure 2.6 presents the contributions of financialization, globalization, welfare state retrenchment and technological change to changes in wage shares in the period 1990/94–2000/04. The impact of financialization is proxied by FINGLOB, globalization by OPEN, welfare state by CG and technological and structural change by GDPPW, AG and IND. The contribution of GROWTH, which was included as a short-term variable, is approximately zero and is therefore omitted in the presentation. The contributions of different factors are calculated as the coefficient estimate multiplied by the change in respective under-

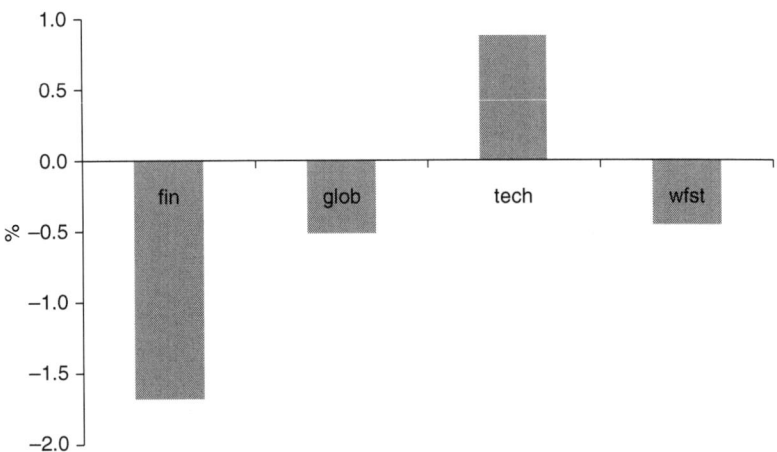

Figure 2.6 Contributions to the change in the wage share for all countries, 1990/94 to 2000/04

lying variable. These calculations are carried out for a hypothetical average country, that is, they are based on the mean of the respective variables across countries. This shows that in this decade financialization has had the largest impact on the adjusted, private wage share, explaining about 1.5 percentage points (Figure 2.6). Globalization and welfare state retrenchment have each contributed about a half percentage point reduction in the wage share. Technological change, broadly defined to include structural change, has had a positive contribution to the wage share of about three-quarters of a percentage point. The picture looks very similar when looking only at developing countries.

2.6   Results for advanced economies

The baseline specification for the sample of advanced countries is:

WSAP = f(GROWTH, FINGLOB, OPEN, TOT, CG, UNION, KL, ICT)

Where WSAP is the adjusted private wage share, growth the real GDP growth, FINGLOB (the logarithm of) financial globalization, OPEN trade openness, TOT the terms of trade, CG government consumption, UNION the union density, KL (the logarithm of) the capital–labour ratio and ICT (the logarithm of) ICT services. Variables definitions and sources are discussed in section 2.4.

For the calculation of medium-run contributions to changes in income distribution this set of variables will be grouped as follows: FINGLOB will measure the effect of financialization, OPEN and TOT will measure the effect of globalization, CG and UNION will measure the effect of welfare state retrenchment, KL and ICT will measure technological change. Note that for the country group of advanced economies we use a narrow concept of technological change, which does not include structural change.

The baseline specification will include union density as a proxy for the bargaining power of labour and the (logarithm of the) capital–labour ratio and the (logarithm of) ICT services as a percentage of GDP. Table 2.2 presents the results for the baseline specification with four estimation methods. Further results below will only be reported for the fixed effects estimator. The four estimation methods give a very similar picture for the statistically significant coefficients, however, not all relevant variables are statistically significant in all specifications. FINGLOB has a negative effect that is statistically significant at the 1 per cent level, OPEN has a negative effect that is statistically significant at the 5 per cent level and TOT has a negative effect that is statistically significant

at the 5 per cent level. CG has a positive effect (statistically significant
at the 1 per cent level), UNION has a positive effect that is statistically
significant at the 10 per cent level. KL has anegative effect (statistically
significant at the 10 per cent level) and ICT has no statistically significant effect. Table 2.2 also reports results for a specification that includes
the unemployment rate. UNEMPL has a statistically significant negative
effect, but the pattern for other variables is not affected. We will follow standard practise and not include unemployment in our baseline
because including it might give rise to endogeneity problems. However,
we note that the coefficient is quite large and unemployment seems to
have strong negative effects on the wage share.

GROWTH has a statistically significant negative effect. Wage shares
behave in a counter-cyclical manner over the business cycle. As the
study is interested in medium-term changes in the wage share, we will
not discuss the effect of GROWTH further.

Figure 2.7 plots the contributions of the financialization, globalization,
welfare state retrenchment and technological change to changes in the
wage share in the period 1980/84 to 2000/04. Financialization has clearly
had the largest contribution, explaining a 3.3 percentage points decline
in the wage share. Welfare state retrenchment explains a decline of –1.9
percentage points and globalization had a contribution of –1.3 percentage
points. Technological change had an impact of –0.7 percentage points.

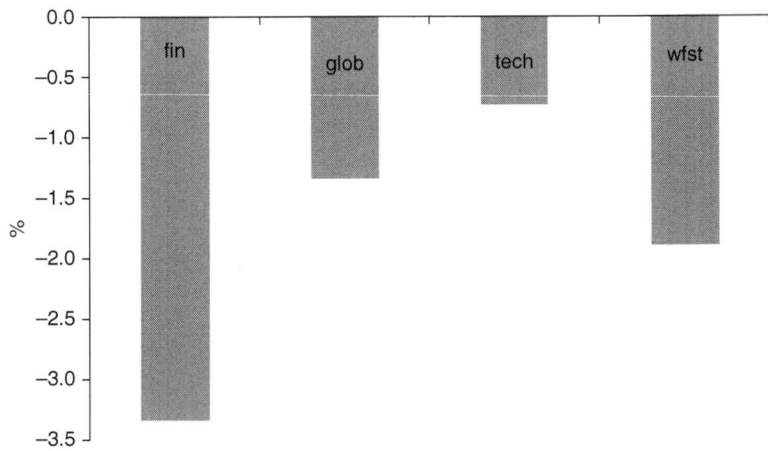

Figure 2.7   Contributions to the change in the wage share for advanced countries, 1980/84–2000/4

2.7 Conclusion

Functional income distribution has changed substantially over the course of the last three decades. Wage shares have declined in all OECD countries. This is part of a broader trend towards greater social inequality. While the picture is somewhat less homogenous in developing and emerging economies, it is clear that in most of these countries wage shares have also declined. Financialization, globalization, welfare state retrenchment and technological change have been identified as possible causes for these changes in income distribution.

The aim of this study has been to investigate the relative impact of financialization, globalization, welfare state retrenchment and technological change on functional income distribution. To this end we constructed a dataset covering up to 71 countries (28 advanced and 43 developing and emerging economies) from 1970 to 2007.

Our results indicate that financialization has been the main cause of the decline in the wage share. There have also been substantial negative effects from globalization and from welfare state retrenchment. Technological (and structural) change has had positive effects in developing countries. Notably, we find that globalization has had negative effects on income distribution in developing as well as in advanced economies, which contradicts the Stolper–Samuelson theorem.

We have also presented further results for advanced economies where the availability of data is better. This confirms our findings for the larger country group. Financialization emerges as the single most important cause for the decline in the wage share. Welfare state retrenchment and globalization has had negative effects on the wage share. For advanced economies we also find modest negative effects of technological change in the wage share.

The results of this study clearly refute two widely held views about income distribution. First the view that changes in income distribution in advanced economies have been driven mainly by technological change. This is not correct. While technological change has had a negative effect on wage shares in developed economies, this effect is smaller than that of other factors and it is also very robust. Second, the Stolper–Samuelson prediction – that globalization would benefit workers in developing and emerging economies – does not hold. We fail to find statistically different effects in advanced and developing economies and we find an overall negative contribution of globalization on wage shares in developing economies. The Stolper–Samuelson theorem does not apply empirically in the past thirty years.

These findings have important implications for economic and social policy. They suggest that income distribution is not primarily determined by technological progress, but rather depends on social institutions and on the structure of the financial system. Strengthening the welfare state, in particular changing union legislation to foster collective bargaining and financial regulation could help increase the wage share with little, if any costs in terms of economic efficiency.

Notes

1. We use 'advanced' economies to include all high income OECD except the Republic of Korea. See section 2.4.
2. Mohun (2006) calculates adjusted profit shares based on the distinction between supervisory and non-supervisory workers. This shows a much sharper increase in profit shares than the raw data. However, the availability of data only allows to perform these adjustments for the United States.
3. We use the term 'developing countries' as short hand for developing and emerging countries and include all countries that are not classified as high-income countries by the World Bank. We include the Republic of Korea in this group as it has been a developing country for much of the sample period and we cannot include it in our advanced countries group for econometric analysis because of data availability.
4. Among developing countries with at least ten years of adjusted wage share data there are 14 countries (Argentina, Botswana, Brazil, Bulgaria, China, Côte d'Ivoire, the Republic of Korea, Mexico, Namibia, Oman, Panama, South Africa, Thailand, Turkey) with declining wage shares, three (Mauritius, Russian Federation, Sri Lanka) with broadly stable wage shares and seven (Belarus, Chile, Colombia, Costa Rica, Hong Kong (China), Kenya, Peru) with increasing wage shares.
5. In the post-Keynesian tradition the (medium-term) interest rate is regarded a distributional variable. Hein and van Treeck (2010) and Hein and Mundt (2012) offer a discussion of the distributional effects of financialization in a Kaleckian framework.
6. They also find that several labour market institutions have 'perverse' effects, that is, higher unemployment benefits and higher employment protection legislation is found to lead to lower wage shares, which is interpreted to be caused by a very elastic labour demand function.

References

Argitis, G. and Pitelis, C. 2001. 'Monetary policy and the distribution of income: evidence for the United States and the United Kingdom', *Journal of Post Keynesian Economics*, vol. 23, pp. 617–38.

Atkinson, A., Piketty, T. and Saez, E. 2011. 'Top incomes in the long run of history', *Journal of Economic Literature*, vol. 49(1), pp. 3–71.

Autor, D., Katz, L. and Krueger, A.B. 1999. 'Computing inequality: Have computers changed the labor market?', *Quarterly Journal of Economics*, vol. 113, pp. 1169–214.

Azmat, G., Manning, A. and Van Reenen, J. 2007. 'Privatization, entry regulation and the decline of labour's share of GDP: A cross-country analysis of the network industries', CEPR Discussion Paper No. DP6348.

Beck, N. and Katz, J.N. 1995. 'What to do (and not to do) with time-series cross-section data', *American Political Science Review*, vol. 89(3), pp. 634–47.

Bentolila, S. and Saint-Paul, G. 2003. 'Explaining movements in the labor share', in *Contribution to Macroeconomics*, vol. 3(1) (Berkeley, CA: Berkeley Press).

Card, D. and DiNardo, J.E. 2002. 'Skill-based technological change and rising wage inequality: some problems and puzzles', *Journal of Labor Economics*, vol. 20(4), pp. 733–83.

Daudey, E. and García-Peñalosa, C. 2007. 'The personal and the factor distributions of income in a cross-section of countries', *Journal of Development Studies*, vol. 43(5), pp. 812–29.

Dreher, A. 2006. 'Does globalization affect growth? Evidence from a new index of globalization', *Applied Economics*, vol. 38(10), pp. 1091–110.

Duménil, G. and Lévy, D. 2001. 'Costs and benefits of Neoliberalism: a class analysis', *Review of International Political Economy*, vol. 8(4), pp. 578–607.

Duménil, G. and Lévy, D. 2004. *Capital Resurgent: Roots of the Neoliberal Revolution* (Cambridge, MA: Harvard University Press).

Epstein, G. and Burke, S. 2001. 'Threat effects and the internationalization of production', Political Economy Research Institute Working Papers 15.

Ertürk, I., Froud, J., Johal, S., Leaver, A. and Williams, K., (eds). 2008. *Financialization at Work: Key Texts and Commentary* (London: Routledge).

European Commission. 2007. 'The labour income share in the European Union', Chapter 5 in *Employment in Europe* (Brussels: European Commission).

Feenstra, R.C. and Hanson, G.H. 1997. 'Foreign direct investment and relative wages: evidence from Mexico's maquiladoras', *Journal of International Economics*, vol. 42(3–4), pp. 371–93.

Feenstra, R.C. and Hanson, G.H. 1999. 'The impact of outsourcing and high-technology capital on wages: estimates for the United States, 1979–1990', *Quarterly Journal of Economics*, vol. 114(3), pp. 907–40.

Goldberg, P. and Pavcnik, N. 2007. 'Distributional effects of globalization in developing countries', *Journal of Economic Literature*, vol. 45(1), pp. 39–82.

Gollin, D. 2002. 'Getting income shares right', *Journal of Political Economy*, vol. 110(April), pp. 458–74.

Harrison, A. 2002. Has globalization eroded labor's share? Some cross-country evidence. Mimeo, University of California, Berkeley.

Hein, E. and Mundt, M. 2012. 'Financialisation and the requirements and potentials for wage-led recovery – a review focussing on the G20'. Paper written for the project 'New perspectives on wages and economic growth: the potentials of wage-led growth'.

Hein, E. and Schoder, C. 2011. 'Interest rates, distribution and capital accumulation – a Post-Kaleckian perspective on the U.S. and Germany', *International Review of Applied Economics*, vol. 25(6), pp. 693–723.

Hein, E. and van Treeck, T. 2010. '"Financialisation" and rising shareholder power in Kaleckian/Post-Kaleckian models of distribution and growth', *Review of Political Economy*, vol. 22(2), pp. 205–33.

Hutchinson, J. and Persyn, D. 2009. 'Globalisation, concentration and foot-loose firms: in search of the main cause of the declining labour share', LICOS Discussion Paper Series, Discussion Paper 229/2009.

International Labour Office (ILO). 2008. *World of Work Report 2008: Income Inequalities in the Age of Financial Globalization* (Geneva: ILO).

International Labour Office (ILO). 2011. 'The labour share of income: determinants and potential contribution to exiting the financial crisis', Chapter 3 in *World of Work Report 2011: Making Markets Work for Jobs* (Geneva: ILO).

International Monetary Fund (IMF). 2007a. 'The globalization of labor', Chapter 5 in *World Economic Outlook*, April 2007 (Washington, DC: IMF).

International Monetary Fund (IMF). 2007b. 'Globalization and inequality', Chapter 4 in *World Economic Outlook*, October 2007 (Washington, DC: IMF).

Jayadev, A. 2007. 'Capital account openness and the labour share of income', *Cambridge Journal of Economics*, vol. 31, pp. 423–43.

Korpi, W. and Palme, J. 2003. 'New politics and class politics in the context of austerity and globalization: Welfare state regress in 18 countries, 1975–95', *American Political Science Review*, vol. 97(3), pp. 425–46.

Krueger, A. 1999. 'Measuring labor's share', *American Economic Review*, vol. 89(2), pp. 45–51.

Lane, P. and Milesi-Ferretti, G. 2007. 'The external wealth of nations mark II: Revised and extended estimates of foreign assets and liabilities', *Journal of International Economics*, vol. 73, pp. 23–250.

Lazonick, W. and O'Sullivan, M. 2000. 'Maximising shareholder value: a new ideology for corporate governance', *Economy and Society*, vol. 29(1), pp. 13–35.

Mohun, S. 2006. 'Distributive shares in the US economy, 1964–2001', *Cambridge Journal of Economics*, vol. 30(3), pp. 347–70.

Organisation for Economic Co-operation and Development (OECD). 2007. 'OECD workers in the global economy: increasingly vulnerable?', Chapter 3 of *OECD Employment Outlook 2007* (Paris: OECD).

Organisation for Economic Co-operation and Development (OECD). 2008. *Growing Unequal? Income Distribution and Poverty in OECD Countries* (Paris: OECD).

Organisation for Economic Co-operation and Development (OECD). 2011. *Divided We Stand: Why Inequality Keeps Rising* (Paris: OECD).

Onaran, Ö. 2009. 'Wage share, globalization and crisis: the case of the manufacturing industry in Korea, Mexico and Turkey', *International Review of Applied Economics*, vol. 23(2), pp. 113–34.

Onaran, Ö. 2011. 'Globalisation, macroeconomic performance and distribution', in E. Hein and E. Stockhammer (eds), *A Modern Guide To Keynesian Macroeconomics and Economic Policies* (Cheltenham: Edward Elgar).

Onaran, Ö., Stockhammer, E. and Grafl, L. 2011. 'Financialization, income distribution, and aggregate demand in the US', *Cambridge Journal of Economics*, vol. 35(4), pp. 637–66.

Pierson, Paul. 1994. *Dismantling the Welfare State? Reagan, Thatcher, and the Politics of Retrenchment* (Cambridge: Cambridge University Press).

Piketty, T. and Saez, E. 2003. 'Income inequality in the United States, 1913–1998', *Quarterly Journal of Economics*, vol. 118 (1), pp. 1–39.

Piketty, T. and Saez, E. 2007. 'Income inequality in the United States, 1913–1998', in A.B. Atkinson and T. Piketty (eds), *Top Incomes in a Global Perspective* (Oxford: Oxford University Press).

Power, D., Epstein, G. and Abrena, M. 2003. 'Trends in the rentier income share in OECD countries 1960–2000', PERI Working Paper 58a.

Rodrik, D. 1997. *Has Globalization Gone Too Far?* (Washington, DC: Institute of International Economics).

Rodrik, D. 1998. Capital mobility and labor. Manuscript. Available online at http://ksghome.harvard.edu/~drodrik/capitalm.pdf.

Rossman, P. 2009. 'Financialization and casualization of labour – building a trade union and regulatory response'. Paper presented at the Global Labour University Conference, Mumbai, February.

Stockhammer, E. 2004. 'Financialization and the slowdown of accumulation', *Cambridge Journal of Economics*, vol. 28(5), pp. 719–41.

Stockhammer, E. 2009. 'Determinants of functional income distribution in OECD countries', IMK Studies 05–2009.

Stockhammer, E. 2010. 'Financialization and the global economy', Political Economy Research Institute Working Paper 242.

Stockhammer, E. 2013. 'Why have wage shares fallen? A panel analysis of the determinants of functional income distribution', Conditions of Work and Employment Series No. 35 (Geneva: ILO).

Stolper, W. and Samuelson, P. 1941. 'Protection and real wages', *Review of Economic Studies*, vol. 9, pp. 58–73.

Wolff, E. and Zacharias, A. 2007. *Class Structure and Economic Inequality*. Levy Economics Institute Working Paper No. 487.

Wooldridge, J. 2002. *Econometric Analysis of Cross Section and Panel Data* (Cambridge, MA: MIT Press).

Datasets

AMECO: Annual macroeconomic database, Directorate General for Economic and Financial Affairs. (link to dataset http://ec.europa.eu/economy_finance/ameco/user/serie/SelectSerie.cfm, accessed 15 June 2011).

Bassanini, A. and Duval, R. 2006. 'Employment patterns in OECD countries: Reassessing the role of policies and institutions', OECD Economics Department Working Papers 486. OECD Publishing.

BGHS: Baker, D., Glyn, A., Howell, D. and Schmitt, J. 2005. 'Labor market institutions and unemployment: a critical assessment of the cross-country evidence', in D. Howell (ed.), *Fighting Unemployment. The Limits for Free Market Orthodoxy* (Oxford: Oxford University Press). Link: http://www.noapparentmotive.org/topics/BGHS_data.html.

ILO/IILS: ILO/IILS data on wage shares, supplied by M. Charpe.

Penn World Tables: Heston, A., Summers, R., Aten, B. 2011. Penn World Table Version 7.0. Center for International Comparisons of Production, Income and Prices, University of Pennsylvania. (link to dataset http://pwt.econ.upenn.edu/Downloads/pwt70/pwt70_06032011version.zip, accessed 25 May 2011).

EU KLEMS: EU KLEMS Growth and Productivity Accounts: November 2009 Release, updated March 2011. (link to dataset http://www.euklems.net/index.html, accessed 17 July 2011).

IMF, 2010. World Economic Outlook Database, October 2010. (link to dataset http://www.imf.org/external/pubs/ft/weo/2010/02/weodata/download.aspx, accessed 21 February 2011).

IMF International Financial Statistics (IFS).

Lane, P.R. and Milesi-Ferretti, G.M. 2007. 'The external wealth of nations mark II: Revised and extended estimates of foreign assets and liabilities, 1970–2004', *Journal of International Economics*, vol. 73(November), pp. 223–50 (link to dataset http://www.imf.org/external/pubs/ft/wp/2006/data/update/wp0669.zip, accessed 15 February 2011).

OECD: OECD.StatExtracts, http://stats.oecd.org/Index.aspx (accessed 18 April 2011).

United Nations Statistics Division, 2011. National Accounts Official Country Data, UNData Explorer. (link to dataset http://data.un.org/Explorer.aspx?d=SNA, accessed 18 April 2011).

UNIDO: INDSTAT3, Industrial Statistics Database (edition: 2006). (link to dataset http://dx.doi.org/10.5257/unido/indstat3/2006, accessed 18 April 2011).

World Bank World Development Indicators (WDI). (link to dataset http://data.worldbank.org/data-catalog/world-development-indicators, accessed 15 February 2011).

Appendix

Table A.1 Variables – all countries

Variable	Description	Source
AG	Agricultural share: value added by forestry, hunting, fishing, the cultivation of crops, and livestock production as a percentage of GDP	World Bank
CG	Government consumption as percentage of GDP	Penn World Tables
FINGLOB	Financial globalization: external assets plus external liabilities divided by GDP	Lane and Milesi-Ferretti
GDPPW	PPP converted GDP per worker at constant prices	Penn World Tables
GROWTH	Growth of real GDP in national currency	World Bank
IND	Industry share: value added in mining, manufacturing, construction, electricity, water, and gas as a percentage of GDP	World Bank
OPEN	Trade openness: exports plus imports divided by GDP	World Bank
POP	Population	Penn World Tables
TOT	Terms of trade	AMECO, IMF IFS, World Bank
UNEMPL	Number of unemployed people as a share of the labour force.	ILO/IILS, AMECO, IMF, World Bank
WSAP	Private adjusted wage share: the total wage share adjusted for government consumption	ILO/IILS, OECD, AMECO, Penn World Tables

Table A.2   Variables – additional variables for advanced countries

Variable	Description	Source
ICT_KLEMS	ICT capital services divided by gross value added	EU KLEMS
KL_KLEMS	Capital-labour ratio: capital services divided by the number of persons engaged	EU KLEMS
UNION	Union density	Bassanini and Duval, BGHS

3
Is Aggregate Demand Wage-led or Profit-led? A Global Model*

Özlem Onaran and Giorgos Galanis

3.1 Introduction

There has been a significant decline in the wage share in both the developed and developing world which has coincided with the introduction of neoliberal policy reforms since the 1980s. The promise of these reforms was to stimulate private investment and exports, which was expected in turn to generate higher growth, more jobs and trickle-down effects. The reasons for this fall have recently been the subject of a growing amount of literature that has tried to pin down the effects of technology, globalization, and changes in labour market institutions (see, inter alia, IMF, 2007; OECD, 2007; EC, 2007; ILO/IILS, 2011; Rodrik, 1997; Diwan, 2001; Harrison, 2002; Onaran, 2009; Rodriguez and Jayadev, 2010; Stockhammer, 2011). This chapter offers a theoretical and empirical assessment of the effects of this pro-capital redistribution of income on growth at both national and global levels.

Mainstream macroeconomic models emphasize the supply side rather than the demand side of the economy; and they assume that demand will follow supply. Most importantly for the purpose of this chapter, they treat wages merely as a component of cost, and neglect their role

* We are grateful to Engelbert Stockhammer, Servaas Storm, Amitava Dutt, Sangheon Lee, Patrick Belser and Marc Lavoie for helpful comments on earlier stages of the research, to Susan Pashkoff for careful language editing, and to Matthieu Charpe, Ricardo Molero Simarro, Uma Rani Amara, Rayaproulu Nagaraj, Juan Graña, Joana Chapa, Araceli Ortega Diaz, Morne Oosthuizen, Claudio Roberto Amitrano, Kazutoshi Chatani and Byung-Hee Lee for their valuable support regarding data. All remaining errors are ours.

as a source of demand. On the contrary, post-Keynesian/post-Kaleckian models, as formally developed by Rowthorn (1981), Dutt (1984), Taylor (1985), Blecker (1989), Bhaduri and Marglin (1990), reflect the dual role of wages affecting both costs and demand, and while they accept the direct positive effects of higher profits on investment and net exports emphasized in mainstream models, they contrast these positive effects with the negative effects on consumption. In these models, consumption is expected to decrease when the wage share decreases, since the marginal propensity to consume out of capital income is lower than that out of wage income. A higher profitability (a lower wage share) is expected to stimulate investment for a given level of aggregate demand. It is also often argued that internal funds are an important source of finance and thus profits may positively influence investment expenditures. Finally, for a given level of domestic and foreign demand, net exports will depend negatively on unit labour costs, which are by definition closely related to the wage share. Thus, the total effect of the decrease in the wage share on aggregate demand depends on the relative size of the reactions of consumption, investment and net exports to changes in income distribution. If the total effect is negative, the demand regime is called wage-led; otherwise the regime is labeled profit-led. Whether the negative effect of lower wages on consumption or the positive effect on investment and net exports is larger in absolute value essentially becomes an empirical question.

We first summarize the effects of the changes in the share of wages in income on aggregate demand in the major developed and developing countries (16 G20 countries, for which data are available) based on the findings in Onaran and Galanis (2012). These countries constitute more than 80 per cent of the global GDP. Thereby we present a global mapping of wage-led demand regimes, where consumption is more sensitive to distribution than investment and domestic demand constitutes a more significant part of aggregate demand, and profit-led demand regimes, where the responsiveness of investment to profits is comparatively strong and foreign trade is an important part of the economy (as is the case in small open economies). Next, we go beyond the nation-state as the unit of analysis and discuss the global effects based on the responses of each country to changes not only in domestic income distribution but also to trade partners' wage share; this affects in turn the import prices and foreign demand for each country. Pro-capital redistribution policies have not taken place in isolation at the nation state level. First, neoliberal policies have been implemented simultaneously in many developed and developing countries in the post-1980s period although the exact timing depended on the national economic and political context. Second, the policy of relying on decreasing labour costs as a core component of international competitiveness in several countries inevitably has had spillover effects to the other countries as countries try to preserve their competitive position in the global markets. Thus we have seen a simultaneous decline in the wage share. So the crucial question is what happens to global demand, when there is a race to the bottom, that is, a simultaneous decline in the wage share in all major developed and developing economies as has been the case in the period since the 1980s. A related question is whether countries that are profit-led in isolation, would stop growing, or even contract, if all other countries were implementing the same wage competition policy simultaneously. Although individual countries can be wage-led or profit-led, the effect of the 'race to the bottom' strategy on global demand can be detrimental, since the competitiveness gains will be lost in individual countries if there is a simultaneous decline in unit labour costs in their trade partners.

The policy conclusions of the analysis shed light on the limits of strategies of international competitiveness based on wage competition in a highly integrated global economy, and point to the possibilities of correcting global imbalances via coordinated macroeconomic and wage policy, where domestic demand plays an important role. There is room for a wage-led recovery in the global economy based on a simultaneous increase in the wage shares, where global GDP – as well as that of all individual countries – can grow.

The rest of the chapter is organized as follows: section 3.2 discusses the stylized facts. Section 3.3 summarizes the empirical findings, and presents the global multiplier effects of a simultaneous decrease in the wage share. Section 3.4 compares these results with the previous findings in the literature. Finally, section 3.5 concludes and derives policy implications.

3.2 Stylized facts

Our aim in this chapter is to present a representative analysis for the global economy. Therefore, we focus on the 16 major developed and developing countries, which are members of G20: the European Union (EU), Germany, France, Italy, the United Kingdom, the United States, Japan, Canada, Australia, Turkey, Mexico, the Republic of Korea, Argentina, China, India and South Africa.[1] As a proxy for the EU, we work with the 12 West European member states of the euro area, since data for the Eastern European new member states do not exist prior to transition.

The United Kingdom is analyzed separately, which is the largest old member state outside the euro area.

Appendix A describes the data sources in more detail. The period of analysis is 1960–2007 for the developed countries, and 1970–2007 for the developing countries (1978–2007 for China). C, I, X, M, Y, W and R are real consumption expenditures, real private investment expenditures, real exports (of goods and services), real imports (of goods and services), real GDP (at market prices), real wages and profits respectively.

Wages are adjusted labour compensation, calculated as real compensation per employee multiplied by total employment. In the national accounts, all income of the self-employed are classified as operating surplus. However, since part of this mixed income is a return to the labour of the self-employed, the simple (unadjusted) share of labour compensation in GDP leads to an underestimation of the labour share. This is a particular problem for developing countries which have a significant share of self-employed workers due to the informal nature of employment. Thus the adjusted wage share allocates a labour compensation for each self-employed person equivalent to the average compensation of the dependent employees.[2] R is also adjusted gross operating surplus, calculated as GDP at factor cost minus adjusted labour compensation.[3] Profit share, π, is defined as adjusted gross operating surplus as a ratio to GDP at factor cost. Wage share, ws, is simply $1 - \pi$; thus it is adjusted labour compensation as a ratio to GDP at factor cost.

There are several data issues regarding the wage share in the developing countries: Due to a lack of long time series data for the number of self-employed we link the data for the unadjusted wage share with the adjusted wage share data for Argentina and South Africa.[4] For China, we use the adjusted wage share data calculated by Zhou et al. (2010), which is reported in Molero Simarro (2011).[5] In India there are no time series data for the number of employees (and self-employed). However, there are data for the mixed income of the self-employed which can be used to calculate adjusted wage share.[6] Gollin (2002) suggests two methods of adjustment using mixed income data: the first method calculates the adjusted wage share as labour compensation as a ratio to GDP at factor cost-mixed income and the second method calculates (labour compensation + mixed income)/GDP at factor cost. Neither of these methods is perfect, and, following Felipe and Sipin (2004) and Jetin and Kurt (2011), we use the average of these two adjusted wage shares.

Appendix B reports the mean values of the variables. The adjusted wage shares in the Republic of Korea and India are relatively high. In both cases a high level of self-employment (measured by the numbers of self-employed in the Republic of Korea and a high share of mixed income in India) leads to a high self-employed income when it is assumed that the self-employed earn the same average wage rate as in the aggregate economy (in the Korean case) or that the share of wage income in the income of the self-employed is the same as in the total economy (in the Indian case). Also in the developing countries, the wages of the self-employed, who to a large extent are working in the informal economy, would be significantly lower than the average wage in the formal economy. Despite these problems associated with the lack of precise data regarding the labour income of the self-employed, we prefer to work with the adjusted wage share. Ignoring the labour income of the self-employed would mean a serious underestimation of the labour income in the developing countries.

Figure 3.1 shows the indices of the adjusted wage share in the developed (1960=100) and developing countries (1970=100).[7] There is a clear secular decline in the wage share in all countries starting from the late 1970s or early 1980s onwards. This downward trend also exists in the unadjusted wage share data. In the developed world the decline is particularly strong in the euro area (this is the case in aggregate, as well as in the three largest economies – France, Germany, Italy – of the euro area) and in Japan with a fall exceeding 15 percentage points in the index value. The fall is lower, but still strong, in the United States and the United Kingdom with decline of 8.9 per cent and 11.1 per cent respectively; however, a correction of the wage share by excluding the high managerial wages, which have increased very steeply in these countries, would have provided a more realistic picture about the loss in labour's income share. However, due to lack of data on managerial wages for the majority of the countries in our sample, except for the United States and the United Kingdom, this adjustment is outside the scope of this chapter.

In the developing world, Turkey and Mexico have experienced the strongest decline in the wage share (31.8 per cent and 37.9 per cent, respectively), where the negative effects of the debt crisis and the initial phases of structural adjustment were compounded by the currency crises of the 1990s and 2000s. Argentina has the most volatile wage share related to the effects of hyperinflation episodes; the country has experienced strong losses after the military dictatorship of 1974, and then the debt crisis in 1982 and then again after the 2001 crisis, but there has been some recovery in the wage share in recent years. In the Republic of Korea the increase in the wage share from mid-1980s onwards was reversed by the crisis in 1997. In India, the secular decline in the wage share since the 1970s has accelerated after the introduction of the liberal reforms in 1990; as of 2007 the wage share index is 17.6 per cent lower as compared to 1980. In China

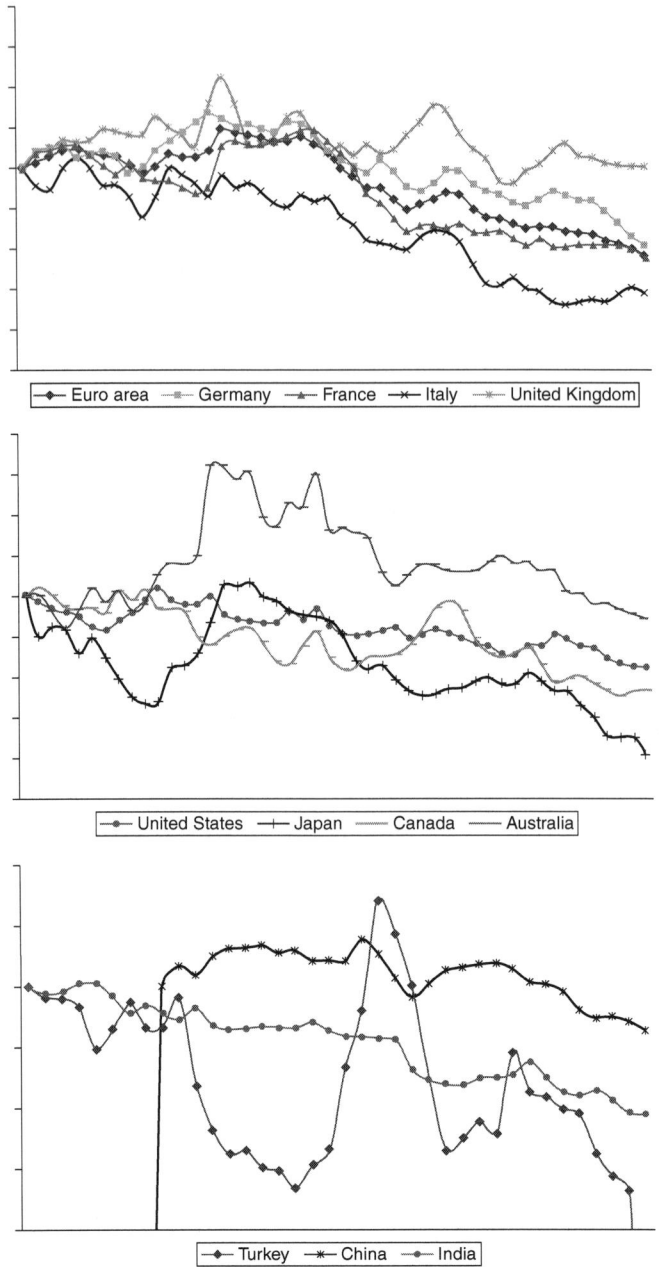

Figure 3.1   Wage share (adjusted, ratio to GDP at factor cost)
Source: Onaran and Galanis (2012). See Appendix A for data sources.

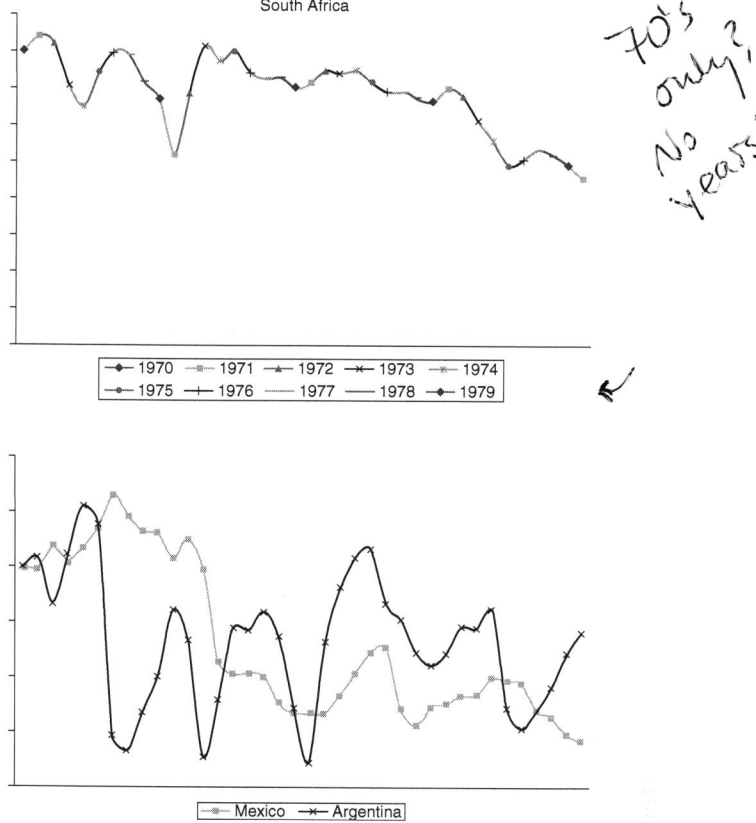

Figure 3.1   (Continued)

the improvement in the wage share in the 1980s was reversed in 1990, cul-
minating in a cumulative decline of 12.8 per cent in the index value. The
wage share in South Africa has been decreasing since the early 1980s with
little change since the end of apartheid.

How did the economies perform during these two to three decades of
decline in the wage share? Tables 3.1a and 3.1b show the average growth
rates in GDP in different periods for the developed and developing countries. In the developed countries, the decline in the wage share was associated with a weaker growth performance in each decade compared to
the previous decade in almost all cases. With the exception of China
and India, all countries in the developing world in the post-1980s period

have lower growth rates as compared to the 1970s. With the exception of the last decade, in Turkey and South Africa there is a continuous deterioration in the growth performance along with the fall in the wage share. In the Republic of Korea, the declining wage share since the Asian crisis corresponds to a clear decline in growth rates. The earlier decline in the wage share coincides with very weak growth performance during the lost decade of the 1980s in Mexico and Argentina. However, while growth recovers in the post-1990s, the wage share does not; thus the direction of the relationship is unclear. In both China and India a strengthening of growth is observed along with falling wage share.

3.3   Summary of the empirical findings

In this section, we summarize the results of the estimations regarding the effects of the changes in the wage share on growth based on Onaran and Galanis (2012), where we estimate single equations for consumption, investment, exports, and imports.

Table 3.1a   Average growth of GDP (%), developed countries

	Euro area-12	Germany	France	Italy	United Kingdom	United States	Japan	Canada	Australia
1961–69	5.30	4.39	5.71	5.77	2.90	4.69	10.14	5.37	5.53
1970–79	3.78	3.27	4.15	4.02	2.42	3.32	5.21	4.11	3.07
1980–89	2.27	1.96	2.31	2.55	2.48	3.04	4.37	3.04	3.35
1990–99	2.15	2.32	1.86	1.43	2.24	3.21	1.46	2.44	3.32
2000–07	2.13	1.53	2.10	1.46	2.73	2.61	1.73	2.92	3.31

Table 3.1b   Average growth of GDP (%), developing countries

	Turkey	Mexico	Korea, Rep. of	Argentina	China	India	South Africa
1970–79	4.86	6.41	10.27	2.92	6.11	2.68	3.03
1980–89	4.08	2.21	8.62	−0.73	9.75	5.69	2.24
1990–99	4.02	3.38	6.68	4.52	9.99	5.63	1.39
2000–07	5.23	3.06	5.20	3.51	10.51	7.26	4.30

Source: Onaran and Galanis (2012). See Appendix A for data sources.

Consumption, C, is estimated as a function of adjusted profits, and adjusted wages. The difference in marginal consumption propensities (between wage and profit incomes) gives the effect of a change in the distribution of income. Our empirical findings verify that the marginal propensity to consume out of profits is lower than that out of wages in all countries; thus, a rise in the profit share leads to a decline in consumption.

Private investment is estimated as a function of output and the profit share. The United States is the only developed country where the profit share has no significant effect on investment (Onaran and Galanis, 2012). However, although gross operating surplus has no significant effect on investment in the United States, Onaran et al. (2011) show that when the effects of financialization are controlled for, that is, the interest and dividend payments are deducted from the operating surplus, there is evidence of some positive effect of the revised profit share (the non-rentier profit share) on investment. Thus, the increase in interest and dividend payments leads to an insignificant effect of the gross operating surplus on investment. Interestingly, in most developing countries the profit share has no statistically significant effect on private investments; we find a positive effect only in Mexico, Argentina, and South Africa (Onaran and Galanis, 2012). The effect of the profit share on private investment in China is also insignificant, although there is a positive effect on total investment, including public investment. In the other countries (Turkey, the Republic of Korea, India), where there is no statistically significant effect of the profit share on private investment, total investment is also not significantly related to the profit share. The lack of evidence for a positive effect of profits on investment is consistent with the previous findings in the literature on developing countries: Onaran and Yentürk (2001) fail to find a statistically significant effect of the profit share on investment in the Turkish manufacturing industry using panel data. Seguino (1999) even finds a negative effect of the profit share on investment in the manufacturing industry in the Republic of Korea based on a single equation estimation. Based on systems estimations using a SVAR model, Onaran and Stockhammer (2005) find a negative effect of the profit share on private investment in both Turkey and the Republic of Korea.

In all countries, GDP has a strong and significant effect on private investment, providing evidence for the significance of an investment–growth nexus (Onaran and Galanis, 2012). Furthermore, we also tested the effects of public investment in the developing countries, and found that in three developing countries (the Republic of Korea, India and China) public investment has a significant positive effect on private investment, which indicates the presence of crowding-in effects.

To estimate the effects of distribution on net exports we followed the stepwise approach of Stockhammer et al. (2009) and Onaran et al. (2011): Exports, X, are estimated as a function of export/import prices, and the GDP of the rest of the world; imports, M, as a function of domestic prices/import prices, and GDP; domestic prices and export prices, are estimated as functions of nominal unit labour costs and import prices. Using the estimated elasticities, the marginal effects of a change in the wage share on exports/GDP and imports/GDP are calculated at the sample average; for example, the total effect of a change in profit share on exports includes the effect of real unit labour cost on nominal unit labour cost, the effect of nominal unit labour costs on prices, the effect of prices on export prices, and the effect of export prices on exports. The effect of the wage share on GDP via the channel of international trade depends not only on the elasticity of exports and imports to prices but also the degree of openness of the economy (that is, on the share of exports and imports in GDP); thus in relatively small open economies net exports may play a major role in determining the overall outcome; the effect becomes much lower in relatively closed large economies.

Table 3.2 summarizes the partial effects of a one percentage point increase in the profit share on consumption, investment and net exports based on the estimations by Onaran and Galanis (2012), and reports the total effect on private demand in column 4. Next, column 5 shows the total effects after the multiplier process, that is, including further effects of changes in private demand on investment, consumption, and imports.

Based on the results summarized in columns (1) and (2), one finding stands out as a robust result for all countries: if we sum up only the effects on domestic private demand (that is, consumption and investment), the negative effect of the increase in the profit share on private consumption is substantially larger than the positive effect on investment in absolute value in all countries. Thus demand in the domestic sector of the economies is clearly wage-led; however, the foreign sector then has a crucial role in determining whether the economy is profit-led.

Overall demand in the euro area (12 countries) is significantly wage-led; a one percentage point increase in the profit share leads to a 0.08 per cent decrease in private excess demand. Unsurprisingly, Germany, France and Italy as individual large members of the euro area are also wage led. The absolute value of the effect of an increase in the profit share in Germany and France is smaller than in the aggregate euro area; the net export effects are higher for the individual countries with a much higher export and import share in GDP due to trade with the other euro area countries as well as non-euro area countries. Previous

Table 3.2 The summary of the effects of a 1 percentage point increase in the profit share

	The effect of a 1%-point increase in the profit share in only one country on					The effect of a simulataneous 1%-point increase on % change in aggregate demand (including effects of Yrw and Pm)
	C/Y	I/Y	NX/Y	private excess demand/Y	% change in aggregate demand (D*multiplier)	
	A	B	C	D (A+B+C)	E	G
Euro area-12	-0.439	0.299	0.057	-0.084	-0.133	-0.245
Germany	-0.501	0.376	0.096	-0.029	-0.031	–
France	-0.305	0.088	0.198	-0.020	-0.027	–
Italy	-0.356	0.130	0.126	-0.100	-0.173	–
United Kingdom	-0.303	0.120	0.158	-0.025	-0.030	-0.214
United States	-0.426	0.000	0.037	-0.388	-0.808	-0.921
Japan	-0.353	0.284	0.055	-0.014	-0.034	-0.179
Canada	-0.326	0.182	0.266	0.122	0.148	-0.269
Australia	-0.256	0.174	0.272	0.190	0.268	0.172
Turkey	-0.491	0.000	0.283	-0.208	-0.459	-0.717
Mexico	-0.438	0.153	0.381	0.096	0.106	-0.111
Korea, Rep. of	-0.422	0.000	0.359	-0.063	-0.115	-0.864
Argentina	-0.153	0.015	0.192	0.054	0.075	-0.103
China	-0.412	0.000	1.986	1.574	1.932	1.115
India	-0.291	0.000	0.310	0.018	0.040	-0.027
South Africa	-0.145	0.129	0.506	0.490	0.729	0.390

Note: The global simulation excludes Germany, France and Italy since they are part of the euro zone.
Source: Onaran and Galanis (2012, Tables 11 and 13).

studies show that small open economies in the euro area, such as the Netherlands and Austria, may be profit-led, when analysed in isolation (Hein and Vogel 2008; Stockhammer and Ederer 2008). However the aggregated euro area is a rather closed economy with low levels of extra-EU trade, albeit a high intra-EU trade in which overall demand is wage-led. Thus wage moderation in the euro area as a whole is likely to have only moderate effects on foreign trade, but it will have substantial effects on domestic demand. Second, if wages were to change simultaneously in all euro area countries, the net export position of each country would change little because extra-euro area trade is comparatively small. Thus, when all euro area countries pursue 'beggar thy neighbour' policies, the international competitiveness effects will be minor, and the domestic effects will dominate the outcome.

The United Kingdom, the United States and Japan are also wage-led; albeit the effect varies depending on the degree of openness of the economy as well as the relative strength of the consumption differentials and investment's response to profits. Overall, the results indicate that large/relatively closed economies are rather wage-led. Canada and Australia are profit-led; as small open economies the net export effects are high; the investment effects are also among the highest in the developed world in these two countries, and the differences in the marginal propensity to consume out of profits and wages are among the lowest.

Among the developing countries, only Turkey and the Republic of Korea are wage-led; consumption effects are very strong and more than offset the rather strong net export effects; there is no significant investment effect in either of the two countries. China is very strongly profit-led with an unusually high distributional effect: a one percentage point increase in the profit share increases private excess demand by 1.57 per cent; however, this effect is not due to investment, but rather results from the very strong export and import effects. South Africa is also profit-led with a relatively high impact of distribution; this is partly related to a very low difference in the marginal propensity to consume out of profits and wages, which may have increased in the period after apartheid. Mexico and Argentina also have a profit-led private demand regime; in Mexico a strong effect of profits on both investment and net exports, and in Argentina a weak effect on consumption, explain the results. India is profit-led but the effect of distribution is rather low; a high net export effect slightly offsets the rather low effect on consumption, and the effect on investment is insignificant.

Column 5 summarizes the multiplier effects of the change in private excess demand on aggregate demand based on the findings in Onaran and Galanis (2012). The initial change in private demand due to a change in income distribution leads to a multiplier mechanism; that is it affects consumption, investment and imports. As expected, when the multiplier effects are taken into consideration the effects of a change in income distribution on aggregate demand become higher. This is, however, only the national effects in isolation, that is, assuming that the change is taking place only in one single country, and ignoring any further feedbacks from the effects on the GDP of the trading partners.

Finally, the last column of Table 3.2 summarizes the total effects of the global multiplier process incorporating both national and international multiplier effects of a simultaneous one percentage point decrease in the wage share in all the 13 large developed and developing economies based on the calculations in Onaran and Galanis (2012).[8] This global multiplier mechanism incorporates the effects of a change in the profit share of other countries on the aggregate demand of each economy; as such it adds the effects of changes in imports prices and the GDP of trade partners on top of the national multiplier effects.

Most interestingly, the profit-led economies of Canada, Mexico, Argentina and India also start contracting when the effects of decreasing import prices and changes in the GDP of the trade partners on net exports are incorporated in a simultaneous 'race to the bottom' scenario. In these countries, the expansionary effects of a pro-capital redistribution of income are reversed, when relative competitiveness effects are reduced and global demand contracts, as all countries are implementing a similar wage competition strategy. Comparing columns five and six, the contraction in private excess demand in the originally wage-led countries (euro zone, the United Kingdom, the United States, Japan, Turkey and the Republic of Korea) is now much deeper. The euro area, the United Kingdom, and Japan contract by 0.18–0.25 per cent and the United States contracts by 0.92 per cent as a result of a simultaneous decline in the wage share. In the developing world, the two wage-led economies of Turkey and the Republic of Korea contract at very high rates – by 0.72 per cent and 0.86 per cent, respectively. Australia, South Africa and China are the only three countries that can continue to grow out of a simultaneous world decline in the wage share. However the growth rates in these countries are also reduced in comparison, for example, in China the growth rate decreases by 0.82 percentage points when all the 13 economies decrease their wage share; China now grows at a rate of only 1.12 per cent.

Overall a one percentage point simultaneous decline in the wage share in these 13 large economies of the world lead to a decline in the global GDP by 0.36 percentage points (the average of the growth rates

Table 3.3 Two wage-led recovery scenarios

	Scenario 1		Scenario 2	
	Change in profit share to preserve the peak wage share	The % change in aggregate demand (includes national and global multiplier effects, i.e. changes in Pm and Yrw)	Change in profit share	The % change in aggregate demand (includes national and global multiplier effects, i.e. changes in Pm and Yrw)
Euro area-12	–11.05	2.49	–11.05	2.36
United Kingdom	–7.83	2.01	–7.83	1.91
United States	–6.31	6.47	–6.31	6.15
Japan	–16.71	1.77	–16.71	1.49
Canada	–7.73	2.44	–3.00	2.84
Australia	–9.02	–1.35	–3.00	0.03
Turkey	–18.41	11.22	–18.41	10.81
Mexico	–22.03	–0.56	–3.00	1.45
Korea, Rep. of	–8.64	7.60	–8.64	7.46
Argentina	–9.12	0.86	–3.00	1.27
China	–8.00	–7.44	–1.00	5.56
India	–15.96	0.05	–3.00	0.43
South Africa	–13.07	–6.29	–1.00	1.93

Source: Onaran and Galanis (2012, Table 14).

in column six of Table 3.2 weighted by the share of each country in the world GDP; Onaran and Galanis 2012). Thus, the world economy in aggregate is wage-led; if there is a simultaneous decline in the wage share in all countries (or as in our case in the 13 major economies of the world), aggregate demand in the world economy also decreases.

Finally we simulate the effects of an alternative scenario of a simultaneous wage-led recovery in these 13 large economies as opposed to a 'race to the bottom'. Obviously if all the countries increase their wage share by one percentage point the global GDP would grow by 0.36 per cent; however, the economies of China, South Africa and Australia would contract. In an alternative scenario shown in Table 3.3, if all 13 countries increase their wage shares to the latest peak levels, the global GDP will increase by 2.81 per cent; however, Mexico and Argentina as well as China, South Africa and Australia would again contract (Onaran and Galanis 2012). Finally, it is possible to find a scenario, where all countries can grow along with an improvement in the wage share; for example, as shown in the second scenario in Table 3.3, if all wage-led countries return to their previous peak wage-share levels, and moreover if all originally profit-led countries increase their wage-share by 1–3 percentage points, all countries could grow, and the global GDP would increase by 3.05 per cent (Onaran and Galanis 2012).

3.4   Comparison with the literature

In this section we compare the country-specific results summarized above with the literature. Consistent with our findings, previous findings for the individual countries in the literature also mostly conclude that domestic demand is wage-led.[9]

In most of the developed country cases analysed in the previous literature, the addition of the foreign demand does not reverse the results with regards to the nature of aggregate private demand. Our results are consistent with Stockhammer et al. (2009) for the euro area; Stockhammer et al. (2011), Hein and Vogel (2008) and Naastepad and Storm (2007) for Germany; Hein and Vogel (2008) and Naastepad and Storm (2007) for France and Italy; with Hein and Vogel (2008), Naastepad and Storm (2007) and Bowles and Boyer (1995) for the United Kingdom; Onaran et al. (2011), Hein and Vogel (2008) and Bowles and Boyer (1995) for the United States, who find evidence of wage-led private demand in these countries. Ederer and Stockhammer (2007) report a wider range of specifications for France, some of which indicate a profit-led demand regime. Bowles and Boyer (1995) find profit-led regimes in Germany, France and Japan, but their results suffer from econometric problems such as unit root issues; they do not apply difference or error correction models. Naastepad and Storm (2007) find profit-led demand regimes in the United States and Japan, but these results are driven by the unconventional finding that the domestic demand regime is profit-led in these countries. These results are rather different from other findings in the literature for these countries as well as ours. Using a different methodology, Stockhammer and Onaran (2004) estimate a structural Vector Autoregression (VAR) model for the United States, United Kingdom and France, where they conclude that the impact of income distribution on demand and employment is very weak and statistically insignificant. Although VAR does well in dealing with simultaneity, it is weak in identifying the effects and individual behavioural equations; thus it is hard to compare the results. Again using VAR methodology Barbosa-Filho and Taylor (2006) find that the US economy is profit-led; however, their estimations suffer from autocorrelation issues. There are no previous studies on the character of the demand regime in Australia and Canada.

The empirical studies on the effects of distribution on demand in the developing countries are remarkably limited. Onaran and Stockhammer (2005) find that Turkey and the Republic of Korea are both wage-led. Molero Simarro (2011) estimates the effects of distribution on domestic demand in China, and Wang (2009) estimates the effects on aggregate demand using regional panel data for China. Both studies use the econometric methodology in Stockhammer et al. (2009). In both studies investment also includes public investment, and therefore they find a positive effect on investment, and thereby a strongly profit-led domestic as well as aggregate demand; however this does not tell us much about the private investment behaviour. Looking only at consumption and private investment, we find that domestic demand is wage-led in China, although aggregate demand, including net exports, is profit-led. To the best of our knowledge, there is no econometric analysis on the effect of functional income distribution on growth in Mexico, Argentina, India, and South Africa. Using a similar methodology as in this chapter, Jetin and Kurt (2011) find that private demand in Thailand is profit-led.

Tables (a) and (b) in Appendix C summarize the literature and compare it with the results of this study.

3.5   Conclusions and policy implications

The dramatic decline in the wage share in both the developed and developing world during the neoliberal era of the post-1980s has accompanied lower growth rates at the global level. The empirical estimations summarized here, which examine the effect of income distribution on growth in 16 large developed and developing countries, offer three important findings to understand this adverse development. First, domestic private demand (that is, the sum of consumption and investment) is wage-led in all countries, because consumption is much more sensitive to an increase in the profit share than is investment; thus, an economy is profit-led only when the effect of distribution on net exports is high enough to offset the effects on domestic demand. Second, foreign trade form only a small part of aggregate demand in large countries, and therefore the positive effects of a decline in the wage share on net exports do not suffice to offset the negative effects on domestic demand. Similarly, if countries, which have strong trade relations with each other (like the euro area with a low trade volume with countries outside Europe), are considered as an aggregate economic area, the private demand regime is wage-led. Finally, the most novel finding is that even if there are some countries, which are profit-led, the global economy is wage-led. Thus, a simultaneous wage cut in a highly integrated global economy leaves most countries with only the negative domestic demand effects, and the global economy contracts. Furthermore most profit-led countries contract when they decrease their wage share, if a similar strategy is implemented also by their trading partners. Thus 'beggar the neighbour' policies cancel out the competitiveness advantages in each country and are counter-productive.

The results indicate that the microeconomic rationale of pro-capital redistribution conflicts with the macroeconomic outcomes at two levels: First, at the national level in a wage-led economy, the consequence of a higher profit share at the macroeconomic level is lower demand; thus, even though a higher profit share at the firm level seems to be beneficial to individual capitalists, at the macroeconomic level a generalized fall in the wage share generates a problem of realization of profits due to deficient demand. Second, even if increasing profit share seems to be promoting growth at the national level in the profit-led countries, at the global level a generalized fall in the wage share leads to a global aggregate demand deficiency. What seems to be rational at the level of an individual firm or a country turns out to be contractionary at the macro or global level.

These results have important policy conclusions. First, at the national level, if a country is wage-led, policies that lead to a pro-capital redistribution of income are detrimental to growth. Even in some wage-led cases, where the effect of distribution on growth is not very large, the results point at the presence of room for policies to decrease income inequality without hurting the growth potential of the economies.

Second, for the large economic areas with a high intra-regional trade and low extra-regional trade, such as the euro area, which tend to be wage-led, macroeconomic policy coordination, in particular with regards to wage policy, can improve growth and employment. Thus the wage moderation policy of the euro area is not conducive to growth.

Third, a global wage-led recovery as a way out of the global recession, that is, a significant increase in the wage share leading to an increase in the global rate of growth, is economically feasible, and growth and an improvement in equality are consistent. This is true not only for the wage-led countries but also for those that are profit-led, although in the latter the room for improving the wage share is more limited unless the structural parameters of the countries change. Thus, even the profit-led countries can grow if there is a simultaneous increase in the wage share. Indeed in the majority of the profit-led countries, it is not at all possible to grow out of a pro-capital redistribution of income, when this strategy is implemented in many other large economies at the same time.

Addressing the problem of income inequality is even more important today with the background of the crisis. A recovery led by domestic demand and increase in the wage share in the global economy would help to reverse a major factor behind the global crisis, that is, increasing inequality. Falling labour's share in the post-1980s has meant a decline in workers' purchasing power, which has limited their potential to consume. Demand deficiency reduced investments, despite increasing profitability in most cases. Debt-led consumption, enabled by financial deregulation and housing bubbles, seemed to offer a short-term solution in the United Kingdom, the United States, or the periphery of Europe. The current account deficits in these countries were matched by an export-led model and significant current account surpluses in countries like Germany in the core, or China in the periphery, where exports had to compensate for the insufficient domestic demand due to a falling or low labour's share. Capital outflows from these countries enabled the credit expansion in the countries driven by debt-led growth. In that respect, inequality in income distribution is one the major causes of the crisis, along with financial deregulation at a national and international scale. In the face of falling wage shares across the world, global stagnation was avoided thanks to an increase in debt (mostly private) and global imbalances. After the collapse of the debt-led model in the wake of the global recession, the wage moderation policies of the last three decades proved to be unsustainable. Reversing inequality would bring us a step closer to eliminating a major cause of the crisis; it would also be a way of making those responsible pay for the crisis.

Furthermore the findings show the danger of the austerity policies, which are pushed by governments across the developed world as a solution to the sovereign debt problem. In this contractionary environment, the wage shares have started to decrease since 2010. This development, along with austerity policies, will only bring further recession. Our results also show that growth in China and a few developing countries alone cannot be the locomotive of global growth.

There is a material basis for a global wage-led recovery, if the coordination problem among the countries can be overcome. However, the coordination problem is a political economy issue related to both international relations and power relations between labour and capital within each country. Given the profit-led structures in some developing countries as well as small open economies in the developed world, the solution to the coordination problem requires a step forward by some large developed economies in terms of radically reversing the pro-capital distribution policies and taking an initiative towards wage and macroeconomic policy coordination. Given that wage competition has been the major policy stance for three decades to date, the credibility of a wage-led recovery scenario will require a stable commitment to the policy by some major countries; only then can we avoid the incentives to resort to wage competition in small open economies, in particular in the developing world. Last but not least, the push for wage-led recovery can only come through a strengthening of the bargaining power of labour. Strengthening the power of the labour unions via an improvement in union legislation, increasing the coverage of collective bargaining, increasing the social wage via public goods and social security, establishing sufficiently high minimum wages, and levelling the global playground through international labour standards are the key elements in creating the balance of power relations in favour of a wage-led global recovery.

Notes

1. Among the G20 countries, there is no wage share data for Saudi Arabia. Wage share data for Brazil start only in 1990 and for Russian Federation in 1989. This is insufficient for reliable time series estimations. In Indonesia, the wage share data exist only for the manufacturing industry; there are no national accounts data based upon income. Therefore these countries could not be included in the analysis.
2. This methodology is used by the OECD and AMECO for calculating adjusted labour share. See Gollin (2002) for more details about the methodology.

3. GDP at factor cost is GDP at market prices minus taxes on production and imports plus subsidies. It is equal to the summation of labour compensation and operating surplus in the national accounts.

4. For Argentina, we use the percentage change in the unadjusted wage share data in Lindenbaum et al. (2011) for 1970–92 and 2006–07 to extend the adjusted wage share data in Charpe (2011) for 1993–2005. Similarly, for South Africa we link the unadjusted wage share data in the UN National Accounts for 1970–88 and 2005–07 with the adjusted wage share data in Charpe (2011) for 1989–2004.

5. Zhou et al. (2010) report that in the national accounts data of the National Bureau of Statistics 'proprietors' income is considered as labor's compensation' before 2004; after 2004 'labor's compensation and operating profits of the proprietors are considered as business profits'. Zhou et al. (2010) correct the problem resulting from this discontinuity in the data by adjusting the wage share after 2004 using self-employment data as suggested by Gollin (2002).

6. However these data are available only until 1999; for 2000–07 we use estimated mixed income based on the sectoral mixed income shares in 1999. We are grateful to Uma Rani Amara for providing the calculations for the mixed income estimates for 2000–07 based on the sectoral mixed income shares in 1999.

7. We prefer to convert the values of the wage share to indices in order to be able to compare the trends and avoid the differences in the levels of the wage share due to methodological differences among the countries in calculating the adjusted wage share.

8. We examine the euro area as a single economic unit, and therefore do not include Germany, France and Italy separately at the national level in the calculation of the global interactions. The 13 large economies constitute more than 80 per cent of the global GDP. In the following, when we are referring to a worldwide increase in the profit share, we refer to an increase in only the 13 large economies with other things being held constant in the rest of the world.

9. See Stockhammer et al. (2009) for the euro area; Stockhammer and Stehrer (2011) for Germany, France, the United States, Japan, Canada, Australia; Naastepad and Storm (2007) for Germany, France, Italy, the United Kingdom; Hein and Vogel (2008) for Germany, France, the United Kingdom, the United States; Bowles and Boyer (1995) for Germany, France, the United Kingdom, the United States, Japan; Stockhammer et al. (2011) for Germany; and Ederer and Stockhammer (2007) for France.

References

Barbosa-Filho, N. and Taylor, L. 2006. 'Distributive and demand cycles in the US economy – a structuralist Goodwin model', *Metroeconomica*, vol. 57(3), pp. 389–411.

Bhaduri, A., and Marglin, S. 1990. 'Unemployment and the real wage: the economic basis for contesting political ideologies', *Cambridge Journal of Economics*, vol. 14, pp. 375–93.

Blecker, R. 1989. 'International competition, income distribution and economic growth', *Cambridge Journal of Economics*, vol. 13, pp. 395–412.

Bowles, S. and Boyer, R. 1995. 'Wages, aggregate demand, and employment in an open economy: an empirical investigation', in G. Epstein and H. Gintis (eds), *Macroeconomic Policy after the Conservative Era. Studies in Investment, Saving and Finance* (Cambridge: Cambridge University Press), pp. 143–71.

Charpe, M. 2011. Adjusted wage share database (Geneva: ILO/IILS).

Diwan, I. 2001. Debt as sweat: labour, financial crises, and the globalisation of capital. Mimeo, the World Bank.

Dutt, A. 1984. 'Stagnation, income distribution and monopoly power', *Cambridge Journal of Economics*, vol. 8, pp. 25–40.

Ederer, S. and Stockhammer, E. 2007. 'Wages and aggregate demand in France: An empirical investigation', in E. Hein and A. Truger (eds), *Money, Distribution, and Economic Policy – Alternatives to Orthodox Macroeconomics* (Cheltenham: Edward Elgar), pp. 119–38.

European Commission. 2007. 'The labour income share in the European Union', Chapter 5 in *Employment in Europe* (Brussels: European Commission).

Felipe, J. and Sipin, G. 2004. 'Competitiveness, income distribution and growth in the Philippines: What does the long-run evidence show?', ERD Working Paper No. 53.

Gollin, D. 2002. 'Getting income shares right', *Journal of Political Economy*, vol. 110(2), pp. 458–74.

Harrison, A.E. 2002. Has globalisation eroded labour's share? Some cross-country evidence. Mimeo, UC Berkeley.

Hein, E. and Vogel, L. 2008. 'Distribution and growth reconsidered – empirical results for six OECD countries', *Cambridge Journal of Economics*, vol. 32, pp. 479–511.

International Labour Office (ILO)/International Institute of Labour Studies (IILS). 2011. *World of Work Report: Making Markets Work for Jobs* (Geneva: ILO/ILLS).

International Monetary Fund (IMF). 2007. 'Spillovers and cycles in the global economy, World Economic and Financial Surveys', *World Economic Outlook*, April (Washington, DC: IMF).

Jetin, B. and Kurt, O. 2011. 'Functional income distribution and growth in Thailand: single equation estimations based on Bhaduri/Marglin model'. Paper presented at the Annual Conference of the Research Network Macroeconomics and Macroeconomic Policies, Berlin, 28–9 October.

Lindenboim, J., Kennedy, D. and Graña, J.M. 2011. 'Wage share and aggregate demand: Contributions for labour and macroeconomic policy'. Paper presented at the Regulating for Decent Work Conference, ILO, Geneva, 6–8 July.

Marglin, S. and Bhaduri, A. 1990. 'Profit squeeze and Keynesian theory', in S. Marglin and J. Schor (eds), *The Golden Age of Capitalism. Reinterpreting the Postwar Experience* (Oxford: Clarendon Press).

Molero Simarro, R. 2011. 'Functional distribution of income and economic growth in the Chinese economy, 1978–2007', School of Oriental and African Studies, Department of Economics Working Papers, No. 168.

Naastepad, C.W.M., and Storm, S. 2007. 'OECD demand regimes (1960–2000)', *Journal of Post-Keynesian Economics*, vol. 29, pp. 213–48.

OECD. 2007. *Employment Outlook* (Paris: OECD).

Onaran, Ö. 2009. 'Wage share, globalisation, and crisis: the case of manufacturing industry in Korea, Mexico, and Turkey', *International Review of Applied Economics*, vol. 23(2), pp. 113–34.

Onaran, Ö. and Yentürk, N. 2001. 'Do low wages stimulate investments? An analysis of the relationship between distribution and investments in Turkish manufacturing industry', *International Review of Applied Economics*, vol. 15(4), pp. 359–74.

Onaran, Ö. and Stockhammer, E. 2005. 'Two different export-oriented growth strategies: accumulation and distribution à la Turca and à la South Korea', *Emerging Markets Finance and Trade*, vol. 41(1), pp. 65–89.

Onaran, Ö., Stockhammer, E. and Grafl, L. 2011. 'The finance-dominated growth regime, distribution, and aggregate demand in the US', *Cambridge Journal of Economics*, vol. 35(4), pp. 637–61.

Onaran, Ö. and Galanis, G. 2012. 'Is aggregate demand wage-led or profit-led? National and global effects', Conditions of Work and Employment Series No. 31.

Rodriguez, F. and Jayadev, A. 2010. 'The declining labor share of income', UNDP Human Development Research Paper 2010/36.

Rodrik, D. 1997. *Has Globalisation Gone Too Far?* (Washington, DC: Institute for International Economics).

Rowthorn, R. 1981. 'Demand, real wages and economic growth', *Thames Papers in Political Economy*, Autumn 1–39; reprinted in *Studi Economici*, 1982(18), pp. 3–54.

Seguino, S. 1999. 'The investment function revisited: disciplining capital in South Korea', *Journal of Post-Keynesian Economics*, vol. 22(2), pp. 313–38.

Stockhammer, E. 2011. 'Decline in wage share: causes and prospects'. Paper presented at the Regulating for Decent Work Conference, ILO, Geneva, 6–8 July.

Stockhammer, E., Onaran, Ö. and Ederer, S. 2009. 'Functional income distribution and aggregate demand in the Euro area', *Cambridge Journal of Economics*, vol. 33(1), pp. 139–59.

Stockhammer, E., and Onaran, Ö. 2004. 'Accumulation, distribution and employment: a structural VAR approach to a Kaleckian macro-model', *Structural Change and Economic Dynamics*, vol. 15, pp. 421–47.

Stockhammer, E., Hein, E. and Grafl, L. 2011. 'Globalization and the effects of changes in functional income distribution on aggregate demand in Germany', *International Review of Applied Economics*, vol. 25(1), pp. 1–23.

Stockhammer, E. and Stehrer, R. 2011. 'Goodwin or Kalecki in demand? Functional income distribution and aggregate demand in the short run', *Review of Radical Political Economics*, vol. 43(4), pp. 506–22.

Stockhammer, E. and Ederer, S. 2008. 'Demand effects of a falling wage share in Austria', *Empirica*, vol. 35(5), pp. 481–502.

Taylor, L. 1985. 'A stagnationist model of economic growth', *Cambridge Journal of Economics*, vol. 9, pp. 383–403.

Wang, P. 2009. Three essays on monetary policy and economic growth in China. Unpublished PhD Thesis, University of Ottawa.

Zhou, M., Xiao, W., and Yao, X. 2010. 'Unbalanced economic growth and uneven national income distribution: Evidence from China', Institute for Research on Labor and Employment Working Paper 2010-11. University of California, Los Angeles.

Appendix A: Data sources and definitions

ws: Adjusted wage share

EU12, Germany, France, Italy, United Kingdom, United States, Japan, Canada, Australia: AMECO

Adjusted wage share = Compensation per employees * number of employed/ GDP at factor costs

Republic of Korea, Mexico, Turkey: OECD STAT online

Adjusted wage share = Compensation per employees * number of employed/ value added at basic prices

Argentina:

1993–2005: Data supplied by Matthieu Charpe at the ILO/IILS in 2011;

Adjusted wage share = (Compensation of employees/GDP at basic prices)*1/ (ratio of employees in total employment)

1970–92 and 2006–07: data supplied by Lindenboim et al. (2011);

Unadjusted wage share = Compensation of employees/GDP at basic prices

The adjusted and unadjusted wage share data are linked using percentage changes.

China:

Zhou et al. (2010)'s adjusted wage share data calculated using the number of self-employed and national accounts data supplied China National Statistics Office, which are reported in Molero Simarro (2011), see also footnote 7.

India:

Own calculations based on data supplied by the Ministry of Statistics and Program Implementation (MOSPI) in the National Factor Income Summary tables for 1970–74 and 1980–99, and estimations supplied by Uma Rani Amara at the ILO/IILS for mixed income for 2000–07 based on sectoral mixed income shares of 1999

Adjusted wage share methodology 1: labour compensation/(national income at factor cost-mixed revenues)

Adjusted wage share methodology 2: labour compensation + Mixed revenues/ National Income at factor cost

Adjusted wage share average = ((adjusted wage share methodology 1)+(adjusted wage share methodology 2))/ 2

1975–79: UN National Account data; Unadjusted Wage share = Compensation of employees/Gross value added at factor cost

The unadjusted wage share data for 1975–79 is linked with the adjusted wage share data based on percentage changes.

South Africa:

1989–2004: Data supplied by Matthieu Charpe at the ILO/IILS in 2011;

Adjusted wage Share = Compensation per employees * number of employed/ value added at basic prices

1970–88 and 2005–07: UN national accounts

Unadjusted wage share = Compensation of employees/Gross value added at factor cost

The two series are linked using percentage changes.

93

Other data

For the following variables, data for the OECD countries are downloaded from the AMECO database (March 2011), and data for the other countries are from the World Bank World Development Indicators (WDI), unless otherwise stated:

Y: GDP in market prices, real

Yf: GDP at factor cost, real

C: Private consumption, real; for Argentina, missing data in WDI is linked with the data supplied by Lindenboim et al. (2011) for 1980–92 based on percentage changes

I: Private Investment, real; for Turkey, AMECO data for 1998–2006 is linked with data in State Planning Organisation for 1970–98; for the Republic of Korea, OECD STAT online; for Mexico, Sistema de Cuantas Nacionales de Mexico, Estadisticas historicas de Mexico 2009; for India Central Statistical Organisation; for South Africa, the South African Reserve Bank; for Argentina, data supplied by Lindenboim et al. (2011); for China, private investment is calculated as total investment – investment by state-owned and collective-owned units based on the national accounts data of the National Bureau of Statistics

P: GDP deflator

PM : Import price deflator

PX : Export price deflator

X: Exports, real

M: Imports, real

Mji: Imports from country J to country I, International Monetary Fund, Direction of Trade Statistics, 1980–2007 for all countries

E: Exchange rate; average of local currency per dollar, euro, and yen; WDI for all countries

YrW: GDP of the rest of world, real; calculated as World GDP (in constant 2000 US$) – Own GDP (in constant 2000 US$), source: World Bank World Development Indicators, 1970–2007 for all countries

W: Adjusted compensation of employees, real; calculated as $W = ws \cdot Y_f$

π: Adjusted profit share; calculated as $\pi = 1 - ws$

R: Adjusted gross operating surplus, real; calculated as $R = \pi \cdot Y_f$

rulc: Real unit labor costs; calculated as $rulc = ws \cdot Y_f / Y$

ulc: Nominal unit labor costs; calculated as $ulc = rulc \cdot P$

Appendix B: Mean values of the sample

	Euro area-12	Germany	France	Italy	United Kingdom	United States	Japan	Canada	Australia
C	2668.752	839.6983	570.3019	488.7716	424.2702	4244.501	188209.9	401.0635	271.7753
I	848.1945	267.3584	163.7691	153.8802	94.02227	906.6983	70709.99	115.6599	94.85458
W	2816.024	876.7782	602.3928	506.6465	435.2017	3928.189	217376.8	410.9098	268.7542
R	1303.102	419.0476	259.8812	285.6084	165.636	1868.476	89226.1	202.3327	139.9816
π	0.307	0.317	0.290	0.316	0.273	0.316	0.279	0.320	0.339
WS	0.693	0.683	0.710	0.684	0.727	0.684	0.721	0.680	0.661
RULC	0.619	0.615	0.615	0.623	0.643	0.634	0.673	0.601	0.597
I/Y	0.187	0.188	0.165	0.182	0.132	0.138	0.214	0.159	0.196
C/Y	0.578	0.580	0.576	0.581	0.613	0.671	0.582	0.582	0.599
X/Y	0.062	0.214	0.171	0.174	0.195	0.068	0.074	0.278	0.140
M/Y	0.068	0.209	0.175	0.172	0.195	0.085	0.070	0.264	0.159

	Turkey	Mexico	Korea, Rep. of	Argentina	China	India	South Africa
C	84	2844	191685	146170113547	3088949091343	1095059644025	62259315789
I	17	633	85641	35762072698	990724329326	2738770457915	129331952120
W	50	1911	245277	111090410472	3295794644564	1201990956938	665629364394
R	54	2060	57782	103315158417	2522921750396	3148272320164	327431252999
π	0.511	0.499	0.155	0.480	0.419	0.176	0.323
WS	0.489	0.501	0.845	0.520	0.581	0.824	0.677
RULC	0.459	0.466	0.753	0.507	0.504	0.753	0.624
I/Y	0.133	0.141	0.234	0.159	0.100	0.139	0.117
C/Y	0.738	0.661	0.610	0.656	0.503	0.697	0.564
X/Y	0.123	0.148	0.237	0.079	0.232	0.091	0.237
M/Y	0.139	0.159	0.255	0.070	0.193	0.112	0.211

Appendix C (a)

	Domestic D		Total D	
	Wage-led	**Profit-led**	**Wage-led**	**Profit-led**
Euro area	Onaran & Galanis 12 Stockhammer, Onaran, Ederer 09		Onaran & Galanis 12 Stockhammer, Onaran, Ederer 09	
Germany	Onaran & Galanis 12 Stockhammer, Hein, Grafl 11 Stockhammer & Stehrer 11 Bowles & Boyer 95 Naastepad & Storm 07 Hein & Vogel 08		Onaran & Galanis 12 Stockhammer, Hein, Grafl 11 Naastepad & Storm 07 Hein & Vogel 08	Bowles & Boyer 95
France	Onaran & Galanis 12 Bowles & Boyer 95 Naastepad & Storm 07 Ederer & Stockhammer 07 Hein & Vogel 08 Stockhammer & Stehrer 11		Onaran & Galanis 12 (Stockhammer, Onaran 04) Naastepad & Storm 07 Hein & Vogel 08HV08	Bowles & Boyer 95 Ederer & Stockhammer 07
Italy	Onaran & Galanis 12 Naastepad & Storm 07		Onaran & Galanis 12 Naastepad & Storm 07	
NL	Naastepad & Storm 07 Stockhammer & Stehrer 11	Hein & Vogel 08	Naastepad & Storm 07	Hein & Vogel 08
Austria	Stockhammer & Ederer 08 Hein & Vogel 08 Stockhammer & Stehrer 11	Stockhammer & Stehrer 11		Stockhammer & Ederer 08 Hein & Vogel 08
United Kingdom	Onaran & Galanis 12 Bowles & Boyer 95 Naastepad & Storm 07 Hein & Vogel 08		Onaran & Galanis 12 Bowles & Boyer 95 Naastepad & Storm 07 Hein & Vogel 08	

	Domestic D		Total D	
	Wage-led	**Profit-led**	**Wage-led**	**Profit-led**
United States	Onaran & Galanis 12 Onaran, Stockhammer, Grafl 11 Bowles & Boyer 95 Hein & Vogel 08 (Stockhammer & Stehrer 11)	Naastepad & Storm 07	Onaran & Galanis 12 Onaran, Stockhammer, Grafl 11 Bowles & Boyer 95 Hein & Vogel 08	(Stockhammer, Onaran 04) Naastepad & Storm 07 Barbosa-Filho & Taylor 08
Japan	Onaran & Galanis 12 Bowles & Boyer 95 (Stockhammer & Stehrer 11)	Naastepad & Storm 07	Onaran & Galanis 12	Bowles & Boyer 95 Naastepad & Storm 07
Australia	Onaran & Galanis 12 (Stockhammer & Stehrer 11)			Onaran & Galanis 12
Canada	Onaran & Galanis 12 (Stockhammer & Stehrer 11)			Onaran & Galanis 12

Appendix C (b)

	Domestic D		Total D	
	Wage-led	**Profit-led**	**Wage-led**	**Profit-led**
Turkey	Onaran and Galanis 12		Onaran and Galanis 12 Onaran, Stockhammer 05	
Korea	Onaran and Galanis 12		Onaran and Galanis 12 Onaran, Stockhammer 05	
Mexico	Onaran and Galanis 12			Onaran and Galanis 12
Argentina	Onaran and Galanis 12			Onaran and Galanis 12
India	Onaran and Galanis 12			Onaran and Galanis 12
China	Onaran and Galanis 12	Molero Simarro 11 Wang 09		Onaran and Galanis 12 Molero Simarro 11
South Africa	Onaran and Galanis 12			Onaran and Galanis 12
Thailand		Jetin and Kurt 11		Jetin and Kurt 11

4
Wage-led or Profit-led Supply: Wages, Productivity and Investment*

Servaas Storm and C.W.M. Naastepad

4.1 A Dutch treat

According to standard writing class instructions, a surefire way of having one's manuscripts ignored is to start off with a lengthy prologue. We deliberately offend this golden rule and take a detour, treating our readers to a perhaps unusual account of a well-known piece of recent economic history – the 'Dutch employment miracle' of the 1980s and 1990s (Blanchard 2000; *The Economist* 2002). What was so miraculous to many was the sharp and sustained drop in the supposedly sclerotic Dutch unemployment rate, which had peaked at more than 11 per cent of the labour force in 1982 – a rate which was 2.1 percentage points *higher* than the average EU-15 unemployment rate in the same year. By 1990, Dutch unemployment had come down to 5.1 per cent, a full 2.1 percentage points *below* the EU-15 unemployment rate in the same year, and it declined further to only 3.1 per cent in 2000, with the EU-15 unemployment rate stuck at 7.7 per cent; the Dutch managed to maintain the momentum, keeping unemployment down at 3.8 per cent of the labour force during the period 2000–10, a full 4 percentage points lower than the unemployment rate in the EU-15. This labour market success is generally ascribed to the Dutch socioeconomic model, colloquially known as the 'Polder Model'.

The label 'Polder Model' is apt, not only because the Netherlands features some 3,000 man-made polders, but also because polder construc-

* We are grateful for comments received from Marc Lavoie, Engelbert Stockhammer, Sangheon Lee, Lance Taylor and participants of the Regulating for Decent Work Conference, held at the ILO, Geneva, 6–8 July 2011.

tion has always involved much employment, including public relief works in the depression years of the 1930s. 'God created the world, but the Dutch created Holland' – with a lot of labour input. In fact, the recent Polder Model has no rival when it comes to employment creation. During the 1960s and 1970s, economic growth in the Netherlands, as in the wider EU-15 area, failed to generate positive growth in employment (measured in hours worked). For the Netherlands this changed drastically after 1982: during the 1980s and 1990s, one percentage point of real GDP growth generated about 0.6 percentage points of employment growth (measured in hours). The change for the EU-15, in contrast, was small: post-1982, one percentage point of real GDP growth in the EU-15 is associated with only about 0.1 percentage point of employment growth. Agnostic observers have tried to argue that the superior employment performance of the Netherlands is a statistical artifact, based on fiddling with the unemployment data and/or definitions or due to a shortening of average work hours as a result of the significant increase in part-time work. Both claims are wrong. The Dutch labour participation rate has been rising steadily after the mid-1980s and is among the highest in the OECD area. And the average work week in the Netherlands is not much shorter than that of other EU countries. So what is the secret of Dutch job creation?

As the by now rather clichéd story goes, the foundations of the employment *renaissance* of the Netherlands were laid in 1982, when employers, unions and the government signed the Wassenaar Agreement, under which the unions promised to deliver pay restraint in exchange for a new emphasis on job creation. Ever since, real wage growth in the Netherlands has been kept below productivity growth and – so the story goes – this allowed firms' profits to increase, led to new investments and thus created new jobs. It must be said that voluntary wage restraint was not done half-heartedly:[1] annual nominal wage growth (per hour), amounting to more than 11 per cent in the 1970s, was brought down to about 2 per cent during 1984–2000; real wage growth (per hour worked) was cut from 4 per cent per year in the 1970s to about zero in the later period. Dutch wage moderation has been exceptional in an international context: on average, annual Dutch real wage growth was 0.5 percentage points below average OECD real wage growth throughout the 1980s and 1990s. As a result and as intended, the Dutch wage share (in GDP at factor cost), which stood at about 65 per cent at the end of the 1970s and in the early 1980s, was brought down to 56 per cent during the period 1984–2000, and the profit share, correspondingly, increased from 35 per cent to slightly more than 44 per cent. It is true that investment (as a proportion of GDP) increased following the recovery in profitability, but the increase was only modest and nowhere near sufficient to give a boost to Dutch economic growth.

It is here where most observers actually go wrong in their analysis of the Jobs Miracle: Dutch real GDP growth post-1982 has been inferior to Dutch growth performance in the 1960s and 1970s, even though there was a restoration of profitability to pre-profit squeeze levels. That growth did not respond to the heavy dose of wage moderation should not have come as a surprise, however: the Dutch economy, after all, is *wage-led* (Naastepad 2006; Naastepad and Storm 2007; Tavani, Flaschel and Taylor 2011). Hence, real wage restraint and the consequent fall in the wage share led to a *net contraction* of aggregate demand which depressed, rather than raised, economic growth. With demand out of wage incomes falling, the Dutch could only sustain – modest – growth after 1982 by means of increased reliance on growing world demand (for Dutch exports) and a growing dependence on (household) debts and (housing) wealth gains as a source of consumption demand. The Dutch central bank has estimated that about half of Dutch GDP growth during 1995–2005 has been due to loan-financed and wealth-gain funded consumption growth. Without these rather dubious sources of growth, the shine of the Dutch employment miracle would have worn off already more than ten years ago.

It is also important to our discussion that Dutch growth performance after 1982 has not been significantly superior to that of the EU-15: between 1984 and 1996, annual Dutch real GDP growth was only slightly higher than that of the EU-15 (2.8 per cent versus 2.7 per cent, respectively). This means that the far better employment growth of the Netherlands (vis-à-vis the EU-15) cannot in any way be attributed to superior growth performance. What remains is just one explanation: the source of the Dutch employment miracle has been inferior labour productivity growth. This is indeed borne out by the data. Annual Dutch labour productivity growth (measured per hour of work) was roughly equal to average productivity growth in the EU-15 in the 1970s. But during the period 1984–2000, average Dutch labour productivity growth was about 0.6 percentage points *lower* than EU-15 productivity growth, and it is this gap in productivity growth which is the cause of relatively rapid Dutch employment growth and its lower unemployment rate (Naastepad 2006; Storm and Naastepad 2011). The flipside of low productivity growth has been a substantial increase in the numbers of Dutch people in low-wage employment, made possible by a policy of labour market deregulation – from less than 10 per cent of total persons employed in the early 1980s to about 18 per cent in the early 2000s.

It is not well understood, and this is rather unfortunate, that the slow-down of Dutch labour productivity growth itself is almost completely due to the widely praised policy of real wage restraint. The reason is (as we will argue below in more detail) that lower real wage growth slows down labour productivity growth in two major ways:

- by depressing the growth of aggregate demand, real wage growth restraint reduces productivity growth through the so-called Kaldor–Verdoorn effect; and
- directly, by retarding the rate of labour-saving technological progress, because lower wage growth reduces firms' incentives to invest in labour-saving R&D.

About 90 per cent of the Dutch productivity growth slowdown after 1982 must be attributed to the policy-engineered decline in real wage growth (Naastepad 2006). And the sharp productivity growth decline, in turn, fully explains the remarkable improvement in Dutch employment growth post-1982. The Dutch Employment Miracle, in other words, is better labelled a 'Productivity Crisis' – and we don't see much ground for urging the rest of Europe to learn from it and adopt a similar model.

This darker side of the miracle is not widely recognized in the Netherlands itself. For example, Dutch unions, in clear defiance of standard insider–outsider models, were happy to give priority to creating jobs for the unemployed over obtaining higher wages for the already employed by means of real wage restraint. Political support for wage moderation has been truly across the board with only the fringe left being a party pooper. The Dutch social democratic party (PvdA) has supported real wage moderation from the outset, while in opposition, and also later, when wage moderation and labour market deregulation became key parts of its own Third Way economic strategy. Tellingly, the motto of the two consecutive governments (1994–2002) under the leadership of social democratic Prime Minister Wim Kok was 'jobs, jobs, jobs' – a motto Mr Kok also gave to the report of the Employment Taskforce, which he chaired in 2003 on behalf of the European heads of state. What the durable Mr Kok, who is a man of few words, actually meant is that full employment, mostly based on low-wage flexible services jobs, should take precedence over inequality as a goal of economic policy – in one blow discarding European social democratic thought in favour of narrow Anglo-Saxon NAIRU logic. In Third Way opinion, it ought to be left to markets to dictate investment and jobs, while government should be used in a traditional liberal manner to make workers more competitive and protect them (within limits) from illness, disability and poverty. Damning the Netherlands with faint praise, we conclude that a major lesson from the Dutch experience is that a policy of real wage restraint can be successful in a wage-led economy – provided, of course, the prime goal is the creation of low-wage flexible (service-sector) jobs in an economy growing mostly as a result of debt-financed demand.

At this point our guided tour to the Low Countries has come to an end. It is fair to ask: what, if any, are its general lessons or broader insights for growth and employment? Cutting out the details, two key lessons emerge. First, in the macro scheme of things, labour productivity growth is an *endogenous variable*, far too important to be ignored, which is influenced by (wage-led or profit-led) demand and real wage growth. Below we investigate how productivity growth interacts with demand and employment growth in a simple (but realistic) demand-led growth model. Second, as the Dutch example illustrates, real wage restraint may generate strong employment growth, even if the economy is wage-led. The Dutch example should stand out as an unforgiving warning signal – cautioning against overoptimistic assessments that there is no trade-off between higher wages and lower unemployment in wage-led economies. Capitalism's internal contradictions cannot be wished away.

4.2   Labour productivity growth

Labour productivity growth is endogenous: it depends – in a structural sense – on aggregate demand growth and real wage growth. The careful reader of this sentence may wonder what we mean by the phrasal adjective 'in a structural sense'. The point here is that in a regime in which trend ('structural') real wage growth is high, for instance, a sudden temporary drop (or rise) in real wage growth will not (significantly) affect productivity growth – because this does not affect firms' R&D investments. However, a more permanent (and credible) change – from a regime with rapid real wage growth to one with low or zero wage growth, as in the Netherlands after 1982 – will affect R&D, investment, the capital intensity of production and hence productivity growth. Our analysis of the macroeconomic effects of real wage changes thus concerns (policy) regime change – and is therefore medium-term in nature. We turn to a discussion of the determinants of productivity growth we have mentioned above: demand growth and real wage growth.

The increase in labour productivity growth caused by growth in aggregate demand and output is known in the literature as the Kaldor–Verdoorn effect. This arises because aggregate demand growth leads to an economy-wide deepening of the division of labour as well as more rapid learning-by-doing (in firms) – and both these processes are eventually reflected in higher labour productivity growth. Moreover, to the extent that demand growth is investment growth, the new investments result in higher labour productivity, because the newly installed equipment embodies the latest state of production technologies and is therefore more productive than older vintages of capital stock. The most comprehensive study on the Kaldor–Verdoorn effect is McCombie, Pugno and Soro (2002), who review 80 empirical studies and conclude that the overwhelming majority of these studies – irrespective of the differences in econometric methods and data employed – find a causal link from demand growth to productivity growth. Table 4.1, which provides evidence on the Kaldor–Verdoorn effect, lists ten more recent studies, which confirm McCombie et al.'s conclusion. The (simple) average value of the Kaldor–Verdoorn coefficient for the group of OECD countries is 0.46: a one percentage point rise in demand growth is thus associated with an increase in labour productivity growth by 0.46 percentage points. We treat this finding as stylized fact.

The second determinant of productivity growth we consider is real wage growth. Its explanation goes back at least to Karl Marx, who argued in *Capital* that high wages lead to a labour-saving bias in innovation and technological progress – because only labour-saving technological progress, which he identifies with rising labour productivity, ensures the reproduction of a positive economic surplus. Higher wages stimulate capital deepening, drive inefficient firms off the market and encourage structural change, increase the proportion of high-skilled workers in the labour force, and, in general, promote labour-saving technological progress. Marx's idea of wage-cost-induced technological progress has gone through various incarnations, including Hicks (1932), Kennedy (1964) and, more recently, Foley and Michl (1999) and Funk (2002). Table 4.2 summarizes recent findings on the impact of real wage growth on labour productivity growth. The statistical evidence assumes that causality runs from wage growth to productivity growth, which appears reasonable in view of the fact that wage growth mostly follows from an institutionalized process of bargaining (as in NAIRU theory, for instance) and therefore 'leads' movements in productivity, as autonomous real wage pressures drive profit-seeking firms to accelerate the pace of labour-saving technological progress. Long-run evidence for 19 OECD countries (1960–2004) provided by Vergeer and Kleinknecht (2010–11) shows that a one percentage point increase in real wage growth raises productivity growth by 0.31—0.39 percentage points.

Table 4.1 Estimates of the impact of (investment) demand growth on productivity growth

	France	Germany	Netherlands	United Kingdom	United States	Nordic countries	OECD countries
McCombie et al. (2002)							0.3–0.6
Cornwall and Cornwall (2002)							0.5
Leon-Ledesma (2002)							0.64–0.67
Knell (2004)	0.43			0.53	0.43	0.40–0.76	
Naastepad (2006)			0.63				
Angeriz et al. (2008)							0.50–0.67
Crespi and Pianta (2008)							0.27–0.38
Hein and Tarassow (2009)	0.54	0.43	0.45	0.23	0.11		
Storm and Naastepad (2011)						0.31	
Alexiadis and Tsagdis (2010)							0.43–0.49
Vergeer and Kleinknecht (2010–11)							0.24–0.37
simple average (standard deviation)	0.49 (0.08)	0.43	0.54 (0.13)	0.38 (0.21)	0.27 (0.23)	0.45 (0.19)	0.46 (0.12)

Notes: McCombie *et al.* (2002): average of 80 empirical studies; Cornwall and Cornwall (2002): based on data for 16 OECD countries (1960–89); Leon-Ledesma (2002): for 18 OECD countries (1965–94); Angeriz, McCombie and Roberts (2008): for European regions (1986–2002); Crespi and Pianta (2008): data cover 22 manufacturing and 10 service industries in France, Germany, Italy, the Netherlands, Portugal and the United Kingdom (1994–2000); Alexiadis and Tsagdis (2010): based on data (1977–2005) for 109 EU-12 regions; Storm and Naastepad (2009): OLS estimates using 5-year average data for 20 OECD countries (1984–2004); and Vergeer and Kleinknecht (2010–11): panel data results based on annual data for 19 OECD countries (1960–2004).

Table 4.2 Estimates of the impact of real wage growth on productivity growth

	France	Germany	Netherlands	United Kingdom	United States	Nordic countries	OECD countries
Rowthorn (1999)	0.11–0.24	0.33–0.87	0.24–0.44	0.25–0.60	0.13–0.28	0.10–0.54	0.24–0.30
Nymoen and Rødseth (2003)						0.50	
Naastepad (2006)			0.52				
Carter (2007)							0.60
Hein and Tarassow (2009)	0.31	0.32	0.33	0.25	0.36		
Storm and Naastepad (2009/2011)							0.29
Vergeer and Kleinknecht (2010–11)							0.31–0.39
simple average (standard deviation)	0.24 (0.10)	0.46 (0.20)	0.43 (0.13)	0.34 (0.12)	0.28 (0.11)	0.41 (0.13)	0.38 (0.15)

Notes: Rowthorn (1999): data are from his Table 2, panel (b); Nymoen and Rødseth (2003): for the four Nordic countries (1965–94); Carter (2007): based on data for 15 OECD countries (1980–96); Storm and Naastepad (2009): OLS estimates using 5-year average data for 20 OECD countries (1984–2004); and Vergeer and Kleinknecht (2010–11): panel data results based on annual data for 19 OECD countries (1960–2004).

Our own finding for 20 OECD countries during 1984–2004 (Storm and Naastepad 2009, 2011) comes close. The simple average of estimates for individual economies including France, Germany, the Netherlands, the United Kingdom, the United States and the Nordic countries is 0.38. Hence, the 'wage-cost induced technological progress effect' holds that an increase in real wage growth by one percentage point is associated with an increase in productivity growth by 0.38 percentage points.

4.3   Wage-led growth

Any model is a heuristic device, a temporary simplification of reality to which excluded features or mechanisms must be added later to make it more realistic. We focus on the impact of the (real) wage rate on economic growth, productivity growth and employment – leaving out, for the moment, other determinants of a country's macroeconomic performance (for example, the interest rate or the fiscal policy stance). The formal, algebraic, model is explained in Storm and Naastepad (2012a, 2012b). Here we use Figures 4.1, 4.2 and 4.3 as a mnemonic device to illustrate its working. Real wage growth is a distributional variable, determined as the outcome of institutionalized negotiation and bargaining between unions and employers' associations. We investigate what happens to growth, productivity and employment when real wage growth is raised by one percentage point. The key variable in the model – as in any model of wage-led or profit-led growth – is the wage share. The wage share depends on the real wage and labour productivity. Higher real wage growth raises the wage share, but higher labour productivity growth reduces the wage share, because one hour of work (at a given wage rate) now generates more output, and hence labour costs per unit of output are reduced. If wages increase more than productivity, the wage share increases, and this automatically means that the profit share is reduced.

Figure 4.1 presents a *wage-led* economy, in which labour productivity growth is exogenous (and constant). Higher real wage growth increases the wage share and this leads to an increase in demand and output. The reason is that a higher wage share redistributes income from (higher-saving) profits to (lower-saving) wages. This raises consumption growth and the increase in consumption growth is larger (in absolute terms) than the decline in investment and export growth, induced by lower profits and higher unit labour costs. There is a consequent expansion in output growth. We assume that a one percentage point rise in wage share growth raises wage-led output growth by 0.3 percentage

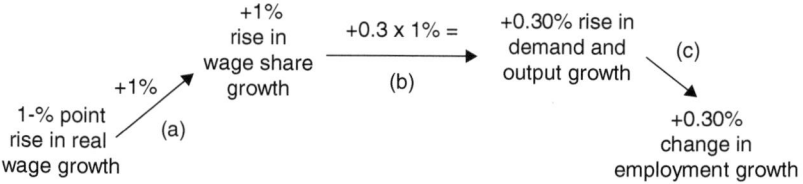

Figure 4.1   A model of wage-led growth with exogenous productivity

points – which is realistic for the EU and individual EU-countries (Stockhammer et al. 2009; Naastepad and Storm 2007, 2012a; Onaran and Galanis 2012). A one percentage point rise in real wage growth raises wage share growth by one percentage point (arrow (a)), raising demand and output growth (arrow (b)) as well as employment growth by 0.3 percentage points (arrow (c)).

This is not the whole story, however, because – as argued above – labour productivity growth is not exogenous, but changes in response to higher real wage growth, directly (through inducing labour-saving innovations) and indirectly (through the Kaldor–Verdoorn effect). Including these direct and indirect effects makes the model of a wage-led economy more complicated, as is illustrated by Figure 4.2. In this figure, arrow (d) captures the wage-cost induced technological progress effect. What it means is that a one percentage point step-up in real wage growth raises productivity growth by 0.38 percentage points. Productivity growth increases even more because of the Kaldor–Verdoorn effect, captured by arrow (e), according to which a one percentage point rise in output growth raises labour productivity growth by 0.46 percentage points. Higher labour productivity growth, as we noted above, reduces wage share growth; this link is given by arrow (f). These are key links in our model: higher real wages induce higher productivity, as a result of which the wage share does not increase as much as the real wage. With our numbers, wage share growth would increase by only 0.54 percentage points in response to a one percentage point hike in real wage growth. This, in turn, has two implications.

First, the smaller rise in wage share growth curtails the acceleration of wage-led output growth to only 0.16 percentage points (as compared to 0.3 percentage points in Figure 4.1). Economic growth thus becomes less strongly wage-led. It follows that the higher is the sensitivity of productivity growth to real wage growth, the more limited will be the strength of the wage-led nature of aggregate demand. The impact of an increase in wage growth on productivity growth is generally ignored in models of demand-led growth which follow the logic of Figure 4.1, and hence the impact of a change in wage growth on demand growth is overestimated.

Second, the impact of higher wage growth on employment growth in the model shown in Figure 4.2 no longer depends solely on what happens to (wage-led) output growth, but also on what happens to productivity growth. This is so, since employment growth is – by definition – the difference between output and productivity growth. Higher real wage growth may now lead to a *reduction* in employment growth, if its stimulus to labour-saving technological progress and productivity growth is strong enough. In Figure 4.2, output growth increases by 0.16 percentage points in response to a one percentage point rise in real wage growth – along arrows (a), (b) and (c). Productivity growth rises by 0.46 percentage points: directly by 0.38 percentage points along arrow (d), and indirectly by another 0.08 percentage points via the Kaldor–Verdoorn effect along arrow (e). This implies that in our prototype wage-led economy, employment growth *declines* by 0.3 percentage points in response to a 1 percentage point increase in real wage growth. The reason is the acceleration of productivity growth implied by higher real wage growth. Conversely, employment growth *rises* if real wage growth is lowered, since real wage growth restraint reduces productivity growth more than output growth – thus creating higher employment, a fact cunningly exploited by the Dutch Polder Model

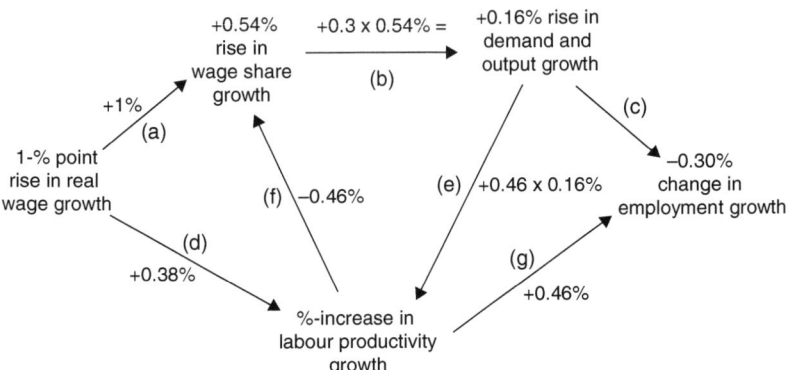

Figure 4.2   A model of wage-led growth

Note: The numbers are realistic for the EU and EU countries. For details, see Storm and Naastepad (2012b).

builders to much international acclaim.[2] The outcome, in that case, may well be lower unemployment, but this is achieved by depressing productivity growth (rather than raising profitability, investment and export and output growth). *Lower* unemployment, in other words, compromises welfare and the overall technological dynamism of the wage-led system.

Our prototypical finding concerns a weakly wage-led economy in which overall growth does not respond strongly to increased wage share growth. It can be shown that if the economy becomes more strongly wage-led, the employment-generating effect of real wage restraint becomes smaller. More strongly wage-led here means that output growth responds much more strongly to wage share growth than we assume in Figure 4.2, where – along arrow (b) – the wage share–output elasticity equals 0.3. However, even in strongly wage-led economies (where the wage-share–output elasticity takes a value of 0.80, as in the Scandinavian countries; see Storm and Naastepad 2012a), lower wage growth still creates more employment – because, also in these economies, productivity growth remains more sensitive to real wage growth than aggregate demand growth. Hence, co-operative wage-led capitalism faces one inescapable problem: lack of employment growth. While this deeper problem may lose importance in the near future (due to the ageing of Europe's labour force), a more proactive approach is to cut annual working hours (as in the 1960s) and/or to expand, often essential, public-sector (tax-financed) employment in health, education and environmental protection ('green jobs') – what Adolph Lowe (1988, 100) aptly called 'planned domestic colonization', the creation of public-sector jobs to strengthen (public) infrastructure and provide essential services in health, education and general welfare. Lowe's proposal, which ties in with the basic income scheme proposed by Andrew Glyn (2006), Richard Sennett (2005) and many others, advocates 'a type of investment that will enlist millions of job-seeking workers, whom the private domain cannot employ, in productive activity'.

4.4 Profit-led growth

When the economy is *profit-led* (rather than wage-led), a higher wage share reduces aggregate demand and output – as along arrow (b) in Figure 4.3. The reason is that higher real wages and a higher wage share depress investments and exports more (in absolute terms) than they actually boost consumption. Aggregate demand contracts following the rise in the wage share – and the decline in the profit share. A higher profit share is therefore 'good' for growth, while a higher wage share is 'bad'. In Figure 4.3, along arrow (b), we assume that a one-percentage point increase in wage share growth reduces output growth by 0.23 percentage points – which is the impact we found for the US economy (Naastepad and Storm 2007; Storm and Naastepad 2012a).[3]

This is not the whole macro story yet – because, also in a profit-led economy, higher wage growth affects productivity growth. First, it directly induces – through induced technological progress – extra productivity growth: the impact is given along arrow (d). Second, lower output growth *reduces* productivity growth through the Kaldor–Verdoorn effect – an effect captured by arrow (e). Using realistic numbers we find that the Kaldor–Verdoorn effect is smaller (in absolute terms) than the wage-cost induced productivity increase and, hence, the net effect of a one percentage point increase in real wage growth is to raise productivity growth by 0.31 percentage points. Higher productivity growth, in turn, reduces the growth of the wage share as illustrated by arrow (f). Going by our numbers, a one percentage point increase in real wage growth does, in effect, lead to an increase in wage share growth by only 0.69 (not one) percentage points. Due to the productivity-growth boost of higher real wage growth, the system becomes less strongly profit-led: the total impact of a one-percentage point increase in real wage growth on (profit-led) output growth is –0.16 percentage points.

Higher real wage growth reduces profit-led output growth while raising productivity growth. This means that employment growth gets

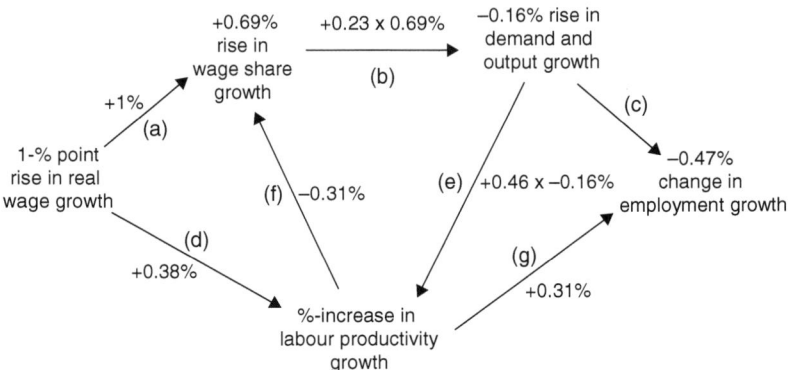

Figure 4.3   A model of profit-led growth

Note: See note to Figure 4.2.

squeezed from both sides: output growth slows down and at the same time firms need fewer workers per unit of output. The estimate for our prototype profit-led economy of Figure 4.3 is that an increase in real wage growth by one percentage point reduces employment growth by almost 0.5 percentage points. Of course, it works the other way around as well: real wage restraint in profit-led systems is pretty effective in raising employment growth. But it must be noted that the employment creation is due more to the slowdown of (endogenous) productivity growth (by 0.31 percentage points) than to the expansion of output growth (by only 0.16 percentage points). Clearly, real wage restraint also hampers productivity growth and technological dynamism in profit-led economies.

4.5   Evidence on OECD employment growth

The message is sobering, perhaps: under realistic assumptions, higher real wage growth does not generate higher employment growth in a wage-led economy. We believe this is a fair conclusion, in line with the fact that the employment elasticity of growth in the OECD countries has increased in recent times, while real wage growth slowed down – as illustrated in Figure 4.4.

Let us consider the historical facts for 11 major OECD economies, appearing in Table 4.3, more closely. It can be seen that average annual employment growth (measured in hours worked) in these countries during the 1990s was low; the unweighted group average is an employment growth rate of 0.3 per cent per year. Hourly employment growth was negative in this period in Finland, Germany, Sweden, and the United Kingdom, and about zero in Belgium, France and Italy. It is only in Denmark, the Netherlands, Spain and the United States that employment growth is higher. Average annual real GDP growth during 1990–99 was 2.2 per cent and average labour productivity growth stood at about 2 per cent per annum. In the second period (2000–08), hourly employment growth increased in almost all countries which featured negative or zero employment growth in the 1990s: in Finland, the employment growth rate increased by a full 2 percentage points, in Belgium and Spain by more than 1 percentage point, and in France, Italy, Sweden and the United Kingdom by more than 0.55 percentage points. Employment growth also increased in Denmark and Germany (where it became less strongly negative) and only in the Netherlands and in the United States did hourly employment growth rates fall after 2000. On average for the 11 countries, employment increased by 0.8 per cent per year during 2000–08.

The rise in employment growth cannot be attributed to an over-all improvement in economic performance. To the contrary, average (unweighted) real GDP growth declined from more than 2.2 per cent per year during the 1990s to less than 2 per cent during 2000–08. This means that the employment elasticity of GDP – defined as the ratio of hourly employment growth to real GDP growth – has increased, as it did, from less than 0.1 in the 1990s to more than 0.4 in the period 2000–08. OECD growth has, in other words, become more employment-intensive. We note that this is not true for the United States, where the employment elasticity of growth declined from a value of 0.44 before 2000 to a value of 0.24 after 2000; this makes it understandable why there is so much discussion in the United States about jobless growth and jobless recovery from the crisis. But for Europe, with the exception of the Netherlands, the post-2000 years were a period of employment growth.

The rise in employment growth (by 0.5 percentage points) and the drop in GDP growth (by about 0.3 percentage points) imply that labour productivity must have declined even more than real GDP growth. Labour productivity growth fell from an unweighted average of 2 per cent in the 1990s to just 1.2 per cent during 2000–08. Employment growth was thus achieved at the cost of productivity growth, closely mimicking the Dutch employment miracle of the 1990s. As we argued in the introduction, the Dutch jobs wonder was based on real wage restraint. What about the European employment growth revival post-2000? As can be seen from Table 4.3, real wage growth was lowered in most countries – most spectacularly in Germany, Belgium, Spain, Denmark and France. Figure 4.4 presents a scatter plot of real wage growth and employment elasticities (of GDP) for the 11 countries in the two periods 1990–99 and 2000–08; the data show, as per the fitted linear curve, that the employment elasticity elasticity of GDP increases, when real wage growth is lowered. In our book *Macroeconomics Beyond the NAIRU* (Storm and Naastepad 2012a) we have analyzed these 11 economies and found that most of them are wage-led economies (the United States is the exception). The reduction in real wage growth did therefore lower real GDP growth – as we can observe in the data of Table 4.3 for most European economies (except Italy and Sweden). This finding matches with the observed increase in employment growth only if there is a considerable (induced) decline in productivity growth, brought about directly and indirectly by real wage moderation. Real wage growth thus has a stronger impact on employment growth than on output growth – in line with our stylized findings. The Dutch employment miracle has definitely gone European.

Table 4.3 Real GDP growth, hourly employment growth, labour productivity growth and real wage growth: 11 OECD countries, 1990–99 and 2000–08

	1990–99				2000–08			
	Real GDP growth	Employment growth	Labour productivity growth	Real wage growth	Real GDP growth	Employment growth	Labour productivity growth	Real wage growth
Belgium	2.06	0.03	2.03	1.67	1.81	1.20	0.61	0.71
Denmark	2.49	0.55	1.94	1.77	1.26	0.75	0.51	1.16
Finland	1.70	-1.12	2.82	1.16	2.98	0.88	2.10	2.06
France	1.78	-0.01	1.79	1.17	1.58	0.54	1.04	0.68
Germany	1.81	-0.23	2.04	1.22	1.37	-0.12	1.49	0.06
Italy	1.35	0.00	1.35	0.21	0.82	0.81	0.01	0.54
Netherlands	3.08	1.36	1.72	1.17	1.96	0.54	1.42	1.11
Spain	2.79	1.32	1.47	0.88	3.09	2.42	0.67	0.05
Sweden	1.83	-0.23	2.06	1.78	2.55	0.55	2.00	1.41
United Kingdom	2.38	-0.18	2.56	1.57	2.23	0.42	1.81	1.49
United States	3.33	1.48	1.85	1.61	2.02	0.48	1.54	1.13

Sources: Employment is measured in total hours worked; GDP is in constant prices. Employment and GDP data are from the Groningen Growth and Development Centre's total economy database. Data on real compensation per employee (GDP deflator, total economy) are from the AMECO Database.

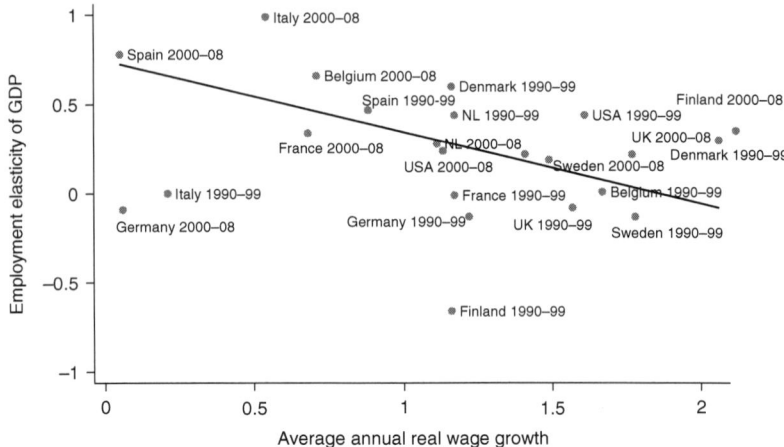

Figure 4.4   The employment elasticity of GDP declines when real wage growth rises. Evidence for 11 OECD economies (1990–2008)

Notes: The fitted curve is based on the following OLS regression (with robust *t*-statistics):

Employment elasticity of GDP = 0.75   –   0.40 real wage growth

$$(4.45)^{***} \qquad\qquad (3.28)^{***}$$

Adjusted $R^2 = 0.27$; F = 10.75; n = 20

Italy (1990–99) and Germany (2000–08) are excluded from the regression. *** = statistically significant at 1 per cent. Employment is measured in total hours worked; GDP is in constant prices. Employment and GDP data are from the Groningen Growth and Development Centre's total economy database. The employment elasticity of GDP is defined as the ratio of average annual (hourly) employment to average annual real GDP growth. Data on real compensation per employee (GDP deflator, total economy) are from the AMECO Database. NL = the Netherlands.

4.6   Wages, productivity and profits

Even in the most strongly wage-led countries in the OECD, wage-led growth is unlikely to be job-creating – because it leads to labour-saving technological progress and productivity growth. One remedy to this problem is an overall reduction of individual working hours (as was done in Scandinavia); ignoring possible organizational complications, no valid objections can be raised so long as wages are reduced in proportion to the reduction in working hours and the growth in labour productivity. Specifically, by sharing available employment (hours), lack of, or even negative, employment growth does not translate into increased unemployment. We believe that successful co-ordinated employment sharing is possible only in a (strongly) *wage-led* economic system that responds to higher wage growth by expanding output and raising productivity; it would not be feasible in a profit-led economy which contracts in reaction to higher real wage growth.

Why is such employment sharing acceptable to private sector firms in a wage-led economy? The answer is that firms' profits are relatively insensitive to higher real wages, and this is in large measure due to the relatively strong response of productivity growth to wage growth. As firms and workers are operating under a fairness constraint, firms obtain more worker commitment, higher productivity as well as more demand, and greater worker willingness to co-operate in engendering technological progress in exchange for the higher wage and a more egalitarian outcome. What is crucial is that the more rapid demand growth and higher productivity growth enables firms to maintain their profitability (in real terms) when facing higher real wages. How can we understand this?

To start, it will be clear that – while keeping all other factors constant – higher real wage growth (say, by one percentage point) must reduce profit growth one-for-one. This we call the *direct profit damage* of higher real wages. But, as we have seen, higher wages have additional *indirect* effects which actually are good for profits:

1. higher real wages raise wage-led output, and this raises total profits (when we assume that profits per unit of output are constant). It follows that the more strongly wage-led the system is, the more output and total profits will grow in response to higher wages.
2. Higher real wage growth provides a boost to productivity growth. This, in turn, translates into higher profit growth, because it reduces wage cost per unit of output.

In a *strongly wage-led* economy, both these effects tend to be so large that the *direct* damage to profits due to higher real wage growth is almost completely offset by its *indirect* effects on profits.[4] This finding is crucial: based on parameter values for a strongly wage-led economy (such as those in Scandinavia), we find that the impact of a one percentage point increase in real wage growth on profit income growth is very small. Elsewhere we argue in more detail that the relative insensitivity of profitability to higher real wages, which is in large measure due to the relatively strong responsiveness of productivity growth to wage growth, provides the foundation for co-operative versions of capitalism such as the Nordic one (Storm and Naastepad 2012a).

If we compare this Nordic model to the Dutch model, closely examined by Naastepad (2006), which arguably is in many ways representative of other *weakly wage-led* EU countries, we find that Dutch profits are much more sensitive to higher wages than Scandinavia profits – the main reason is that weakly wage-led Dutch output growth does not respond very strongly to higher wages (as in Figure 4.2), which limits the productivity–growth stimulus (provided by higher wage growth). As a result, higher real wage growth does depress Dutch profit growth very significantly. It follows that granting workers higher real wages is not an option for Dutch firms as their profitability will suffer. This sharp trade-off between real wage growth and profit growth helps to explain why Dutch unions did not push for higher pay but instead decided to bargain for more jobs by means of a social compromise, entailing a long-term (voluntary) commitment to real wage growth restraint (as we explained in the introduction). Predictably, this real wage restraint did lead to the recovery of firm profitability as well as to the so-called 'Dutch employment miracle', which has been the by-product of a wage-moderation-induced productivity growth slowdown. The contrast with the technologically more dynamic Nordic model being obvious, we may call the Nordic model 'social-productivist', while labelling the Dutch model 'social-stagnationist'.

The label 'social-stagnationist' applies to most other EU economies, including France, Germany, Italy and Spain. This is apparent from Figure 4.5 which shows that the more strongly wage-led the economy in question is, the lower is the sensitivity of profit income growth to increases in real wage growth. It can be seen that for Germany the sensitivity of profit growth to real wage growth is similar (–0.62) to that of the Netherlands, while for Italy it is lower (–0.56), and for France and Spain it would take a value of about –0.4. These European continental countries feature similarly weakly wage-led aggregate demand as the Dutch one and have also opted for high employment growth (and low wage growth) rather than high productivity growth, high wage growth and employment sharing. Figure 4.5 also features the profit-led US economy: with profit-led demand, a one percentage point increase in real wage growth translates into a decline in profit income growth by one percentage point; nowhere in the OECD is the conflict between wage growth and profit growth more pronounced than in the United States.

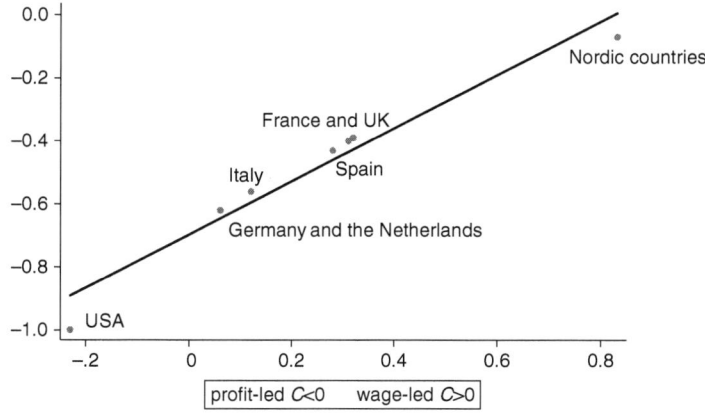

Figure 4.5 The more strongly wage-led the economy, the less sensitive is profit income growth to real wage growth

Note: The scatter points indicate the sensitivity of profit income growth to a change in real wage growth by 1 percentage point.

Source: Storm and Naastepad (2012a), Figure 7.3.

4.7   Wages and economic recovery

What can we say – based on the preceding discussion – about the role of wages in the economic recovery or, more broadly, in long-run growth? Perhaps we best start with what should *not* be done.

First, governments, especially in the euro area, are pressed to drastically reform their economies, sharply cut public (social) spending and deregulate their supposedly 'rigid' labour markets. IMF economists, for example, claim that a full decentralization of wage bargaining and a reduction of the employment protection of permanent workers would bring the Spanish unemployment rate (currently over 23 per cent) down by as much as 7–10 percentage points – with no further macro action required and Spanish aggregate demand still in the doldrums of debt insolvency. Similarly, in August 2011 the European Central Bank sent a letter to the Spanish government asking for wage cuts and the creation of 'mini jobs' to fight youth unemployment in exchange for buying Spanish government bonds in the secondary market; mind you: the 'mini jobs' would pay wages of €400 a month, well below the Spain's official minimum wage of €541 per month. But all this will not work: if the economy is wage-led, as is true for Spain and for most of the European Union (Storm and Naastepad 2012a), real wage cuts and further deregulation of labour markets will not create the conditions for a viable, sustained economic recovery. Rather they are a recipe for prolonged stagnation of output and productivity growth – especially now, with households, firms, and governments burdened by debts, there no longer exists an escape route through carefree borrowing as the one taken by the Dutch as well as the Americans before the crisis (Palma 2009; Palley 2009). However, real wage restraint may generate some employment growth, because it likely depresses labour productivity growth more than output growth – but in this process it will mostly create low-wage, precarious 'not-so-decent' services-sector jobs. What must be understood is that this strategy amounts to 'working many more hours' in return for 'less income' – neither an attractive nor a sensible proposition, and politically potentially self-destructive, especially since labour forces are about to become smaller because of demographic reasons (ageing).

Second, if the economy is profit-led, as is the United States (Naastepad and Storm 2007), lowering real wage growth does raise output growth – but not very strongly so, because productivity growth drops off and technological progress becomes bogged down. Profitability and investment will rise – but again not very strongly because lower productivity growth reduces the (expected) rate of return on investment. Employment growth will rise (and to a considerable extent), but here also mostly in the form of low-productive, low-wage jobs. This is a scenario of 'working more' in return for 'a somewhat higher income' – which is also not an altogether agreeable prospect. Moreover, lowering real wages, by depressing investment demand and consumption, combined with the debt overhang, introduces a deflationary bias and creates a non-negligible risk of debt deflation in both wage-led and profit-led systems.

This much is clear, therefore: lowering wages will not get us on the road to economic recovery. But what about *raising* real wages: will this help? Surely, one could argue, higher real wages will stimulate output if the system is wage-led, and this may in turn create a virtuous cycle of higher investment, higher productivity and further growth – eventually also of employment. But as we argued, while higher real wages do raise output, they increase labour productivity even more, and hence employment is likely to fall. Higher unemployment, combined with high debts in very uncertain times, means reluctant and wary consumers and investors and ultimately lacklustre demand growth. Higher real wages (per se) are no panacea – a cure for all economic diseases – not even in a wage-led economy. What is needed for recovery is a *broader* policy package to protect wages as well as profits, jobs as well as technological progress, and egalitarian outcomes as well as international *non-price* competitiveness (Storm and Naastepad 2012a). Such a package should entail: (1) a fair sharing of the gains of labour productivity growth between business and labour; (2) an allowance for high enough profits to stimulate investment; and (3) a commitment to providing employment security both at the level of the firm and as a (full-employment) macroeconomic strategy. Real wages could (and should) be raised, but in combination with supportive macroeconomic policy, for example, a low real interest rate and a system of taxation which progressively taxes the high-saving income groups to finance public-sector employment and R&D. For profit-led economies, a similar approach will also pay off in terms of growth, productivity and employment. Higher real wages here depress output – but this can be compensated by appropriate output-enhancing interest rates and fiscal policy. The conclusion of our analysis is a sobering asymmetry: lowering real wages will be unambiguously counterproductive, but the opposite policy of raising real wages will unlikely (and all by itself) put the economy on the road to recovery. This may sound depressing.

But let our key message not be misunderstood: the argument that lower wages and further deregulation of (supposedly) rigid labour markets, all in the name of 'increasing cost competitiveness', are the only possible way out of the recession, is dead wrong – especially for wage-led Europe – even though, as we made clear, the advocates of real wage restraint can claim that it may generate 'jobs, jobs, jobs' (but very low-wage jobs and the aggregate economy remains otherwise stagnant). Neither the social democrats nor the labour unions in Europe have grasped this point – and in the past this has led them to accept real wage restraint and labour market deregulation in exchange for lower unemployment, as has happened in the Netherlands (and later on Germany). They should no longer accept this, and demand both fair real wage increases and a credible commitment in macroeconomic policy-making to full employment (rather than low inflation) – demands which do not need to conflict with productivity growth and profitability (if properly managed). However, if these demands are to effectuate, they should be accompanied by the imposition of strict compulsions on capital – forcing shareholders to become more committed long-term investors (Lazonick 2009; Palma 2009; Storm and Naastepad 2012a).

Notes

1. All data in this section are from Naastepad (2006).
2. In our model, higher real wage growth leads to a fall in employment growth. However, technological progress may have an independent impact on accumulation and growth which our model does not take into account (see Lavoie 1992, pp. 316–26), because 'waves of innovations' can shift the investment function up. If this independent impact on investments is sufficiently large, faster productivity growth will raise output growth and hence an increase in real wages in a wage-led demand regime could have a more neutral effect on employment. While the effect may exist – especially following the introduction of new general-purpose technologies – we think it is unlikely to be of empirical importance for the OECD countries (1960–2010), because in that case demand would have been found to be strongly wage-led – the impact of wage share growth on demand growth would have to equal 0.7, much higher than what econometric studies find (Onaran and Galanis 2012).
3. We must note here that the empirical evidence on the nature of the US demand regime is mixed. On the one hand, Bowles and Boyer (1995), Barbosa-Filho and Taylor (2006), Tavani, Flaschel and Taylor (2011), Storm and Naastepad (2012a). and Nikiforos and Foley (2012) find that US demand is profit-led (as we assume here). On the other hand, Hein and Vogel (2008), Onaran, Stockhammer and Grafl (2011) and Onaran and Galanis (2012) conclude that US demand is wage-led. While the issue is empirically unresolved, we provide a theoretical case why profit-led demand is consistent with the US stock-market based financial system (Storm and Naastepad 2012a, chapter 5).
4. For the empirical analysis, see Storm and Naastepad (2012b).

References

Alexiadis, S. and Tsagdis, D. 2010. 'Is cumulative growth in manufacturing productivity slowing down in the EU12 regions?', *Cambridge Journal of Economics*, vol. 34(6), pp. 1001–17.

Angeriz, A., McCombie, J.S.L. and Roberts, M. 2009. 'Increasing returns and the growth of industries in the EU regions: paradoxes and conundrums', *Spatial Economic Analysis*, vol. 4(2), pp. 127–48.

Barbosa-Filho, N.H. and Taylor, L. 2006. 'Distributive and demand cycles in the US economy – a structuralist Goodwin model', *Metroeconomica*, vol. 57(3), pp. 389–411.

Blanchard, O. 2000. 'The Dutch jobs miracle'. Available at: http://www.project-syndicate.org/commentary/bla5/English.

Bowles, S. and Boyer, R. 1995. 'Wages, aggregate demand, and employment in an open economy: an empirical investigation', in Gerald Epstein and Herbert E. Gintis (eds), *Macroeconomic Policy after the Conservative Era – Studies in Investment, Saving and Finance* (Cambridge: Cambridge University Press), pp. 143–71.

Carlin, W., Glyn, A. and van Reenen, J. 2001. 'Export market performance of OECD countries: an empirical examination of the role of cost competitiveness', *The Economic Journal*, vol. 111(468), pp. 128–62.

Carter, S. 2007. 'Real wage productivity elasticity across advanced economies, 1963–1999', *Journal of Post Keynesian Economics*, vol. 29(4), pp. 573–600.

Cornwall, J. and Cornwall, W. 2002. 'A demand and supply analysis of productivity growth', *Structural Change and Economic Dynamics*, vol. 13(2), pp. 203–29.

Crespi, F. and Pianta, M. 2008. 'Demand and innovation in productivity growth', *International Review of Applied Economics*, vol. 22(6), pp. 655–72.

The Economist, 2002. 'Model makers. A survey of the Netherlands', 2 May.

Foley, D.K. and Michl, T.R. 1999. *Growth and Distribution* (Cambridge, MA: Harvard University Press).

Forslund, A., Gottfries, N. and Westermark, A. 2008. 'Prices, productivity and wage bargaining in open economies', *Scandinavian Journal of Economics*, vol. 110(1), pp. 169–95.

Funk, P. 2002. 'Induced innovation revisited', *Economica*, vol. 69(273), pp. 155–71.

Glyn, A. 2006. *Capitalism Unleashed: Finance, Globalization and Welfare* (Oxford: Oxford University Press).

Hein, E. and Tarassow, A. 2010. 'Distribution, aggregate demand and productivity growth-theory and empirical results for six OECD countries based on a post-Kaleckian model', *Cambridge Journal of Economics*, vol. 34(4), pp. 727–54.

Hein, E. and Vogel, L. 2008. 'Distribution and growth reconsidered: Empirical results for six OECD countries', *Cambridge Journal of Economics*, vol. 32(3), pp. 479–511.

Hicks, J.R. 1932. *The Theory of Wages* (London: Macmillan).

Kennedy, C. 1964. 'Induced bias in innovation and the theory of distribution', *The Economic Journal*, vol. 74, pp. 541–7.

Knell, M. 2004. 'Structural change and the Kaldor–Verdoorn law in the 1990s', *Revue d'économie industrielle*, vol. 105(1), pp. 71–83.

Lavoie, M. 1992. *Foundations of Post-Keynesian Analysis* (Aldershot: Edward Elgar).

Lazonick, W. 2009. 'The New Economy Business Model and the crisis of US capitalism', *Capitalism and Society*, vol. 4(2). On-line article 4. Available at: http://www.strongwindpress.com/pdfs/TuiJian/LazonickNewEconomyCrisis.pdf.

Leon-Ledesma, M. 2002. 'Accumulation, innovation and catching-up: an extended cumulative growth model', *Cambridge Journal of Economics*, vol. 25(2), pp. 201–16.

Lowe, A. 1988. *Has Freedom a Future?* (New York: Praeger Publishers).

McCombie, J.S.L., Pugno, Maurizio and Soro, Bruno (eds). 2002. *Productivity Growth and Economic Performance: Essays on Verdoorn's Law* (London: Macmillan).

Naastepad, C.W.M. 2006. 'Technology, demand and distribution: a cumulative growth model with an application to the Dutch productivity growth slowdown', *Cambridge Journal of Economics*, vol. 30(3), pp. 403–34.

Naastepad, C.W.M. and Storm, S. 2007. 'OECD demand regimes (1960–2000)', *Journal of Post Keynesian Economics*, vol. 29(2), pp. 211–46.

Nikiforos, M. and Foley, D.K. 2012. 'Distribution and capacity utilisation: conceptual issues and empirical evidence', *Metroeconomica*, vol. 63(1), pp. 200–29.

Nymoen, R. and Rødseth, A. 2003. 'Explaining unemployment: some lessons from Nordic wage formation', *Labour Economics*, vol. 10(1), pp. 1–29.

Onaran, Ö. and Galanis, G. 2012. 'Is aggregate demand wage-led or profit-led? National and global effects'. Project Report for the Project 'New Perspectives on Wages and Economic Growth: The Potentials of Wage-Led Growth', International Labour Office, Geneva.

Onaran, Ö., Stockhammer, E. and Grafl, L. 2011. 'The finance-dominated growth regime, distribution and aggregate demand in the US', *Cambridge Journal of Economics*, vol. 35(4), pp. 637–61.

Palma, J.G. 2009. 'The revenge of the market on the rentiers. Why neo-liberal reports of the end of history turned out to be premature', *Cambridge Journal of Economics*, vol. 33(4), pp. 829–69.

Palley, T. 2009. *America's Exhausted Paradigm: Macroeconomic Causes of the Financial Crisis and the Great Recession*. New American Contract Policy Paper (Washington, DC: New America Foundation).

Rowthorn, R.E. 1999. 'Unemployment, wage bargaining and capital–labour substitution', *Cambridge Journal of Economics*, vol. 23(4), pp. 413–25.

Sennett, R. 2005. *The Culture of the New Capitalism* (New Haven, CT: Yale University Press).

Stockhammer, E., Onaran, Ö. and Ederer, S. 2009. 'Functional income distribution and aggregate demand in the Euro area', *Cambridge Journal of Economics*, vol. 33(1), pp. 139–59.

Storm, S. and Naastepad, C.W.M. 2011. 'The productivity and investment effects of wage-led growth', *International Journal of Labour Research*, vol. 3(2), pp. 197–218.

Storm, S. and Naastepad, C.W.M. 2012a. *Macroeconomics beyond the NAIRU* (Cambridge, MA: Harvard University Press).

Storm, S. and Naastepad, C.W.M. 2012b. 'Wage-led or profit-led supply: wages, productivity and investment', *WLG Project Report* (Geneva: ILO).

Tavani, D., Flaschel, P. and Taylor, L. 2011. 'Estimated non-linearities and multiple equilibria in a model of distributive-demand cycles', *International Review of Applied Economics*, vol. 25(5), pp. 519–38.

Taylor, L. 2010. *Maynard's Revenge: Keynesianism and the Collapse of Free Market Macroeconomics* (Cambridge, MA: Harvard University Press).

Vergeer, R. and Kleinknecht, A. 2010–11. 'The impact of labor market deregulation on productivity: a panel data analysis of 19 OECD countries (1960–2004)', *Journal of Post Keynesian Economics*, vol. 33(2), pp. 369–405.

5
The Role of Income Inequality as a Cause of the Great Recession and Global Imbalances[1]

Simon Sturn and Till van Treeck

5.1 The Rajan hypothesis and the renewed interest in income inequality as a macroeconomic risk

Is there a link between rising inequality and the 'Great Recession' of 2008? As noted by *The Economist* (22 January 2011, p. 11), '[s]everal prominent economists now reckon that inequality was a root cause of the financial crisis'. Similarly, IMF-ILO (2010, p. 8) conclude: 'In the wake of the current crisis there is an emerging view about the importance of growing inequality as one of the causes of global crises past and present.' Indeed, in recent years there has been a proliferation of analyses supporting this view (see, inter alia, UN Commission of Experts, 2009; Rajan, 2010; Reich, 2010; Kumhof and Rancière, 2010; Galbraith, 2012; Palley, 2012). The explanation is straightforward: As the benefits of rising income over the past decades were confined to a relatively small group of households at the top of the income distribution, the consumption of the lower- and middle-income groups was largely financed through rising credit rather than rising incomes. This process was facilitated by government action, both directly through credit promotion policies and indirectly through the deregulation of the financial sector. But with the downturn in the housing market and the subprime mortgage crisis starting in 2007, the overindebtedness of the US personal sector finally became apparent and the debt-financed private demand expansion came to an end. We refer to this line of argument as the 'Rajan hypothesis', because of the impetus his book *Fault Lines* (2010) has given to the renewed interest in inequality as a macroeconomic risk. Rajan succinctly summarizes his argument as follows:

> [T]he political response to rising inequality – whether carefully planned or an unpremeditated reaction to constituent demands – was

to expand lending to households, especially low-income ones. The benefits – growing consumption and more jobs – were immediate, whereas paying the inevitable bill could be postponed into the future. [...] In the United States, the expansion of home ownership – a key element of the American dream – to low and middle-income households was the defensible linchpin for the broader aims of expanding credit and consumption. But when easy money pushed by a deep-pocketed government comes into contact with the profit motive of a sophisticated, competitive, and amoral financial sector, a deep fault line develops. (Rajan, 2010, p. 9)

While Rajan places considerable emphasis on government failure and the political economy of income inequality and financial market deregulation, the central implication of his analysis is the rejection of the mainstream theories of consumption, which see no link between the inequality of (permanent) income and aggregate personal consumption, and hence no need for government action to stimulate consumption and jobs. Moreover, while more conventional views of the crisis point to the crucial role of deregulated financial markets, asset bubbles and debt accumulation (for example, Shiller, 2008; Reinhart and Rogoff, 2010), '[t]hat does not however seem to be the end of the matter, since inequality could have had an indirect effect in contributing to the asset bubble' (Atkinson and Morelli, 2010, p 58). In essence, thus, the Rajan hypothesis posits that given the rise in inequality the credit expansion in the personal sector were both necessary for supporting aggregate demand and employment and at the same time unsustainable.

The Rajan hypothesis has a further implication, linking the debt-fuelled consumption demand in the United States to the strong increase in the US current account deficit during the period leading up to the crisis:

There are usually limits to debt-fueled consumption, especially in a large country like the United States. The strong demand for consumer goods and services tends to push up prices and inflation. A worried central bank then raises interest rates, curbing both households' ability to borrow and their desire to consume. Through the late 1990s and the 2000s, though, a significant portion of the increase in U.S. household demand was met from abroad, from countries such as Germany, Japan, and, increasingly, China, which have traditionally relied on exports for growth and had plenty of spare capacity to make more. (Rajan, 2010, p. 9)

This causal link between US inequality and the global current account imbalances is noteworthy, because the latter are generally considered an important contributing factor to the Great Recession at the global level (for example, Caballero et al., 2008; Palley, 2012). Yet there is an emerging view that growing income inequality also contributed to the emergence of export-led growth in other countries (see, inter alia, Fitoussi and Stiglitz, 2009; Horn et al., 2009; Broer, 2010; IMF-ILO, 2010; Kumhof et al., 2012; Galbraith, 2012). The argument is that in advanced, especially Anglo-Saxon, economies with highly developed financial markets, rising inequality has led to a deterioration of savings–investment balances, as the poor and middle class borrowed from the rich and from foreign lenders to finance consumption. In emerging economies, especially China, inequality has also increased, but financial markets are less developed and hence do not allow the lower and middle classes to respond to lower shares in aggregate income by borrowing. This leads to weak domestic demand and an export-oriented growth model, with wealthy creditors effectively lending to foreign rather than domestic borrowers (Kumhof et al., 2012). In the European context, it has been argued that the weak wage growth and strongly rising inequality in Germany have improved the price competitiveness of German exports while at the same time constraining domestic demand, as private households reacted to falling incomes and increased income uncertainty not by borrowing more, but rather by higher precautionary savings (see, for example, Deutsche Bundesbank, 2007a; Carlin and Soskice, 2007; Fitoussi and Stiglitz, 2009).

While Rajan's (2010) analysis relies often on narrative and sometimes rather anecdotal evidence, some recent theoretical and empirical work has assessed the potential link between rising inequality, the US financial crisis, and the global imbalances more systematically. On the theoretical side, Kumhof and Rancière (2010) present a theoretical DSGE model where the increase in the top income share leads to higher leverage for the remainder of the population, and eventually triggers a financial and real crisis. Kumhof et al. (2012) extend this analysis and develop a DSGE model where the current account surpluses of emerging economies are attributed to the financial constraints of workers, so that investors choose to deploy their surplus funds abroad. Similarly, Broer (2010) calibrates a theoretical model to match the observed rise in household indebtedness in the United States as a result of higher income risk and the higher precautionary saving by households in China due to increased income volatility in the context of less developed financial markets. A somewhat different but related approach is followed by the 'wage-led recovery' project of the ILO, with its focus on the macroeconomic implications of the functional distribution of income between labour (households) and capital (corporations) (Lavoie and Stockhammer, 2013). This perspective is important because in many countries with current account surpluses not only did the distribution of household incomes become more unequal, but households' incomes as a share of national income also declined, with potentially negative consequences for private consumption (see also ILO, 2011). Kumhof et al. (2012) estimate a panel of 18 OECD countries for the period 1968–2008 and find that a rise in top (5 or 1 per cent) income shares are associated with a weaker current account, after controlling for standard fundamental variables. Therefore they posit that rising inequality contributed to the global imbalances, which in turn fuelled the build-up of the crisis. However, the generality of these results is called into question by the findings of Bordo and Meissner (2012) who estimate a panel of 14 advanced economies for the period 1920–2008 and conclude that while financial crises are typically preceded by credit booms, inequality rises only occasionally during periods of credit expansion. Similarly, Atkinson and Morelli (2010, p. 66) conclude, after investigating several financial crises in detail, that '[o]utside the United States, the history of systemic banking crises in different countries around the world does not suggest that either rising or high inequality has been adduced as a significant causal factor'. Yet, these assessments do not take into account that not only domestic credit expansions but also excessive current account surpluses can give rise to macroeconomic instability, and both can be linked to income inequality.

Our work contributes to the literature in two main respects. First, focusing on the United States, we summarize the available empirical literature in support of the Rajan hypothesis. We also discuss how far the Rajan hypothesis contradicts previous findings on the link between income inequality and household leverage that were informed by the dominant permanent income and life-cycle theories of consumption.

Second, we review the debates about the macroeconomic consequences of changes in the distribution of income in China and Germany. We choose these two countries because the rise in income inequality has been particularly strong here during the period leading up to the Great Recession, and because China and Germany have had the largest current account surpluses worldwide during the 2000s. While the bilateral trade balance between the United States and China has been the subject of widespread debate, Germany plays a crucial role for the current account imbalances within the European Monetary Union. However, there is as yet no consensus as to the underlying causes of the global and European imbalances, and it has proven difficult in panel regression analyses to explain the widening of current accounts during the decade or so before the Great Recession with standard fundamentals, especially in the cases of the United States, China and Germany (Chinn et al. 2011).

In sum, we agree with Bordo and Meissner (2012) that while the Rajan hypothesis cannot simply be applied to all other economies without reference to the country-specific historical and institutional circumstances, additional narrative evidence is necessary to investigate the link between inequality and macroeconomic crises.

5.2   Was the US financial crisis caused by the secular rise in inequality?

5.2.1   Conventional thinking about inequality and household debt

According to the dominant theories of household consumption current consumption is proportionally related to the household's permanent, or life-cycle, income, and does not depend on the level or distribution of permanent income. Inspired by the standard theory, a very influential view up until the Great Recession was that despite the dramatic rise in measured income inequality, the distribution of permanent incomes has remained largely stable over the past thirty years or so. Indeed, as the available survey data suggested that the inequality of consumption between households had not increased substantially, the rise in measured inequality was interpreted as reflecting mainly a higher dispersion in the transitory components of income, which households could insure against through credit markets. Hence, the idea was not that 'easy credit has been been used as a palliative [...] by governments' (Rajan, 2010, p. 39), but 'that the structure of the credit markets in an economy is endogenous and may evolve in response to higher income volatility' (Krueger and Perri, 2006, p. 164). In the words of Alan Greenspan, the chairman of the Federal Reserve from 1987 to 2006:

> [I]ncome disparities, as measured by Gini coefficients, climbed steadily through 1994. [...] But [...] there is a surprising difference between trends in the dispersion of holdings of claims to goods and services (that is, income and wealth) and trends in the dispersion of actual consumption. [...] I do not wish to disparage income as a partial antidote to insecurity. Nevertheless, some aspects of economic well-being may be more accurately discerned by examining consumption. (Greenspan, 1996, p. 176)

The work by Krueger and Perri (2003, 2006) responded to Greenspan's request for research along these lines. Krueger and Perri (2006) construct different measures of consumption using survey data and find that the variance of consumption has increased by only 5 per cent in 1980–2003, whereas the variance of income has increased by 21 per cent. They distinguish between 'between-group' and 'within-group' inequality by regressing income and consumption on the following characteristics of the reference person and the spouse (if present): sex, race, years of education, experience, interaction terms between experience and education, dummies for managerial/professional occupation, and region of residence. The authors denote the cross-sectional variance explained by these characteristics as 'between-group' inequality and the residual variance as 'within-group' inequality. Based on these definitions, they find that for consumption, the between-group component displays an increase similar in magnitude to that of income. But for the within-group component, the increase in consumption inequality is much smaller than the increase in income inequality. They interpret the within-group inequality as being mainly transitory or somehow insurable, whereas changes in between-group inequality reflect permanent, or uninsurable, changes in distribution. Finally, based on the finding of a strong correlation between the ratio of unsecured consumer credit to disposable income and the Gini coefficient, the authors conclude that this 'may suggest that consumers could, and in fact did, make stronger use of credit markets exactly when they needed to (starting in the mid-1970's), in order to insulate consumption from bigger income fluctuations' (Krueger and Perri, 2006, p. 187; see also Kruger and Perri, 2003, p. 15; Blundell et al., 2008; Heathcote et al., 2010). These results were literally treated as stylized facts by the press (see, for example, *The New York Times*, 11 July 2002; *The Economist*, 19 December 2007; *Wall Street Journal*, 15 December 2006), as indeed they were strongly encouraged by the political climate of the time that downplayed concerns about inequality and highlighted the importance of the availability of credit as an integral part of the American Dream.

5.2.2   Rising inequality in permanent or transitory incomes?

The distinction between 'between-group' and 'within-group' inequality in Krueger and Perri (2003, 2006) is conceptually problematic, if inequality is also driven by other factors apart from education and sex. The most frequently discussed candidate explanations of the rise in US inequality include: skill-biased technological change (for example, Autor et al., 1998); globalization including increasing trade, immigration, and offshoring (Roberts, 2010); the emergence of superstars and 'winner-takes-all' markets (for example, Frank and Cook, 1995); rent-seeking behaviour by top executives, especially in the financial sector (for example, Philippon and Resheff, 2009); deficiencies in the educational system (for example, Goldin and Katz, 2008); changes in labour market institutions, including the erosion of the real minimum wage and the decline of the trade unions (for example, Levy and Temin, 2007); changes in the tax system (for example, Piketty and Saez, 2007); and social norms, including, for instance, the political orientation of the government (for example, Hacker and Pierson, 2010). In other words, Krueger and Perri (2003, 2006) may underestimate the degree of 'between-group' inequality.

The explosion of top incomes is certainly the most peculiar aspect of the rise in inequality in the United States. Most strikingly, the increase in the share of top incomes is driven mainly by that within the top 1 per cent, or even the top 0.5 and 0.1 per cent, of all households. Interestingly, top income shares have remained fairly stable in continental Europe over the past three decades, at least until very recently (Piketty and Saez, 2006), but the decline in the wage share, especially in Germany, has been much more pronounced than in the United States. We will return to this issue below. But even below the top 10 per cent, the increase in income dispersion has been very substantial in the United States. In the bottom half of the distribution, individual wage and household income inequality increased sharply in the early 1980s; wage inequality then has remained roughly constant since the early 1990s, while income inequality at the household level has started to increase again since the early 2000s. By contrast, wage and income inequality has increased steadily in the top half of the distribution since the early 1980s; it has been more pronounced for income than for hourly wages, partly because high-income households receive a larger fraction of their income from capital. Moreover, due to government transfers the increase in inequality was less pronounced for income than for hourly wages at the bottom of the distribution (Heathcote et al., 2010).

Statistical studies on income mobility show that the variance of both permanent and transitory earnings has risen in the 1980s, but the variance of transitory earnings is found to have declined in the 1990s (Moffitt and Gottschalk, 2002; Sabelhaus and Song, 2009). Bradbury and Katz (2002a, 2002b) analyse family income mobility by examining the percentage of families that change from one quintile to another by comparing the distribution of income in the first and the last year of a given time period. They find that mobility patterns were very similar in the 1970s and 1980s, but that mobility declined noticeably in the 1990s. Kopczuk et al. (2010) compare Gini coefficients based on annual earnings and 5-year to 20-year average earnings and conclude that 'increases in annual earnings inequality are driven almost entirely by increases in permanent earnings inequality, with much more modest changes in the variability of transitory earnings' (p. 125). Only very long-term income mobility has somewhat increased (though not after the late 1970s), but this is entirely due to the increased labour force participation and higher wages of women.

These results conflict with the view that the rise in inequality was driven by insurable temporary income shocks over the 1990s and are clearly evidence in favour of the Rajan hypothesis, which implies that consumption inequality has risen less than income inequality in spite of substantial and permanent changes in income inequality.

5.2.3   Coping with rising inequality

There are various 'coping mechanisms' (Reich, 2010) through which households can attempt to prevent a decline in (relative) consumption in the face of an adverse development in individual hourly wages. First, individual working hours can be increased; second, family labour supply can be raised, that is, an additional household member can enter the paid labour force; third, taxes and transfers, although beyond the control of the individual household, provide an additional mechanism by which the effect of lower wages on consumption is alleviated; and, finally, households can reduce saving and increase debt as a means of financing consumption.

There is considerable evidence supporting the view that labour supply, saving and financial decisions were indeed strongly influenced by changes in income distribution during the decades prior to the crisis. It seems reasonable for our purpose to consider these coping mechanisms together because it is likely that households respond to rising inequality in a variety of ways, and the excessive use of credit may imply that other, seemingly less problematic coping mechanisms have become overstretched.

To begin with, it seems obvious that higher earnings inequality creates an incentive to work longer hours, especially at the top of the wage distribution. Freeman (2007, p. 63) points to the fact that more Americans than Europeans say that they want to increase rather than decrease their number of working hours at given wage rates and that they work hard even if it interferes with the rest of their life. This phenomenon may indeed be linked to higher inequality in the United States, leading to a 'tournament style economic system that gives the person who puts in an extra hour of work a potentially high return' (Freeman, 2008, p. 137). Stiglitz (2008) also emphasizes the link between long working hours, consumerism and inequality.

Bowles and Park (2005), after estimating a panel data model for 10 European and North American countries for the period 1963–98, conclude that greater inequality is indeed strongly associated with longer work hours, controlling for other factors typically included in labour supply models.

Neumark and Postlewaite (1998) find that women whose sister's husband had a higher income than their own husband were between 16 and 25 per cent more likely to participate in the paid labour force. The comparison of labour supply decisions of relatives is interesting because it might be anticipated that relatives are typically members of a person's social reference group. Frank (2007) quotes evidence that traffic delays for rush-hour commuters in major US cities roughly tripled between 1983 and 2003. Also, official working time statistics do not capture the effects of additional hours worked on the quality of leisure time. For instance, there is evidence that Americans sleep considerably less today than in past decades – by some estimates as much as one to two hours per night less than in the 1960s (McCoy, 2004). Similarly, Americans spend less time with families and friends today than in the past (Putnam, 2000; Neumark-Sztainer et al., 2003).

Schor (1998) asked workers how their 'financial status' compared to that of those in their reference group (as defined by respondents themselves, consisting primarily of co-workers, friends, relatives and persons of the same religion). She found that, after controlling for a measure of permanent income as well as a set of other control variables the financial status compared to the self-defined reference group had a significantly negative impact on household saving.

Bertrand and Morse (2011) estimate the effects of the expenditures of rich households (above the 80th income percentile) on those of non-rich households. They find clear evidence of 'top-down consumption spillover effects' and argue that their results are 'most consistent with the view that visible increased consumption by the rich induces status-seeking or status-maintaining consumption by the less rich' (Bertrand and Morse, 2011, p. 1).

Frank et al. (2010) provide indirect evidence for the 'expenditure cascades' hypothesis, that is, that rising incomes and consumption at the top lead to increased pressure for those below the top to maintain their relative spending (particularly with regard to 'positional' goods). To begin with, they point to the fact that the median size of a newly constructed house in the United States has increased more than twice as rapidly as the increase in the median family earnings from 1980 to 2001, although at the same time one in five households had zero or negative net worth. They go on to examine the relationships between various measures of financial distress and measures of income inequality. They find that income inequality, after controlling for standard explanatory variables, increases the likelihood of filing for bankruptcy, average commute times, and the likelihood of marriages ending in divorce. Frank et al. (2010) also quote evidence suggesting that median house prices were substantially higher in school districts with higher levels of income inequality, even after controlling for median income.

Barba and Pivetti (2009) provide descriptive evidence in favour of the view that credit has been effectively operating as a sort of palliative in the face of stagnating median real wages. Iacoviello (2008) describes a similar mechanism within a formal model in which credit serves as a substitute for income growth in the financing of consumption.

Finally, there is also some tentative econometric evidence suggesting that there is a direct relation between the rise in income inequality and household debt in the United States (Pollin, 1988, 1990; Christen and Morgan 2005; Boushey and Weller, 2006).

5.2.4   Concluding remarks

There is strong evidence that lower- and middle-income households have attempted to compensate for the decline in their relative permanent incomes by a higher labour supply, reduced saving, and higher personal debt. The incentives for households to work more, save less and go into debt are particularly strong in the United States due not only to the easy access to credit but also to other country-specific factors such as the importance of homeownership, partly as a substitute for social policy, and the reliance of the education system on private financing in the context of low and declining intergenerational income mobility. In sum, we find substantial evidence against the 'Greenspan–Krueger–Perri argument' of higher household indebtedness due to merely increased insurance demand as a result of higher transitory income dispersion and strong evidence for the Rajan hypothesis. In this sense, then, the rise in inequality is indeed one of the structural causes of the Great Recession and of the rising current account deficit in the United States.

5.3 Export-led growth in the emerging superpower: the case of China

Since the 1990s China's growth has relied increasingly on investment and net exports. Between 2002 and 2007 alone, gross national saving increased by more than 10 per cent of GDP, and since then the gross national saving rate has been persistently higher than 50 per cent of GDP. The decline in the private consumption-to-GDP ratio in the 2000s was accompanied by a decline in personal disposable income as a share of GDP, which is in turn almost entirely explained by the decline in labour income, and by an increase in households' saving rate. The latter peaked at the extremely high level of 38 per cent in 2007. For the period 2002–2007, the rise in the personal saving rate accounts for almost 70 per cent, and the decline in household income for the remaining 30 per cent of the total decline in the private consumption-to-GDP ratio.

There is a broad consensus among economists, international organizations and the Chinese government that China's export- and investment-led growth model is unsustainable and therefore needs to become more balanced. In the public debate it is often argued that exchange rate manipulation in China is the primary cause of the massive trade imbalances with the United States (for example, Goldstein and Lardy, 2006; Krugman, 2011). There is no consensus, however, about the extent to which the Renminbi is actually undervalued, with estimates ranging from close to zero (Cheung et al., 2011) to up to 20 or even 50 per cent vis-à-vis the US dollar (for example, Goldstein and Lardy, 2006; Ferguson and Schularick, 2011). Questions have also been raised about the notion that more exchange rate flexibility would significantly decrease China's current account surplus (McKinnon, 2006; Reisen, 2010; Song et al., 2011), at least if not accompanied by structural changes in social and economic policy boosting consumption. In sum, although exchange rate policy is likely to play a significant role, there is clearly more to the Chinese export-led growth model than merely an undervalued currency.

5.3.1 Low growth in household and wage incomes

According to a broadly held view, the declining share of household incomes, together with the strong reliance of economic growth on business investment, is linked to a number of institutional distortions that affect the allocation of capital, labour and natural resources.

Li and Zhou (2005) present empirical evidence that the provincial leaders are rewarded and punished by the central government according to their economic performance, which motivates them to promote the local economy. This incentive system increases competition to attract capital at the local level and results in low tax rates, hidden subsidies in energy use, and low or negative rents on land use (Yongding, 2007). But several distortions or hidden subsidies also exist at the national level. For example, Prasad argues that:

> [A] substantial fraction of this investment in China has been financed by credit provided by state-owned banks at low interest rates. Indeed, cheap capital has played a big part in skewing the capital–labor ratio and holding down employment growth [...]. In addition, local governments provide subsidized land in order to encourage investment. And energy prices continue to be administered and made available to enterprises at prices below international levels. Hence, the prices of the factors of production that serve as complementary inputs to physical capital – land and energy – are also cheap. (Prasad, 2009, p. 106)

Yang et al. (2011, p. 9) see the 'suppression of wages, low interest payments on loans, and low land rentals' behind the Chinese saving and investment puzzle, while Dooley et al. (2007) argue the Chinese government influences wages, interest rates, and international financial transactions so as to boost export-led growth. According to Huang and Tao (2010, p. 4), various 'subsidies' on capital, labour, energy, land and environment 'artificially increase producer incentives, raise investment returns, and improve the international competitiveness of Chinese products. [...] In addition, they also distort the broad income distribution pattern in favor of the government and the corporate sector, but at the expense of household income. This weakens consumption and further boosts external sector surplus'. Huang and Tao also present crude estimates on the size of such factor market distortions for the years 2000–2009. According to their results, the biggest quantitative impacts stem from distortions on the cost of capital, followed by energy and land use, and labour.

5.3.2 The role of high households saving rates

In 2007, household saving amounted to more than 20 per cent of GDP and thus contributed the largest fraction to China's national saving rate. In OECD countries, the bulk of national saving is attributable to business saving, although the private household sector appropriates a larger share of national income in OECD countries than in China. Hence, the high and rapidly rising personal saving rate plays a very important role in explaining the weak development of private consumption as a share of GDP in China, especially during the 2000s. Kraay (2000) reports that household saving was only about 7 per cent of GDP in the late 1970s, making cultural norms an unlikely explanation for high savings.

Following Chamon and Prasad (2010), most promising as an explanation of high and rising household saving in recent years are the rapid privatization of the housing stock (combined with very limited availability of household credit) and the rising private burden of education and health expenditures, together with precautionary motives stemming from the reforms of state-owned enterprises and market-oriented reforms more generally. These issues are pursued further by Chamon et al. (2010). They show that income uncertainty has increased strongly since the 1990s: The transition rate from employment to unemployment and from state-owned companies to non-state-owned companies increased sharply. Further, a pension reform in 1997 reduced the pension replacement rate, leading to higher saving by households approaching retirement. They proceed by arguing and presenting econometric evidence that 'greater uncertainty in earnings at the microeconomic level can have macroeconomic implications. One important channel is the impact of greater household-specific uncertainty on precautionary savings. In the absence of a strong social safety net and an underdeveloped financial system, this could lead households to self-insure by increasing their savings' (Chamon et al., 2010, p. 13).

But doubts remain as to whether the strong rise in income inequality in China merely reflects higher income uncertainty. Note that personal income inequality has increased strongly over the past decades. While China was characterized by very low inequality three decades ago, today '[i]nequality is relatively high in China by international standards' (OECD, 2010a, p. 147). The Gini coefficient is even higher than in the United States. One reason for this is the very pronounced rural–urban income gap. However, urban inequality has also been steadily increasing since the 1980s, and in 2007 the Gini coefficient for urban incomes in China was nearly as high as the Gini for total household income in the United States (OECD, 2010a, figure 5.1, p. 130).

Chamon et al. (2010, p. 11) report that none of their income measures shows evidence of a clear trend in the variance of permanent shocks, while they find a clear upward trend in the variance of transitory shocks. However, Gong et al. (2010) provide evidence that intergenerational mobility in China is very low by international standards. However, it is well-known that countries with a more unequal distribution of income at a given point in time typically also exhibit lower income mobility across generations (OECD, 2008a, ch. 8). One reason for this is the self-reinforcing positive relationship between inequality and the private returns on education. Education gives access to relatively well-paid jobs and, on the other hand, the ability to take advantage of the high returns on education will typically be limited to children of richer households (OECD, 2008a, p. 214). Moreover, it is a rather difficult task to distinguish changes in transitory and permanent income inequality. This is all the more true in the Chinese context of strongly rising inequality, high intergenerational inequality and rapid overall income growth. Due to its relation with educational success, an initial increase in transitory earnings dispersion can quickly turn into higher individual lifetime inequality and further reduced intergenerational mobility.

Jin et al. (2011), using household data for 1997 to 2006, present direct econometric evidence that rising inequality rather than uncertainty has positively affected household saving even when controlling for other potential explanatory factors discussed above. Their estimations explain consumption (net of education expenditures) and the average propensity to consume (ratio of consumption to disposable income) with household income, a set of control variables and a measure for income inequality. Overall, they find a strong, robust and statistically significant negative impact of a rise in the Gini on consumption. They also control for the increase of income risk; however, the inclusion of this variable does not show the expected sign and the coefficient of the Gini is even higher for this specification. Jin et al. (2011) further include two measures for the quality of the provincial social security net. These variables are both statistically significant and stimulate consumption, but do not affect the coefficient and significance of the Gini variable.

Jin et al. (2011) attribute these results to status-seeking motives. Due to the limited access of private households to credit, social status depends to a large extent on the family's position in the wealth distribution and related indicators which are closely associated with wealth when credit markets are imperfect:

> As a result, in order to ascend in the status hierarchy or keep the social status in the 'Rat Race', families try to accumulate wealth by increasing savings. When income inequality increases, the benefit gap between the high-status and low-status groups widens, which in turn strengthens the incentives of status-seeking savings. [...] Furthermore, rising income inequality also raises the entry wealth level for the high-status group, which means that more savings are needed for one to enter the high-status group. (Jin et al., 2011, p. 192)

5.3.3 Concluding remarks

Private consumption, and hence domestic aggregate demand, in China has been weakened by rising inequality. The declining share of household – and especially labour – income in national income can largely be attributed to a number of distortions in the labour and financial markets. Subdued household income growth, relative to productivity, has led to weak domestic consumption and strong reliance on exports and on investment financed largely out of retained profits. While the absence of deep and liberalized credit markets has contributed to the rise in the personal saving rate in a context of strongly rising inequality, as argued by Kumhof et al. (2012), private consumption demand was further weakened by high precautionary saving due to high income uncertainty and a weak social safety net. Moreover, there is evidence that higher income inequality has contributed to an increasing intensity of status seeking. However, as the access to credit is still highly limited for households in China, the status-seeking motive appears to have led to increased wealth accumulation, e.g. for education-related purposes, rather than higher debt-financed consumption as in the United States.

5.4 Growing inequality and domestic stagnation in the heart of Europe: the case of Germany

In Germany, the strong improvement in the current account since the early 2000s is reflected in a decrease in private consumption and residential investment as a share of GDP, but also in a lower share of government consumption and investment. While the private household financial balance has improved somewhat despite the declining share of private households' income in the national income, the improvement in the current account is reflected mainly in a very strong improvement in the corporate financial balance and the improvement in the government balance. Even more strikingly, real private household expenditures have almost completely stagnated in level terms after 2000. During the period 2001–2007, the wage share declined by more than 5 percentage points. The share of disposable income in GDP only started to decline after 2003, with the drop of 4 percentage points in 2003–2007 being much larger than that of the drop in the wage share during the same period. Personal income inequality in Germany has increased very strongly over the past decade or so. OECD (2008b) found, for the period until 2005, that '[s]ince 2000, income inequality and poverty have grown faster in Germany than in any other OECD country'.

There is wide agreement, at least outside Germany, that the German economy has been overly export-dependent during the past decade, and that stronger domestic demand in Germany would help to reduce the current account imbalances in Europe and globally (for example, OECD, 2010a, 2012; European Commission, 2010; GCEE, 2011). There is less agreement as to how Germany's large current account surplus relates to the very weak development of wages and the rapid increase in inequality since the early 2000s.

Some have argued that the German economy still suffers from structural problems, although significantly deregulating labour and product markets in the last decade, and that a continuation of this deregulation process is necessary to strengthen domestic demand and, in particular, private investment activity:

> While many of the recently elected government's initiatives address the right issues in a sensible way, some might have gone in the wrong direction. The lack of a specified strategy for fiscal consolidation and remaining deficiencies of product and labour market regulation need to be tackled in order to boost potential growth. Improving economic dynamism and increasing the attractiveness of Germany as a location for investment through structural reforms would also contribute to a reduction of external imbalances. (OECD, 2010b, p. 12)

However, several recent empirical studies investigate the effects of labour and product market regulation on the size and speed of adjustment of the current account. Most of these studies are unable to find any robust effects of product and labour market regulations on the current account, or their results contradict the policy conclusion cited above (Ivanova, 2012, for a survey). Moreover, unlike public and residential investment, private equipment investment throughout the 2000s was not weak by either historical or international standards (Dullien and Schieritz, 2011). We therefore prefer an alternative explanation of the weak domestic demand and large current account surplus in Germany.

5.4.1   Stagnating wages and the current account surplus

In a fixed exchange rate regime like the European Monetary Union, nominal unit labour costs are strongly related to real effective exchange rates and relative real interest rates. An argument that is sometimes made in the public debate is that the wage restraint of the 2000s was a reaction to the loss of international competitiveness and the strong real appreciation of the Deutsche Mark after reunification. But standard estimates, for example, by the German Council of Economic Experts (2004, Para. 840ff.) find that Germany's real effective exchange rate was in line with its fundamental value in 1999 (also see Boss et al., 2009). Similarly, the price competitiveness indicator of the Deutsche Bundesbank suggests that international competitiveness was already high by historical standards in 1999, and further improved thereafter. Estimations by the European Commission (2010, p. 29) suggest that the real effective exchange rate of Germany was undervalued by more than 11 per cent in 2008. When price competitiveness had last been at such a high level in 1983/4, the Deutsche Mark subsequently underwent a rather long period of pronounced nominal appreciation, and the indicator of price competitiveness worsened by more than 20 per cent even before reunification. The persistently low real effective exchange rate after 2002, despite the substantial appreciation of the euro, is due to the continuing real depreciations vis-à-vis the other euro area member countries, linked to the divergence of unit labour costs. And yet, as nominal unit labour costs in Germany stagnated completely, firms were able to increase their profit margins, resulting in a decline in real hourly compensation, while still improving price competitiveness.

An intriguing issue that clearly requires more research are the very large excess corporate savings in Germany. The European Commission (2007) tentatively suggests that the German corporate sector had to undergo a process of balance sheet consolidation during the first half of the 2000s due to a somewhat larger financing deficit in 1998–2000 compared to the euro area average. But the European Commission (2007, p. 65) already interpreted the 'slight increase in the debt to GDP ratio in 2005' as tentative evidence that 'overall balance sheet positions have significantly improved and corporations are now in a good position to embark on new ventures'. Yet the corporate financial balance has remained positive ever since 2004.

It has also been noted that the German corporations have strongly increased their foreign direct investments (FDIs) during the 2000s (OECD, 2012, pp. 13–14). While there has been much discussion in Germany about the 'flight of capital and talent' (Hans-Werner Sinn, *Wirtschaftswoche*, 22 June 2009, p. 38), the Deutsche Bundesbank has always emphasized the fact that the overwhelming majority of all German FDIs are directed towards other rich industrialized countries and that sales-oriented motives dominate cost-saving motives (Deutsche Bundesbank, 2007b, 2008). It may therefore simply be the case that investment decisions are primarily driven by relative demand.

In sum, a somewhat higher nominal and real wage growth, both absolute and relative to productivity growth, would likely have contributed to more dynamic private consumption demand. Moreover, with higher household incomes and with lower real interest rates (at higher inflation), aggregate investment activity and especially residential and non-residential construction investment, would have likely been more dynamic.

5.4.2   Inequality and the rise in personal savings

The increase in the personal saving rate during 2000–2004 was clearly exceptional in historical comparison. In previous cyclical downturns, private consumption developed more positively than income, consistent with the habit persistence hypothesis (see Deutsche Bundesbank, 2007a). Hence, it is important to discuss the recent rise in the personal saving rate in a broader macroeconomic context. In 2001–2002 economic growth in Germany, as in any other advanced economy, was adversely affected by the burst of the New Economy bubble. Yet while the downturn was rather short-lived in most economies, Germany entered a long period of stagnation and only started to grow again significantly in 2006. Initially, the failure of the German economy to overcome the downturn after 2001 was in part due to the high real interest rates especially during the period 2001–2004, associated with low inflation compared to the euro are average and the pro-cyclical fiscal policy especially during 2002–2004 (Hein and Truger, 2007; Dullien and Schwarzer, 2009). Moreover, in such a context of depressed aggregate demand, the political debates about and subsequent implementation of labour market and welfare state reforms, such as the semi-privatization of the old-age pension system, led to both rising inequality and increased uncertainty. Hence, there seems to be a general consensus that the untypical behaviour in the saving rate after 2000 can be partly attributed to precautionary saving in the face of higher income insecurity, policy uncertainty and a widespread fear of status loss (Deutsche Bundesbank, 2007a; Bartzsch, 2008; Giavazzi and McMahon, 2008).

It is sometimes argued that a high degree of labour and product market regulation may be associated with higher precautionary saving due to a higher probability of unemployment (see Ivanova, 2012, for a discussion). However, given the institutional specificities of the German labour market, this mechanism is unlikely to apply in Germany. Streeck (1991) and Soskice (1997), for instance, argue from a 'varieties of capitalism' perspective that the German model of 'diversified quality production', characterized by high-quality industrial production, incremental innovation and product differentiation and long-term customer relations, requires a high level of firm- or industry-specific skills. Relatively strict employment protection legislation thus helps to reduce labour turnover and hence the devaluation of skills during cyclical downturn. Relatively high unemployment benefits are a further incentive for workers to accept the risk of highly specific human capital. The availability of these firm- and industry-specific skills in turn rewards firms with high-quality, skill-intensive production. In this sense, employment- and income-protecting institutions are favourable for both employees and employers (for cross-country evidence, see Estevez-Abe et al., 2001, and Bassanini and Ernst, 2001).

Therefore, even if the German labour market were found to be 'rigid' as defined by the standard indicators, it is not clear whether labour market deregulation would lead to an improvement in the employment performance. Interesting in this respect are the results by Eichhorst et al. (2009), who construct a quantitative indicator for 16 European countries in 2003, which includes measures of both external and internal flexibility. Internal flexibility refers to adjustment mechanisms within firms such as overtime during booms, labour hoarding and advanced vocational training during downturns. On this account, the German labour market is one of the most flexible in the euro area and even more flexible than the labour market in the United Kingdom, although rather inflexible when looking only at external flexibility.

As argued by Carlin and Soskice (2009, p. 68), 'the implementation of reforms to make the labour market more flexible may have interacted with the behaviour of workers with specific skills to increase precautionary savings and therefore contributed to depressed domestic demand'. The higher precautionary savings motive can be attributed both to the worries about expected future income from the public pension system (for example, Meinhardt et al., 2009) and to 'widespread uncertainty about the effects of labour market reforms' (Deutsche Bundesbank, 2007b, p. 50; see also Carlin and Soskice, 2007, 2009).

A further explanation of the higher precautionary saving as a result of the labour market and welfare state reforms are the relatively low female participation rate and especially the very large gender pay gap in Germany, which is amongst the highest in the OECD (OECD, 2008c). As noted by Carlin and Soskice:

The dramatic growth in the prevalence of marginal part-time jobs [...] has taken place in the context of a tax and benefit regime in which spouses acquire access to social security through their husband and face a very high marginal tax rate if they exceed a limited number of hours of work. This structure undermines the development of a potentially important insurance mechanism within the household for families with risk-averse male workers who have specific skills. (2009, p. 86)

Moreover, there are reasons to believe that, in addition to the pro-cyclical fiscal policy even in times of high unemployment in the aftermath of the 2001 downturn, the more structural retrenchment of the (welfare) state has also contributed to higher precautionary saving. For instance, Fuchs-Schündeln and Schündeln (2005), using household survey data, suggest that self-selection of risk-averse individuals into the civil service plays an important role in explaining saving behaviour and significantly decreases aggregate precautionary wealth holdings in Germany. However, this may also imply that a reduction of jobs in the civil service (or similarly secure jobs in the private sector) below the number of risk-averse individuals will have a positive effect on aggregate precautionary saving.

It has also been argued that higher income inequality has directly contributed to the rise in aggregate saving, as a result of differential household saving rates (Klär and Slacalek, 2006; Deutsche Bundesbank, 2007a; Meinhardt et al., 2009). Brenke (2011, p. 10) reports evidence from the GSOEP that households in the bottom half of the distribution have actually slightly reduced their saving rates after 2000. Households in the bottom decile have even reduced their saving rate by half in the period from the early 2000s to 2007, although it has always remained positive. Households in the upper half of the distribution have slightly increased their saving rates, especially within the top decile, and this has overcompensated for the constant or falling saving rates in the lower parts of the distribution.

'Expenditure cascades', as observed in the United States, were rather limited in Germany because, firstly, shifts in the distribution of income did not affect the middle class as strongly and, secondly, the extent to which households at the bottom were able to reduce their saving and go into debt was likely limited by credit constraints. As a result, both the percentage of households with positive consumer or mortgage debt holdings and the average amount of debt outstanding have remained remarkably constant since the mid-1990s (see Karl and Schäfer, 2011). Yet the mortgage and other credit markets are actually rather developed in Germany, although certainly not as 'innovative' as in the United States.

Overall, it is perfectly conceivable that the same cause, rising inequality, leads to completely different reactions by private households depending on country-specific institutions, that is, lower savings and rising debt in the United States but higher precautionary saving in Germany. Social norms and myths ('from dishwasher to millionaire' versus 'German angst') are certainly important in this respect, but they also correspond to institutional realities, as sketched above.

5.4.3 Concluding remarks

The weakness of domestic demand in Germany and the increase in the current account are in an important way linked to changes in the distribution of income, most importantly the very weak development of real wages and household disposable income, which stagnated in absolute terms and declined strongly as a share of national income. However, the persistently high corporate excess savings are somewhat puzzling and require further investigation. At the same time, the effects of rising household inequality on personal saving have been very different compared to the United States, which cannot be fully explained within the framework of Kumhof et al. (2012), since Germany is a rich country with a developed financial system, at least in comparison with the emerging economies. Rather, we attribute the rise in the personal saving rate since the early 2000s in part to the fact that 'expenditure cascades' have been limited as the rise in inequality has occurred mainly in the bottom half (and only far less at the very top) of the income distribution, where households were likely liquidity constrained. However, while there was less pressure for the middle class to keep up with consumers at the top, the implementation of reforms to make the labour market more flexible and unemployment and old-age benefits less generous has contributed not only to rising inequality but also to the higher precautionary savings of middle-class workers. The rise in precautionary saving motive can partly be attributed to the prevalence of vocational, that is, firm-specific rather than general, qualifications of workers, implying that policies aiming at raising the 'external flexibility' of the labour market increase the perceived and actual risk of skill depreciation (Carlin and Soskice, 2007). This risk is corroborated by a low reactivity of monetary and fiscal policy to business cycle fluctuations, which is due in part to the economic policy regime of the euro area but also to the specificities of fiscal policy in Germany. In fact, since the early 2000s large cuts in government spending have further contributed to both higher inequality and low domestic demand.

5.5   Conclusion

We have reviewed the potential macroeconomic effects of rising income inequality in three very different countries, which have experienced strongly widening inequality and substantial macroeconomic imbalances in the years – or even decades – before the Great Recession. Because the United States, China and Germany together accounted for nearly 40 per cent of global GDP (in current US$) in 2010 (World Bank's World Economic Indicators), the macroeconomic trends in these three countries are of obvious importance for the past and future development of the world economy.

While the three countries under investigation differ considerably in terms of both the average standard of living and the financial, product and labour market institutions, there are also several similarities when it comes to the macroeconomic effects of rising inequality. Most importantly, perhaps, labour supply, saving and financing decisions of private households are to a considerable extent affected by changes in income distribution, although the precise household responses depend on factors such as the deepness and regulation of the credit markets, the quality of the social safety net, the educational system (private versus public financing), the functioning of the labour market (internal versus external flexibility), workers' qualifications (specific/vocational skills versus general skills) and the reactivity of monetary and fiscal policy to cyclical unemployment. For example, education-related expenses, in combination with higher inequality, appear to give rise to higher debt in the United States but higher saving in China, due to differences in the credit market. And precautionary savings, related to labour market deregulation and rising income uncertainty, appear to play more of a role in Germany (due in part to the specific skills of workers and more passive macroeconomic stabilization policies) and China (due to a very weak social safety net) than in the United States. Likely, country-specific social norms also play an important role.

While the rise in the private consumption-to-GDP ratio in the United States is almost exclusively due to the lower personal saving rate, in China and especially in Germany changes in the functional distribution between business income, or profits, and household income, or wages, also have important effects on overall macroeconomic trends.

As an overall policy conclusion, the governments of these countries will have to 'address the deeper anxieties of the middle class directly' (Rajan, 2010, p. 35), rather than relying on seemingly easy solutions such as either the promotion of credit for households below the top of the income distribution or a policy of export-led growth.

Note

1. This chapter is a short version of van Treeck and Sturn (2012) 'Income inequality as a cause of the Great Recession? A survey of current debates', Conditions of Work and Employment Series. No. 39 (Geneva: ILO)

References

Atkinson, A. and Morelli, S. 2010. 'Inequality and banking crises: A first look'. Paper prepared for the European Labour Forum in Turin organized by the International Training Centre of the ILO.

Autor, D.H., Katz, L.F. and Krueger, A.B. 1998. 'Computing inequality: have computers changed the labor market?', *The Quarterly Journal of Economics*, vol. 113(4), pp. 1169–213.

Barba, A. and Pivetti, M. 2009. 'Rising household debt: Its causes and macroeconomic implications – a long-period analysis', *Cambridge Journal of Economics*, vol. 33, pp. 113–37.

Barnes, S., Lawson, J. and Radziwill, A. 2010. 'Current account imbalances in the Euro Area: A comparative perspective', OECD Economics Department Working Paper No. 826.

Bartzsch, N. 2008. 'Precautionary saving and income uncertainty in Germany – new evidence from microdata', *Jahrbücher f. Nationalökonomie u. Statistik*, vol. 228(1), pp. 5–25.

Bassanini, A. and Duval, R. 2006. 'The determinants of unemployment across OECD countries: Reassessing the role of policies and institutions', OECD Economic Studies (42), pp. 7–86.

Bassanini, A. and Ernst, E. 2001. 'Labour market regulation, industrial relations, and technological regimes: A tale of comparative advantage', CEPREMAP Working Papers (Couverture Orange) (0117).

Bertrand, M. and Morse, A. 2011. 'Consumption contagion: Does the consumption of the rich drive the consumption of the less rich?' Available online at http://faculty.chicagobooth.edu/adair.morse/research/NBER_reporter_sum-maryAug2011.pdf.

Blundell, R., Pistaferri, L. and Preston, I. 2008. 'Consumption inequality and partial insurance', *American Economic Review*, vol. 98(5), pp. 1887–921.

Bordo, M.D. and Meissner, C.M. (forthcoming) 'Does inequality lead to a financial crisis?', NBER Working Papers 17896 (Cambridge, MA: National Bureau of Economic Research).

Boss, A., Dovern, J., Gern, K.-J., Jannsen, N., Meier, C.-P., van Roye, B. and Scheide, J. 2009. *Ursachen der Wachstumsschwäche in Deutschland 1995–2005* (Kiel: Kiel Institute for the World Economy).

Boushey, H. and Weller, C.E. 2006. 'Inequality and household economic hardship in the United States of America', Working Papers 18, United Nations, Department of Economics and Social Affairs.

Bowles, S. and Park, Y. 2005. 'Emulation, inequality and work hours: Was Thorsten Veblen right?', *The Economic Journal*, vol. 115, pp. F397–F412.

Bradbury, K. and Katz, J. 2002a. 'Issues in economics: Are lifetime incomes growing more unequal? Looking at new evidence on family income mobility', *Regional Review*, Q4, pp. 2–5.

Bradbury, K.L. and Katz, J. 2002b. 'Women's labor market involvement and family income mobility when marriages end', *New England Economic Review*, Q4, pp. 41–74.

Brenke, K. 2011. 'Einkommensumverteilung schwächt privaten Verbrauch', *DIW-Wochenbericht*, vol. 8/2011, pp. 2–12.

Broer, T. 2010. Domestic or global imbalances? Rising inequality and the fall in the US Current Account, IIES mimeo 2010. Available online at http://people. su.se/~tbroe/Tobias_Broer_Domestic_or_global_imbalances_October_2010.pdf.

Caballero, R.J., Farhi, E. and Gourinchas, P.-O. 2008. 'Financial crash, commodity prices, and global imbalances', *Brookings Papers on Economic Activity*, vol. 2(2008), pp. 1–55.

Carlin, W. and Soskice, D. 2007. Reforms, macroeconomic policy and economic performance in Germany, CEPR Discussion Paper No. 6415. Also published as W. Carlin and D. Soskice (2008), 'Reforms, macroeconomic policy and economic performance in Germany', in R. Schettkat and J. Langkau (eds), *Economic Policy Proposals for Germany and Europe* (Abingdon, UK and New York: Routledge), pp. 72–118.

Carlin, W. and Soskice, D. 2009. 'German economic performance: disentangling the role of supply-side reforms, macroeconomic policy and coordinated economy institutions', *Socio-Economic Review*, vol. 7, pp. 67–99.

Chamon, M.D. and Prasad, E.S. 2010. 'Why are saving rates of urban households in China rising?', *American Economic Journal: Macroeconomics*, vol. 2(1), pp. 93–130.

Chamon, M., Liu, K. and Prasad, E.S. 2010. 'Income uncertainty and household savings in China', NBER Working Papers 16565 (Cambridge, MA: National Bureau of Economic Research).

Cheung, Y., Chinn, M. and Fujii, E. 2011. 'A note on the debate over Renminbi undervaluation'. Available online at http://www.ssc.wisc.edu/~mchinn/ cheung_chinn_fujii_2011.pdf.

Chinn, M., Eichengreen, B. and Ito, H. 2011. 'A forensic analysis of global imbalances', NBER Working Papers 17513 (Cambridge, MA: National Bureau of Economic Research).

Christen, M. and Morgan, R.M. 2005. 'Keeping up with the Joneses: analyzing the effect of income inequality on consumer borrowing', *Quantitative Marketing and Economics*, vol. 3(2), pp. 145–73.

Deutsche Bundesbank. 2007a. 'Private consumption in Germany since reunification', Monthly Report No. 9.

Deutsche Bundesbank. 2007b. 'Die deutsche Zahlungsbilanz für das Jahr 2006', Monthly Report No. 3.

Deutsche Bundesbank. 2008. 'Die deutsche Zahlungsbilanz für das Jahr 2007', Monthly Report No. 3.

Deutsche Bundesbank. 2010. 'On the problems of macroeconomic imbalances in the Euro Area', Monthly Report No. 7.

Dooley, M., Folkerts-Landau, D. and Garber, P. 2007. 'Direct investment, rising real wages and the absorption of excess labor in the periphery', in *G7 Current Account Imbalances: Sustainability and Adjustment* (Cambridge, MA: National Bureau of Economic Research), pp. 103–32.

Dube, A., Lester, T.W. and Reich, M. 2011. 'Do frictions matter in the labor market? Accessions, separations, and minimum wage effects', Institute for Research on Labor and Employment, Working Paper Series 1622839. Berkeley, CA: Institute of Industrial Relations, University of California, Berkeley.

Dullien, S. and Schieritz, M. 2011. 'Die deutsche Investitionsschwäche: Die Mär von den Standortproblemen', *Wirtschaftsdienst, Zeitschrift für Wirtschaftspolitik*, vol. 91(7), pp. 458–64.

Dullien, S. and Schwarzer, D. 2009. 'Fiskalpolitik im Euroraum: Reformbedarf und Reformoptionen', *WSI-Mitteilungen*, vol. 62(9), pp. 498–504.

Eichhorst, W., Marx, P. and Tobsch, V. 2009. 'Institutional arrangements, employment performance and the quality of work', IZA Discussion Papers 4595.

Estevez-Abe, M., Iversen, T. and Soskice, D. 2001. 'Social protection and the formation of skills – A reinterpretation of the welfare state', in D. Hall and P. Soskice (ed.), *Varieties of Capitalism – The Institutional Foundations of Comparative Advantage* (Oxford: Oxford University Press), pp. 145–83.

European Commission. 2007. 'Raising Germany's growth potential', Occasional Paper 28 (February). Available online at http://ec.europa.eu/economy_finance/publications/publication_summary7530_en.htm.

European Commission (2010) 'Surveillance of intra-euro-area competitiveness and imbalances', *European Economy* 1 (May). Available online at http://ec.europa.eu/economy_finance/publications/european_economy/2010/ee1_en.htm.

Faruqee, H. and Lee, J. 2009. 'Global dispersion of current accounts: Is the universe expanding?', *IMF Staff Papers*, vol. 56, pp. 574–95.

Ferguson, N. and Schularick, M. 2011. 'The end of Chimerica', *International Finance*, vol. 14(1), pp. 1–26.

Fitoussi, J.-P. and Stiglitz, J.E. 2009. 'The ways out of the crisis and the building of a more cohesive world', Document de Travail, OFCE (17), pp. 471–82.

Frank, R.H. and Cook, P. 1995. *The Winner-take-all Society: How More and More Americans Compete for Ever Fewer and Bigger Prizes, Encouraging Economic Waste, Income Inequality, and an Impoverished Cultural Life* (New York: Free Press).

Frank, R.H. 2007. *Falling Behind: How Rising Inequality Harms the Middle Class* (Berkeley, CA: University Of California Press).

Frank, R.H., Levine, A.S. and Dijk, O. 2010. 'Expenditure cascades, social science research network'. Available online at http://ssrn.com/abstract=1690612.

Freeman, R.B. 2007. 'Labor market institutions around the world', NBER Working Papers 13242.

Freeman, R.B. 2008. 'Why do we work more than Keynes expected?', in L. Pecchi and G. Piga (eds), *Revisiting Keynes: Economic Possibilities for Our Grandchildren* (Cambridge, MA: MIT Press), pp. 135–42.

Fuchs-Schündeln, N. and Schündeln, M. 2005. 'Precautionary savings and self-selection: Evidence from the German reunification experiment', *The Quarterly Journal of Economics*, vol. 120(3), pp. 1085–120.

Galbraith, J.K. 2012. *Inequality and Instability: A Study of the World Economy Just Before the Great Crisis* (Oxford: Oxford University Press).

German Council of Economic Experts (GCEE). 2004. 'External successes – internal challenges: annual report 2003/04' (Wiesbaden: German Council of Economic Experts).

German Council of Economic Experts (GCEE). 2011. 'Chances for a stable upturn: annual report 2010/11' (Wiesbaden: German Council of Economic Experts).

Giavazzi, F. and McMahon, M. 2008. 'Policy uncertainty and precautionary savings', NBER Working Paper 13911.

Goldin, C. and Katz, L.F. 2008. 'The evolution of U.S. educational wage differentials, 1890 to 2005', in *The Race Between Education and Technology* (Cambridge, MA: Harvard University Press).

Goldstein, M. and Lardy, N. 2006. 'China's exchange rate policy dilemma', *American Economic Review*, vol. 96(2), pp. 422–6.

Gong, C.H., Leigh, A. and Meng, X. 2010. 'Intergenerational income mobility in urban China', IZA Discussion Papers 4811.

Greenspan, A. 1996. 'Address: job insecurity and technology', *Conference Series; Proceedings*, (June), pp. 173–81.

Hacker, J.S. and Pierson, P. 2010. *Winner-Take-All Politics: How Washington Made the Rich Richer – and Turned Its Back on the Middle Class* (New York: Simon & Schuster).

Heathcote, J., Perri, F. and Violante, G.L. 2010. 'Unequal we stand: An empirical analysis of economic inequality in the United States: 1967–2006', *Review of Economic Dynamics*, vol. 13(1), pp. 15–51.

Hein, E. and Truger, A. 2007. 'Germany's post 2000 stagnation in the European context – a lesson in macroeconomic mismanagement', in P. Arestis, E. Hein and E. Le Heron (eds), *Aspects of Modern Monetary and Macroeconomic Policies* (Basingstoke: Palgrave Macmillan), pp. 223–47.

Horn, G., Dröge, K., Sturn, S., van Treeck, T. and Zwiener, R. 2009. 'From the financial crisis to the world economic crisis. The role of inequality', IMK Policy Brief (10). Institut für Makroökonomie und Konjukturforschung (IMK).

Huang, Y. and Tao, K. 2010. 'Factor market distortion and the current account surplus in China', *Asian Economic Papers*, vol. 9(3), pp. 1–36.

Iacoviello, M. 2008. 'Household debt and income inequality, 1963–2003', *Journal of Money, Credit and Banking*, vol. 40(5), pp. 929–65.

International Labour Organization (ILO) and International Monetary Fund (IMF). 2010. 'The challenges of growth, employment and social cohesion. Discussion document, International Labour Organization and International Monetary Fund'. Proceeding from the joint ILO–IMF conference held in Oslo, Norway, 13 September.

Ivanova, A. 2012. 'Current account imbalances: Can structural policies make a difference?', IMF Working Papers 12/61.

Jin, Y., Li, H. and Wu, B. 2011. 'Income inequality, consumption, and social-status seeking', *Journal of Comparative Economics*, vol. 39(2), pp. 191–204.

Karl, M. and Schäfer, D. 2011. 'Verschuldung der privaten Haushalte in der Krise nicht erhöht', *DIW-Wochenbericht*, vol. 22/2011, pp. 3–9.

Klär, E. and Slacalek, J. 2006. 'Entwicklung der Sparquote in Deutschland: Hindernis für die Erholung der Konsumnachfrage', *DIW-Wochenbericht*, vol. 40/2006, pp. 537–43.

Kopczuk, W., Saez, E. and Song, J. 2010. 'Earnings inequality and mobility in the United States: Evidence from social security data since 1937', *The Quarterly Journal of Economics*, vol. 125(1), pp. 91–128.

Kraay, A. 2000. 'Household saving in China', *World Bank Economic Review*, vol. 14(3), pp. 545–70.

Krueger, D. and Perri, F. 2003. 'On the welfare consequences of the increase in inequality in the United States', NBER Working Paper.

Krueger, D. and Perri, F. 2006. 'Does income inequality lead to consumption inequality? Evidence and theory', *Review of Economic Studies*, vol. 73, pp. 163–93.

Krugman, P. 2011. 'Holding China to account', *The New York Times*, 3 October 2011, p. A25. Accessed at http://www.nytimes.com/2011/10/03/opinion/holding-china-to-account.html?_r=1&scp=3&sq=krugman%20china&st=cse.

Kumhof, M. and Ranciere, R. 2010. 'Inequality, leverage and crises', IMF Working Papers 268 (Washington, DC: International Monetary Fund).

Kumhof, M., Lebarz, C., Ranciere, R., Richter, A.W. and Throckmorton, N.A. 2012. 'Income inequality and current account imbalances, IMF Working Papers 12/08 (Washington, DC: International Monetary Fund).

Lavoie, M. and Stockhammer, E. 2013. 'Wage-led growth: Concept, theories and policies', in M. Lavoie and E. Stockhammer (eds), *Wage-Led Growth: An Equitable Strategy for Economic Recovery* (Basingstoke: Palgrave Macmillan).

Levy, F. and Temin, P. 2007. 'Inequality and institutions in 20th century America', Working Paper 17.

Li, H. and Zhou, L.-A. 2005. 'Political turnover and economic performance: the incentive role of personnel control in China', *Journal of Public Economics*, vol. 89(9–10), pp. 1743–62.

McCoy, K. 2004. 'Sleeping less than eight hours a night may stimulate your appetite', Goldlite Hypnosis Institute. Available online at http://www.goldlite-hypnosisinstitute.com/Sleep_Less_Making_U_Hungry.html.

McKinnon, R. 2006. 'China's exchange rate trap: Japan redux?', *American Economic Review*, vol. 96(2), pp. 427–31.

Meinhardt, V., Rietzler, K. and Zwiener, R. 2009. 'Konjunktur und Rentenversicherung – gegenseitige Abhängigkeiten und mögliche Veränderungen durch diskretionäre Maßnahmen, Forschungsbericht im Auftrag Deutsche Rentenversicherung Bund', IMK Studies, 3/2009.

Moffitt, R.A. and Gottschalk, P. 2002. 'Trends in the transitory variance of earnings in the United States', *Economic Journal*, vol. 112(478), pp. C68–C73.

Neumark, D. and Postlewaite, A. 1998. 'Relative income concerns and the rise in married women's employment', *Journal of Public Economics*, vol. 70, pp. 157–83.

Neumark-Sztainer, D., Nahhan, P., Story, M., Croll, J. and Perry, C. 2003. 'Family meal patterns: associations with sociodemographic characteristics and improved dietary intake among adolescents', *Journal of the American Dietetic Association*, vol. 103, pp. 317–22.

Organisation for Economic Co-operation and Development (OECD). 2008a. *Growing Unequal? Income Distribution and Poverty in OECD Countries* (Paris: OECD).

Organisation for Economic Co-operation and Development (OECD). 2008b. 'Growing unequal?: Income distribution and poverty in OECD countries, country note: Germany'. Available online at http://www.oecd.org/datao-ecd/45/25/41525346.pdf.

Organisation for Economic Co-operation and Development (OECD). 2008c. *Women and Men in OECD Countries* (Paris: OECD).

Organisation for Economic Co-operation and Development (OECD). 2009. *Employment Outlook – Tackling the Jobs Crisis* (Paris: OECD).

Organisation for Economic Co-operation and Development (OECD). 2010a. *OECD Economic Surveys of China* (Paris: OECD).

Organisation for Economic Co-operation and Development (OECD). 2010b. *Economic Survey of Germany* (Paris: OECD).

Organisation for Economic Co-operation and Development (OECD). 2012. *Economic Survey of Germany* (Paris: OECD).

Palley, T.I. 2012. *From Financial Crisis to Stagnation: The Destruction of Shared Prosperity and the Role of Economics* (Cambridge: Cambridge University Press).

Philippon, T. and Resheff, A. 2009. 'Wages and human capital in the US finance industry: 1909–2006', NBER Working Paper 14644.

Piketty, T. and Saez, E. 2006. 'The evolution of top incomes: A historical and international perspective', *American Economic Review*, vol. 96(2), pp. 200–5.

Piketty, T. and Saez, E. 2007. 'How progressive is the US federal tax system? A historical and international perspective', *Journal of Economic Perspectives*, vol. 21(1), pp. 3–24.

Pollin, R. 1988. 'The growth of U.S. household debt: Demand-side influences', *Journal of Macroeconomics*, vol. 10(2), pp. 231–48.

Pollin, R. 1990. *Deeper In Debt: The Changing Financial Conditions of US Households* (Washington, DC: Economic Policy Institute).

Prasad, E.S. 2009. 'Is the Chinese growth miracle built to last?', *China Economic Review*, vol. 20(1), pp. 103–23.

Putnam, R. 2000. *Bowling Alone: The Collapse and Revival of American Community* (New York: Simon & Schuster).

Rajan, R. 2010. *Fault Lines: How Hidden Fractures Still Threaten the World Economy* (Princeton, NJ: Princeton University Press).

Reich, R. 2010. *Aftershock: The Next Economy and America's Future* (New York: Knopf).

Reinhart, C.M. and Rogoff, K.S. 2010. *This Time is Different: Eight Centuries of Financial Folly* (Princeton, NJ: Princeton University Press).

Reisen, H. 2010. 'Is China's currency undervalued?' Available online at http://www.voxeu.org/index.php?q=node/4845.

Roberts, P. 2010. *How the Economy Was Lost* (Oakland, CA: AK Press).

Sabelhaus, J. and Song, J. 2009. 'Earnings volatility across groups and time', *National Tax Journal*, vol. 62(2), pp. 347–64.

Schor, J.B. 1998. *The Overspent American: Upscaling, Downshifting, and the New Consumer* (New York: Basic Books).

Shiller, R.J. 2008. *The Subprime Solution: How Today's Global Financial Crisis Happened, and What to Do about It* (Princeton, NJ: Princeton University Press).

Song, Z., Storesletten, K. and Zilibotti, F. 2011. 'Growing like China', *American Economic Review*, vol. 101(1), pp. 196–233.

Soskice, D. 1997. 'German technology policy, innovation, and national institutional frameworks', *Industry & Innovation*, vol. 4(1), pp. 75–96.

Stiglitz, J.E. 2008. 'Toward a general theory of consumerism: Reflections on Keynes' economic possibilities for our grandchildren', in L. Pecchi and G. Piga (eds), *Revisiting Keynes: Economic Possibilities for Our Grandchildren* (Cambridge, MA: MIT Press), pp. 41–86.

Stiglitz, J.E. 2009. 'The global crisis, social protection and jobs', *International Labour Review*, vol. 148(1–2), pp. 1–13.

Streeck, W. 1991. 'On the institutional conditions of diversified quality production', in W. Streeck and E. Matzner (eds), *The Socio-Economics of Production and Employment* (Cheltenham: Edward Elgar).

United Nations Commission of Experts. 2009. *Report of the Commission of Experts of the President of the United Nations General Assembly on Reforms of the International Monetary and Financial System* (New York: United Nations).

Yang, D.T., Zhang, J. and Zhou, S. 2011. 'Why are saving rates so high in China?', NBER Working Papers 16771.

Yongding, Y. 2007. 'Global imbalances and China', *Australian Economic Review*, vol. 40(1), pp. 3–23.

6
Financialization, the Financial and Economic Crisis, and the Requirements and Potentials for Wage-led Recovery*

Eckhard Hein and Matthias Mundt

6.1 Introduction

In 2008/09 the world economy was hit by a decline in real GDP, the scale of which had not been seen for generations. The so-called 'Great Recession' started with the collapse of the subprime mortgage market in the United States in summer 2007, and it gained momentum following the collapse of Lehman Brothers in September 2008. Under the conditions of deregulated and liberalized international financial markets, the financial and real crisis spread rapidly across the world, reaching another climax with the euro crisis which began in 2010. Although recovery has already started in late 2009 – albeit with different speeds in different countries – the world economy is far from having overcome the causes of the crisis which are rooted in long-run developments since the early 1980s. We hold that the severity of the present crisis is due to the following medium- to long-run developments, in particular in the advanced capitalist economies but also affecting the emerging market economies: the inefficient regulation of financial markets; an increasing inequality

* Many thanks go to Matthieu Charpe, of the International Labour Office and the International Institute for Labour Studies, for providing data on functional income distribution for non-OECD countries. A preliminary version of the paper was presented at the Regulating for Decent Work Network Conference on 'Regulating for a Fair Recovery', 6–8 July 2011, ILO, Geneva, and at a workshop of the project 'New Perspectives on Wages and Economic Growth', 9 July 2011, ILO, Geneva. We are grateful to the participants for helpful comments and suggestions, in particular by the other contributors to this project, Marc Lavoie, Özlem Onaran, Engelbert Stockhammer, Servaas Storm, Simon Sturn and Till van Treeck, and, most importantly, to Sangheon Lee. We have also benefitted from comments by Jens Christiansen. Remaining errors are, however, exclusively ours.

in the distribution of income; and rising imbalances at the global (and at the euro area) level.[1] These developments have been dominated by the policies aimed at the deregulation of labour markets, the reduction of the level of government intervention in the market economy and of government demand management, the redistribution of income from (lower) wages to profits and top management salaries, and the deregulation and liberalization of national and international financial markets. In what follows, we will give this broad policy stance the label 'neoliberalism', describing the policies implemented – to different degrees in different capitalist economies – since the early 1980s. 'Financialization' or 'finance-dominated capitalism' (we use these terms interchangeably) is interrelated and overlaps with 'neoliberalism', but is not identical with it.[2] Epstein (2005: 3) has presented a widely accepted definition, arguing that '[...] financialization means the increasing role of financial motives, financial markets, financial actors and financial institutions in the operation of the domestic and international economies'.

From a macroeconomic perspective, financialization has affected long-run economic developments through the following channels (Hein 2012; Hein and van Treeck 2010):

1. With regard to distribution, financialization has been conducive to a rising gross profit share, including retained profits, dividends and interest payments, and thus a falling labour income share, on the one hand, and to an increasing inequality of wages and top management salaries, on the other hand. The major reasons for this have been the decreasing bargaining power of trade unions, increasing profit claims imposed, in particular, by increasingly powerful rentiers and a change in the sectoral composition of the economy in favour of the financial corporate sector (Hein and Mundt 2012).

2. Regarding investment, financialization has been characterized by increasing shareholder power vis-à-vis management and workers, an increasing rate of return on equity and bonds held by rentiers, and an alignment of management with shareholder interests through short-run performance-related pay schemes, bonuses, stock option programmes, and related measures. On the one hand, this has imposed short-termism on management and has caused decreasing managements' 'animal spirits' with respect to real investment in capital stock and the long-run growth of the firm. On the other hand, it has drained internal means of finance for real investment purposes from the corporations, through increased dividend payments and share buybacks in order to boost stock prices and thus shareholder

value, and through risky financial investments aimed at maximizing short-run profits. These 'preference' and 'internal means of finance' channels have each had partially negative effects on the real investment of firms in capital stock and hence on the long-run growth of the economy.

3. Regarding consumption, financialization has generated an increasing potential for wealth-based and debt-financed consumption, thus creating the potential to compensate for the depressing demand effects of financialization in some countries, which were imposed on the economy via redistribution and the impact on real investment. Stock market and housing price booms have each increased notional wealth against which households were willing to borrow. Changing financial norms, new financial instruments (credit card debt, home equity lending), a deterioration in the standards of creditworthiness, triggered by the securitization of mortgage debt and 'originate and distribute' strategies of commercial banks, made increasing amounts of credit available to low-income, low-wealth households, in particular. This allowed consumption to rise faster than medium income and thus to stabilize aggregate demand. But it also triggered increasing debt–income ratios of private households and thus increasing financial fragility.

4. Whereas some countries relied on soaring consumption demand as the main driver of aggregate demand and GDP growth, others focussed on mercantilist export-led strategies as an alternative to generate demand in the face of redistribution at the expense of (low) labour incomes, stagnating consumption demand and weak real investment. However, this strategy contributed to rising global current account imbalances prior to the Great Recession.

This chapter is intended to contribute to the understanding of the long-run effects of financialization on the financial and economic crisis, on the one hand. On the other hand, we attempt to outline the requirements and the potentials for a long-run sustainable recovery strategy after the crisis, and we will argue that such a recovery strategy will have to be (mass) income- or wage-led. We will concentrate here on the G20 economies – that is, on Argentina, Australia, Brazil, Canada, China, France, Germany, India, Indonesia, Italy, Japan, the Republic of Korea, Mexico, Russian Federation, Saudi Arabia, South Africa, Turkey, the United Kingdom and the United States.[3]

Since the developments of income distribution in these countries and its determinants have already been discussed extensively in the previous chapters of this book by Lavoie/Stockhammer, Stockhammer and Sturn/van Treeck,[4] we will focus here on the effects of financialization and redistribution on aggregate demand and on global and regional imbalances. The countries examined so far in the empirical literature are dominated by 'wage-led' domestic demand regimes, and most of them also by wage-led overall demand regimes – and probably also by 'wage-led' growth regimes (as shown in the contribution to this book by Onaran/Galanis), although some of them might turn profit-led when the net export channel is included. A falling wage share and increasing inequality should hence have been detrimental to domestic demand in most of the cases, and also to total demand as well as to growth in many countries. However, the three further effects of financialization mentioned above have to be taken into account when assessing the effects of financialization on the macroeconomy and on the crisis.

The direct effects on investment of the business sector, via 'preference' (shareholder value orientation and short-termism of management) and 'internal means of finance' channels (rising dividend payments and share buybacks), have been found to be negative in the theoretical and empirical literature.[5] The effects on consumption demand of private households, however, can be positive and potentially overcompensate the partially negative demand effects of financialization through the decrease in the labour income share and the fall in real investment. The conditions for this are considerable wealth effects on consumption and an increase in financial and/or housing wealth.[6] If these conditions are met, liberalization of financial markets, financial innovation and deterioration of creditworthiness standards may generate 'debt-led consumption booms', which, however, suffer from internal contradictions regarding sustainability due to increasing debt–income ratios of private households in particular.[7] The counterpart to the 'debt-led consumption boom' type of development is the 'export-led mercantilist' type, which is driven by export surpluses compensating for weak domestic demand. In section 6.2 of this chapter we will examine the demand regimes of the G20 economies along these lines and the concomitant global imbalances in more detail. Given that the crisis has proven that neither the 'debt-led consumption boom' type nor the 'export-led mercantilist' type are sustainable, we will then draw the economic policy conclusions from our analysis in section 6.3 and we will argue that a sustainable recovery strategy from the crisis has to be (mass) income- or wage-led and has to be embedded into a 'Global Keynesian New Deal' which, more broadly, will have to address the three main causes for the severity of the crisis: inefficient regulation of financial markets, increasing inequality in the distribution of income and rising imbalances at the global (and at the euro area) level. Section 6.4 will summarize and conclude.

6.2 Financialization, aggregate demand and global imbalances

Against the background of rising inequality in personal income distribution and falling labour income shares, associated with financialization and neoliberalism since the early 1980s in the developed capitalist economies in particular, and the restrictive effects of 'financialization' on real investment, two extreme 'types of capitalism under financialization' have developed,[8] which are complementary and which have fed rising current account imbalances in the world economy.[9] On the one hand, we have the 'debt-led consumption boom' type generating a 'profits without investment' regime. Since this type has been characterized by considerable current account deficits, there has developed a necessary counterpart at the global level, the 'strongly export-led mercantilist' type, on the other hand, which may also give rise to a 'profits without investment' regime. In the former it is debt-financed consumption demand which allows for the realization of rising profits. In the latter it is export surpluses which have to take care of the realization of profits in the face of relatively weak domestic demand, either investment and/or consumption in the face of redistribution at the expense of labour. Note that from national accounting we obtain Kalecki's (1971: 82) famous profit equation:

Gross profits net of taxes = Gross investment
+ Export surplus
+ Government budget deficit   (6.1)
– workers' saving
+ Capitalists' consumption.

As the G20 current account imbalances have exploded in particular since the early 2000s in the course of recovery from the burst of the new economy boom of the late 1990s (Figure 6.1), we take cyclical average data for the trade cycle of the early 2000s in order to distinguish the two extreme types, the 'debt-led consumption boom' and the 'strongly export-led mercantilist' types, and two intermediate types of capitalism, the 'domestic demand-led' and the 'weakly export-led' types, and allocate the G20 countries to them. It goes without saying that classifying such a heterogeneous set of economies as the G20

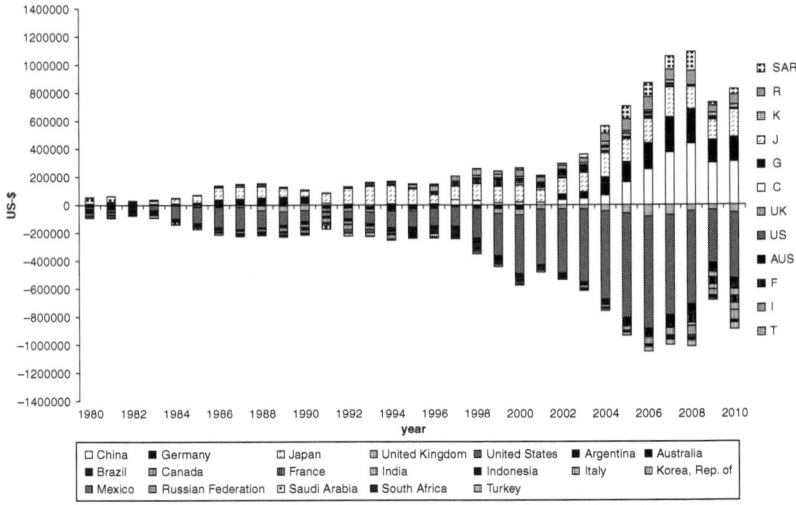

Figure 6.1   Current accounts of G20 economies, 1980–2012, in millions of US$
Source: IMF (2011).

into four categories is of necessity a somewhat arbitrary exercise. It should also be noted that the cycle of the early 2000s had dynamic growth rates in the emerging market economies, which exceeded the growth rates of the previous cycles, whereas in the developed capitalist economies real GDP growth fell short of the rates of the previous cycles (Table 6.1).

In the cycle of the early 2000s, the 'debt-led consumption boom' type of capitalism can be found in the United Kingdom and the United States, in particular, but Australia and Mexico also show tendencies towards this type (Table 6.2a). Real GDP growth in all of these countries was driven by domestic demand, and, in particular, these countries saw considerable growth contributions of private consumption in the face of declining labour income shares. The growth contributions of net exports were negative throughout, although Mexico, the United Kingdom and the United States managed to improve price competitiveness, indicated by a negative rate of change in the real effective exchange rate, mainly through a nominal depreciation of their currencies, whereas there was a deterioration in price competitiveness in Australia.[10] The countries were characterized by considerable deficits in their balances of goods and services and current accounts were also in deficit. Financial balances of the respective external sectors were therefore positive, whereas the domestic sectors were in deficit, either the private or the public sector, or both.

Table 6.1 Real GDP growth, average values over the trade cycle, early 1980s–2008, in percentages

	1. Early 1980s–early 1990s	2. Early 1990s–early 2000s	3. Early 2000s–2008	Change (3 – 2), percentage points
Argentina [a]	−0.49	2.50	5.72	2.22
Australia	3.58	3.58	3.20	−0.38
Brazil [a]	2.31	1.94	4.21	2.27
Canada	2.77	2.94	2.28	−0.66
China [a]	9.97	9.85	10.66	0.81
France	2.21	2.15	1.61	−0.60
Germany	2.75	1.50	1.46	−0.04
India [a]	5.67	5.48	7.37	1.89
Indonesia [a]	6.48	3.93	5.19	1.26
Italy	2.20	1.59	0.73	−0.86
Japan [a]	4.30	0.97	1.22	0.25
Korea, Rep. of [a]	9.74	6.15	3.99	−2.16
Mexico [a]	1.85	3.44	2.43	−1.01
Russian Federation [a]	...	−0.34	6.79	7.13
Saudi Arabia [a]	0.43	1.45	3.96	2.51
South Africa [a]	1.05	2.16	4.24	2.08
Turkey [a]	5.25	3.77	4.46	0.69
United Kingdom	2.77	2.54	2.21	−0.33
United States	3.33	3.44	2.08	−1.36

Notes: The beginning of a trade cycle is given by a local minimum of annual real GDP growth in the respective country.
[a] adjusted to fit in three-cycle pattern.
Source: European Commission (2011); World Bank (2011), authors' calculations.

There is some indication that the development in the 'debt-led consumption boom' economies was driven by considerable increases in residential property prices and/or in wealth–income ratios in the cycle of the early 2000s. The United Kingdom and the United States each show negative financial balances of the private household sector on average during the trade cycle of the early 2000s and Australia, the United Kingdom and the United States have each seen significant

Table 6.2a Key macroeconomic variables for 'debt-led consumption boom' economies, average values for the trade cycle from the early 2000s–2008

	Australia	United Kingdom	United States	Mexico
Financial balances of external sector as a share of nominal GDP, per cent	**4.84**	**2.24**	**4.96**	**1.15**
Financial balances of public sector as share of nominal GDP, per cent	0.73	–3.26	–3.50	–0.78 [a]
Financial balance of private sector as a share of nominal GDP, per cent	–5.57	1.02	–1.47	–1.35 [a]
Financial balance of private household sector as a share of nominal GDP, per cent	...	–2.37	–1.68	3.10 [a]
Financial balance of the corporate sector as a share of nominal GDP, per cent	...	3.55	0.21	–4.44 [a]
Real GDP growth, per cent	**3.20**	**2.21**	**2.08**	**2.43**
Growth contribution of domestic demand including stocks, percentage points	4.69	2.43	2.15	2.77
Growth contribution of private consumption, percentage points	**2.05**	**1.52**	**1.75**	**2.41**
Growth contribution of public consumption, percentage points	0.56	0.47	0.36	0.04

Growth contribution of gross fixed capital formation, percentage points	2.14	0.51	0.13	0.86
Growth contribution of the balance of goods and services, percentage points	–1.37	–0.23	–0.07	–0.37
Net exports of goods and services as a share of nominal GDP, per cent	–1.43	–2.83	–4.88	–1.67
Change in labour income share, as percentage of GDP at current factor costs, from previous cycle, percentage points	–3.19	–1.26	–1.25	–0.19
Growth rate of nominal unit labour costs, per cent	3.36	2.44	2.05	5.04
Inflation (rate of change of consumer price index), per cent	3.17	2.04	2.83	4.67
Growth rate of nominal effective exchange rates (relative to 52 countries), per cent	2.68	–1.25	–2.15	–2.84
Growth rate of real effective exchange rates (relative to 52 countries), per cent	3.49	–1.90	–2.05	–1.07

Notes: The beginning of a trade cycle is given by a local minimum of annual real GDP growth in the early 2000s in the respective country, [a] average value only for 2001–02.

Sources: European Commission (2011); IMF (2011); World Bank (2011), authors' calculations.

Table 6.2b Key macroeconomic variables for 'domestic demand-led' economies, average values for the trade cycle from the early 2000s–2008

	France	Italy	India	South Africa	Turkey
Financial balances of external sector as a share of nominal GDP, per cent	**1.16**	**1.59**	**0.22**	**3.24**	**4.41**
Financial balances of public sector as share of nominal GDP, per cent	–3.18	–3.16	–7.23	–0.47	–4.52
Financial balance of private sector as a share of nominal GDP, per cent	2.02	1.57	7.01	–2.77	0.41
Financial balance of private household sector as a share of nominal GDP, per cent	3.78	4.04	...	...	...
Financial balance of the corporate sector as a share of nominal GDP, per cent	–1.80	–2.36	...	...	...
Real GDP growth, per cent	**1.61**	**0.73**	**7.37**	**4.24**	**4.46**
Growth contribution of domestic demand including stocks, percentage points	2.12	0.82	7.70	5.45	4.82
Growth contribution of private consumption, percentage points	**1.21**	**0.44**	**4.02**	**2.99**	**3.30**
Growth contribution of public consumption, percentage points	0.39	0.27	0.54	0.93	0.37

Growth contribution of gross fixed capital formation, percentage points	0.54	0.09	3.32	1.61	1.17
Growth contribution of the balance of goods and services, percentage points	−0.51	−0.08	−0.33	−1.21	−0.40
Net exports of goods and services as a share of nominal GDP, per cent	−0.49	−0.09	−2.52	0.13	−1.99
Change in labour income share, as percentage of GDP at current factor costs, or wage share in GDP from previous cycle, percentage points	−1.01	−0.88	−0.07[a]	−4.69[a]	−3.78
Growth rate of nominal unit labour costs, per cent	1.99	2.97	...	...	17.65
Inflation (rate of change of consumer price index), per cent	1.98	2.36	5.10	6.09	21.89
Growth rate of nominal effective exchange rates (relative to 52 countries), per cent	1.80	1.71	−1.94	−3.88	−10.87
Growth rate of real effective exchange rates (relative to 52 countries), per cent	1.18	1.25	0.49	−1.62	2.32

Notes: The beginning of a trade cycle is given by a local minimum of annual real GDP growth in the early 2000s in the respective country, [a] wage share in GDP, no complete trade cycle.

Sources: Charpe (2011), European Commission (2011), IMF (2011), World Bank (2011), authors' calculations.

Table 6.2c Key macroeconomic variables for 'strongly export-led mercantilist' economies, average values for the trade cycle from the early 2000s–2008

	Germany	Japan	China	Indonesia	Korea, Rep. of
Financial balances of external sector as a share of nominal GDP, per cent	**-5.51**	**-3.45**	**-5.86**	**-2.24**	**-1.34**
Financial balances of public sector as share of nominal GDP, per cent	-2.06	-5.15	-1.41	-0.74	2.47
Financial balance of private sector as a share of nominal GDP, per cent	**7.57**	**8.60**	**7.26**	**2.98**	**-1.13**
Financial balance of private household sector as a share of nominal GDP, per cent	5.89	2.56	…	…	…
Financial balance of the corporate sector as a share of nominal GDP, per cent	1.69	4.96	…	…	…
Real GDP growth, per cent	**1.46**	**1.22**	**10.66**	**5.19**	**3.99**
Growth contribution of domestic demand including stocks, percentage points	0.83	0.75	8.15	4.82	2.89
Growth contribution of private consumption, percentage points	0.23	0.61	3.11	2.52	1.40
Growth contribution of public consumption, percentage points	0.15	0.29	1.31	0.60	0.66

Growth contribution of gross fixed capital formation, percentage points	0.46	–0.19	4.47	1.61	0.68
Growth contribution of the balance of goods and services, percentage points	**0.63**	**0.46**	**2.52**	**0.37**	**1.11**
Net exports of goods and services as a share of nominal GDP, per cent	5.60	1.24	4.90	5.15	1.81
Change in labour income share, as percentage of GDP at current factor costs, or wage share in GDP, from previous cycle, percentage points	**–2.67**	**–4.73**	**–2.28[a]**	**...**	**–3.56**
Growth rate of nominal unit labour costs, per cent	0.03	–2.12	...	...	1.89
Inflation (rate of change of consumer price index), per cent	1.79	–0.06	2.37	9.44	3.21
Growth rate of nominal effective exchange rates (relative to 52 countries), per cent	1.97	–1.21	0.55	–3.48	–0.42
Growth rate of real effective exchange rates (relative to 52 countries), per cent	**0.92**	**–4.07**	**0.57**	**3.41**	**0.18**

Notes: The beginning of a trade cycle is given by a local minimum of annual real GDP growth in the early 2000s in the respective country, [a] wage share in GDP, no complete trade cycle.

Sources: Charpe (2011), European Commission (2011), IMF (2011), World Bank (2011), authors' calculations.

Table 6.2d Key macroeconomic variables for 'weakly export-led' economies, average values for the trade cycle from the early 2000s–2008

	Canada	Argentina	Brazil	Russian Federation	Saudi Arabia
Financial balances of external sector as a share of nominal GDP, per cent	-1.60	-3.72	-0.62	-8.50	-21.22
Financial balances of public sector as share of nominal GDP, per cent	0.77	-4.01	-3.13	4.94	16.03
Financial balance of private sector as a share of nominal GDP, per cent	0.83	7.73	3.74	3.55	5.18
Financial balance of private household sector as a share of nominal GDP, per cent	...	...	...	...	...
Financial balance of the corporate sector as a share of nominal GDP, per cent	...	...	...	...	...
Real GDP growth, per cent	2.28	5.72	4.21	6.79	3.96
Growth contribution of domestic demand including stocks, percentage points	3.46	5.92	4.66	10.38	8.32
Growth contribution of private consumption, percentage points	1.92	3.72	2.68	5.84	2.50
Growth contribution of public consumption, percentage points	0.55	0.43	0.59	0.29	2.48

Growth contribution of gross fixed capital formation, percentage points	1.04	2.30	1.19	2.58	2.83
Growth contribution of the balance of goods and services, percentage points	-1.16	-0.20	-0.46	-3.59	-4.36
Net exports of goods and services as a share of nominal GDP, per cent	3.50	7.47	2.50	11.24	26.91
Change in labour income share, as percentage of GDP at current factor costs, or in wage share in GDP, from previous cycle, percentage points	-4.05	-5.63[a]	-3.69[a]	-0.31[a]	...
Growth rate of nominal unit labour costs, per cent	2.73	...	...	...	...
Inflation (rate of change of consumer price index), per cent	2.26	11.67	6.96	12.26	2.58
Growth rate of nominal effective exchange rates (relative to 52 countries), per cent	3.53	-14.21	5.17	-2.41	-3.62
Growth rate of real effective exchange rates (relative to 52 countries), per cent	3.03	-9.03	8.33	6.56	-3.68

Notes: The beginning of a trade cycle is given by a local minimum of annual real GDP growth in the early 2000s in the respective country, [a] wage share in GDP, no complete trade cycle.

Sources: Charpe (2011), European Commission (2011), IMF (2011), World Bank (2011), authors' calculations.

increases in the gross debt–income ratios of private households (Table 6.3). These were based on increases in (notional) net wealth and on considerable increases in residential property prices in each of these three countries (Figure 6.2a). In Mexico, residential property prices have increased since 2005, too, but there is no information on private household debt–income or net wealth–income ratios. Available data on

Table 6.3 Household debt and net wealth, per cent of annual disposable income

	Debt			Net wealth		
	1995	2000	2005	1995	2000	2005
Argentina	...	...	...	...	...	...
Australia	83	120	173	514	567	734
Brazil	...	...	...	...	...	...
Canada	103	114	124	370	527	640
China	...	...	...	...	...	...
France	66	78	89	461	547	752
Germany	97	111	107	541	575	578 [a]
India	...	...	...	...	...	...
Indonesia	...	...	...	...	...	...
Italy	32	46	59	702	820	936 [a]
Japan	130	136	132 [a]	736	750	725 [a]
Korea, Rep. of	...	...	...	...	...	...
Mexico	...	...	...	...	...	...
Russian Federation	...	...	...	...	...	...
Saudi Arabia	...	...	...	...	...	...
South Africa	...	...	...	...	...	...
Turkey	...	...	...	...	...	...
United Kingdom	106	118	159	569	750	790
United States	93	107	135	510	575	573

Notes: [a] for 2004 instead of 2005. Debt refers to total liabilities outstanding at the end of the period. Net wealth is defined as non-financial and financial assets minus liabilities. Data is from national statistics. Shaded grey means an increase of debt–income ratios of more than 20 percentage points and of net wealth–income ratios of more than 50 percentage points relative to previous value.

Source: Girourard et al. (2007: 9).

private household financial balances until 2002 indicate that private household deficits and debt were not a general problem up to that year, so that classifying this country as a 'debt-led consumption boom' economy may be premature. During the trade cycle of the early 2000s, the 'debt-led consumption boom' economies were the world demand engines.

Also the economies of the second type, the 'domestic demand-led' economies, were drivers of world demand (Table 6.2b). This group consists of such different countries as France and Italy, on the one hand, and India, South Africa and Turkey, on the other hand. The 'domestic demand-led' economies display similar characteristics as the 'debt-led consumption boom' economies: The respective external sectors show positive financial balances, that is, the current accounts of these countries were in deficit, and, with the exception of South Africa, the same holds true for the balances of goods and services. Growth contributions of net exports were negative throughout. Despite falling labour income shares, growth in these countries was therefore driven exclusively by domestic demand. However, these countries did not experience debt-led consumption booms in the face of redistribution at the expense

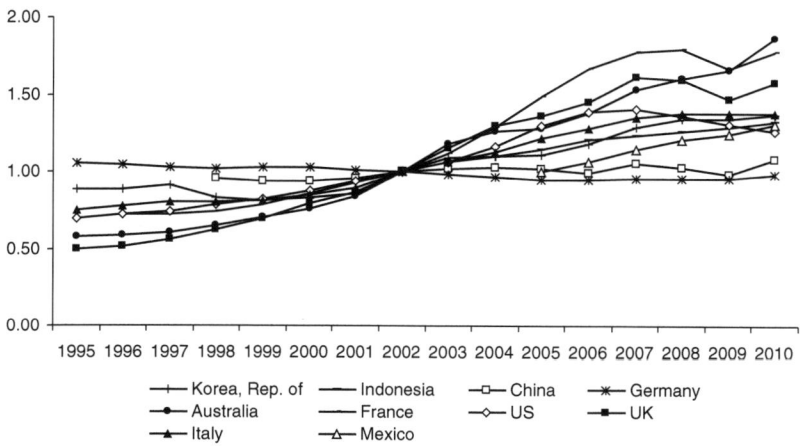

Figure 6.2a Residential property prices in nine G20 economies, 1995–2012, index: 2002 = 1 (Mexico: 2005 = 1)

Notes: Data are on residential property prices, all or existing dwellings for all countries but China, Indonesia and United States. China: land prices (residential and commercial), Indonesia: new houses (big cities), United States: existing one-family houses.

Source: BIS (2011), authors' calculations.

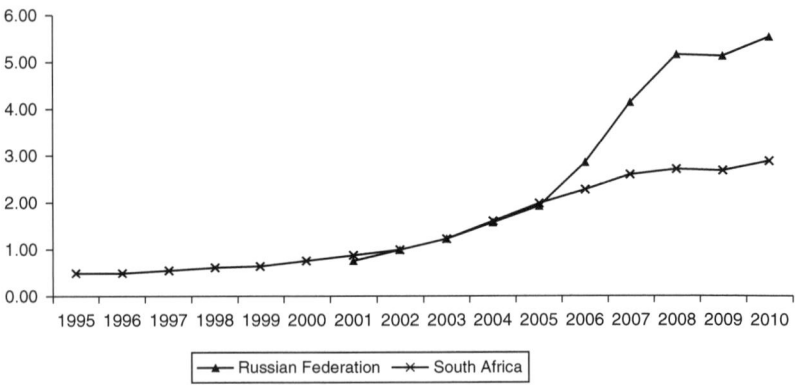

Figure 6.2b   Residential property prices, Russian Federation and South Africa, 1995–2010, index: 2002 = 1

Notes: Data are on residential property prices existing dwellings for Russian Federation and all middle-segment houses for South Africa.

Source: BIS (2011), authors' calculations.

of labour. In the mature European economies of France and Italy net wealth–income ratios and residential property prices also increased (Table 6.3, Figure 6.2a), however, without feeding debt-financed consumption demand. Household gross debt–income ratios increased only slightly and the financial balances of the private household sectors remained positive, as did the financial balances of the private sector as a whole. With falling labour income shares, growth contributions of private consumption demand remained weak and with weak investment in capital stock, real GDP growth in these countries was only meagre. The emerging economies in this group, India, South Africa and Turkey, however, have seen strong real GDP growth during the cycle of the early 2000s, which was driven by private consumption but also by considerable growth contributions of investment in capital stock. Due to the lack of data, there is no indication yet that private consumption was mainly wealth-driven and debt-financed. The financial balances of the private sector as a whole remained positive in India and Turkey, whereas in South Africa this balance was negative. South Africa also experienced significant increases in residential property prices since the early 2000s (Figure 6.2b), but more data would be required to identify a debt-led consumption boom in this country.

The counterparts to the 'debt-led consumption boom' and the 'domestic demand-led' economies at the world level were the 'export-led' economies with both positive net exports of goods and services and current account surpluses – that is, negative financial balances of the respective external sectors. We distinguish two types of export-led economies, first the 'strongly export-led mercantilist' type, and second the 'weakly export-led' type.

The 'strongly export-led mercantilist' type contains Germany, Japan, China, Indonesia and the Republic of Korea (Table 6.2c). These countries have not only seen positive net exports and current accounts, but also gained from positive growth contributions of net exports in the course of the cycle of the early 2000s, which means that they managed to increase net exports on average during this period. The slowly growing mature economies of Germany and Japan, with particularly weak domestic demand in the face of falling labour income shares and small, and in the case of Japan even negative, growth contributions of fixed capital formation, derived more than one-third of their meagre growth from increasing external surpluses. But also the more dynamic Asian economies of China and the Republic of Korea, with more considerable growth contributions of private consumption and fixed capital formation, derived more than one-quarter of their growth from rising external surpluses. Only Indonesian growth has relied less on still increasing net exports.

Although Indonesia and the Republic of Korea have seen considerable increases in residential property prices (Figure 6.2a), there is no indication in the available data that this has stimulated debt-driven consumption. In China, Germany and Japan no such increase in residential property prices could be observed, and in the cases of Germany and Japan we find that household net wealth has either only increased slightly (in the case of Germany) or declined (in Japan), so that household gross debt–income ratios in these two countries have rather declined around 2005 as compared to 2000 (Table 6.3).

The basis for external surpluses were thus particularly weak domestic demand in the cases of Germany and Japan, on the one hand, but also low unit labour cost growth, low inflation, and, in the case of Japan, nominal depreciation of the currency, on the other hand.[11] Also in China and the Republic of Korea, where domestic demand was far more dynamic, net exports gained from low inflation and even nominal depreciation in the case of the Republic of Korea. Of this group, only Indonesia has seen a considerable real appreciation of its currency and respective losses in price competitiveness, mainly due to high inflation, which however, have not turned growth contributions of net exports negative.

The second type of 'export-led' economies, the 'weakly export-led' type, can be found in Canada, Argentina, Brazil, the Russian Federation and Saudi Arabia during the trade cycle of the early 2000s (Table 6.2d). Although these countries, in particular the fossil energy-exporting countries of the Russian Federation and Saudi Arabia, have seen considerable surpluses in their balances of goods and services and in their current accounts, and thus negative financial balances of their respective external sectors, growth contributions of net exports were negative throughout. These countries have therefore experienced falling net exports on average over the trade cycle prior to the Great Recession. This was due to dynamic domestic demand in all of these countries with significant growth contributions of private consumption and gross fixed capital accumulation, and to a loss of price competitiveness in the cases of Brazil, Canada and the Russian Federation, whereas Argentina and Saudi Arabia managed to increase competitiveness through nominal devaluation. Again, from the available data we have no indication that in these countries dynamic consumption was driven by wealth effects and household debt. The financial balances of the private sectors remained positive in all of these countries, although in the case of the Russian Federation there has been a dramatic increase in residential property prices (Figure 6.2b). And in the case of Canada, household net wealth–income ratios have increased considerably, without, however, triggering a significant increase in household gross debt–income ratios (Table 6.3).

From our analysis so far we can conclude that the escalating current account imbalances in the world economy during the trade cycle of the early 2000s were mainly driven and dominated by the two extreme types of capitalism, the 'debt-led consumption boom' type, on the one hand, and the 'strongly export-led mercantilist' type, on the other hand. These two types are mainly composed of developed capitalist economies which have been subject to the processes of financialization – starting in the early 1980s in particular. However, they also include Mexico as a presumably 'debt-led consumption' boom economy and China and Indonesia as 'strongly export-led mercantilist' economies. The two intermediate types of capitalism, the 'weakly export-led' and the 'domestic demand-led' types, including most of the emerging market G20 countries, but also Canada, France and Italy, contributed less to the global imbalances, because either their net exports were shrinking during the early 2000s trade cycle, or they had relied on domestic demand without building it on unsustainable private household debt.

Focussing on the two extreme types of capitalism, we can argue that against the background of financialization and its effects on income distribution, fixed capital formation and consumption, a highly fragile constellation at national and global levels had developed in the course of the trade cycle of the early 2000s. On the one hand, the dynamic 'debt-led consumption boom' type of the United States and other countries following this type had to rely on the willingness and ability of private households to go into debt, and thus on ever-rising notional wealth, in particular rising residential property prices, (seemingly) providing collateral for credit, and on the willingness of the rest of the world to run current account surpluses and thus to increasingly supply credit, notably the 'strongly export-led mercantilist' countries, in order to finance the related current account deficits in the 'debt-led consumption boom' economies. On the other hand, in particular the slowly growing or stagnating 'strongly export-led mercantilist' economies such as Germany and Japan, but also the more dynamic China, Indonesia and the Republic of Korea, had to rely on the willingness and the ability of their respective external sectors, in particular the 'debt-led consumption boom' economies, to go into debt, because their growth, which was very weak in the cases of Germany and Japan, but was highly dynamic in the cases of China, Indonesia, and the Republic of Korea, was dependent on the dynamic growth of world demand and their export markets.

A collapse of a 'debt-led consumption boom' type of development, as was triggered by the collapse of the subprime mortgage market in the United States in 2007, therefore affected not only the 'debt-led consumption boom' economies themselves – only Australia did not experience negative growth in 2009 –,[12] but also the 'strongly export-led mercantilist' economies. In particular, Germany and Japan experienced a considerable reduction in real GDP, whereas China, Indonesia and the Republic of Korea only saw a slowdown in real GDP growth.[13] On the one hand, export markets collapsed in the crisis and in particular the low-growth economies of Germany and Japan were facing serious aggregate demand problems. On the other hand, they were infected through the financial markets, because their capital exports became drastically devalued if they were directed towards the risky and now collapsing financial markets of the 'debt-led consumption boom' economies. Also the 'weakly export-led' economies were affected through these two channels;real GDP growth collapsed and even became negative in Brazil, Canada and the Russian Federation.[14] Finally, also the 'domestic demand-led' economies were hit by the crisis in the financial markets and the collapse of major parts of the world economy. In particular, the European economies, France, Italy and Turkey, but also South Africa faced shrinking real GDP whereas India only saw a slowdown in its real GDP growth.[15]

6.3 Wage-led recovery embedded in a Global Keynesian New Deal

From our analysis in the previous section it follows that a medium-to long-run sustainable recovery strategy for major parts of the world economy can follow neither the 'debt-led consumption boom' type nor the 'strongly export-led mercantilist' type,[16] in particular in those economies which are characterized by wage-led demand and growth regimes. Tendencies towards overindebtedness of private households have to be avoided, as do persistent current account surpluses or deficits which are not attributable to productivity growth catch-up processes of less developed economies.[17] This implies that also profit-led economies which turn profit-led via the export channel need to give up export-led strategies because their strategy has to rely on current account deficits in other countries and thus contributes to world wide imbalances.

A medium- to long-run recovery strategy has thus to be (mass) income- or wage-led. This means that wages will have to rise broadly in line with (potential) output. Labour income shares have to be at least roughly stable in the medium to long run, and may even rise if distribution claims of firms, rentiers, the state or the foreign sector are falling and permit the increase of the labour income share without triggering cumulative inflationary processes. In this case, the economy may also benefit from wage-push effects on productivity growth, that is, rising real wages and labour income shares pushing firms to speed up the introduction of labour-saving innovation into the production process and thus increasing potential growth.[18] A wage-led recovery strategy would therefore also contribute to overcoming the tendencies towards dampened productivity growth inherent to financialization and neoliberalism (Hein 2012, chapter 4). These tendencies have been imposed through the long-run depressing effects of financialization and neoliberalism on the labour income share, thus dampening the wage-push effect on productivity growth, through the dampening effect on capital accumulation, with a negative effect on capital embodied technical progress and thus productivity growth, and on aggregate demand growth, thus restricting the 'Verdoorn' effect.

A wage-led recovery strategy requires the addressing of the three main causes for the fall in the labour income share in the period of neoliberalism and financialization: First, the bargaining power of trade unions needs to be stabilized and enhanced; second, the overhead costs of firms, in particular top management salaries and interest payments, as well as profit claims of financial wealth holders have to be reduced;

and third, the sectoral composition of the economy has to be shifted away from the high profit share financial corporations towards the non-financial corporate sector and the public sector.

Although reversing the trends in primary functional distribution is the key for a wage-led recovery strategy, distribution policies should not only address primary functional distribution. They should also focus directly on reducing the inequality of personal distribution of income, in particular of disposable income. This means that the tendencies towards increasing wage dispersion have to be contained and, in particular, that progressive tax policies and social policies need to be applied in order to reduce inequality in the distribution of disposable income.

Distribution policies are at the core of, and are thus embedded in, a 'Global Keynesian New Deal',[19] which will have to address more broadly the three main causes for the severity of the crisis: the inefficient regulation of financial markets, the increasing inequality in the distribution of income and the rising imbalances at the global (and at the euro area) level. The three main pillars of the policy package of a 'Keynesian New Deal at the Global and the European Level' are (Hein/Truger 2011):

- first, the re-regulation of the financial sector in order to prevent future financial excesses and financial crises;
- secondly, the reorientation of macroeconomic policies, in particular in the current account surplus countries; and
- thirdly, the reconstruction of international macroeconomic policy co-ordination and a new world financial order.

In what follows we briefly sketch the main building blocks of such a Global Keynesian New Deal and highlight the role of distribution policies.

6.3.1 Re-regulation of the financial sector

The re-regulation of the financial system requires a host of measures which should aim at orienting the financial sector towards financing *real* economic activity, namely real investment and real GDP growth.[20] This has at least three dimensions: First, measures which increase transparency in financial markets should be introduced, in order to reduce the problems of uncertainty, asymmetric information, moral hazard and fraud, which are inherent to this sector in particular. These measures include the standardization and supervision of all financial products in order to increase transparency in the market. Off-balance sheet operations should be abolished and national and international regulation and supervision of all financial intermediaries (banks, insurance companies, hedge funds, private equity funds, etc.) should be introduced. Since rating can be considered a public good, independent public rating agencies will have to be introduced replacing the private ones. Diversity in the banking sector should be increased in order to increase resilience. Therefore public and cooperative banks supplying credit to households and small firms, and thus competing with private banks, should be strengthened. Financial institutions with systemic relevance should be in public ownership, because stability of these institutions can be considered a public good, too.

Secondly, re-regulation should generate incentives for economic actors in the financial and non-financial sectors encouraging them to focus on long-run growth rather than short-run profits. This includes the reduction of securitization in order to prevent 'originate and distribute' strategies which were at the root of the US subprime mortgage crisis. Banks should be induced to do what banks are supposed to do, that is, evaluate potential creditors and their investment projects, grant credit and supervise the fulfilment of payment commitments by the debtor. For the financial and non-financial corporate sector, share buybacks in order to drive share prices up should be reduced or even abolished. The short-termism of managers in the corporate sector should be minimized by means of reducing stock option programmes and by extending minimum holding periods. Generally, co-determination on the firm level and improving the rights of other stakeholders in the firm, in particular workers and trade unions, should be strengthened in order to overcome short-termism and to increase the importance of investment into long-term projects improving productivity and developing new products.

Third, measures directed at containing systemic instability, like asset-based reserve requirements and counter-cyclical capital requirements for all financial intermediaries, and a general financial transactions tax should be implemented. Furthermore, commercial banks (savings and loans) should be strictly separated from investment banks in order prevent contagion in the case of speculation crises in the latter sector.

Apart from stabilizing and orienting the financial sector towards financing real economic activity, these measures should affect distribution and thus positively feed back on aggregate demand and growth through the following channels: First, since these measures imply a downsized financial sector they will contribute to an increasing labour income share through the change in the sectoral composition of the economy. Second, reducing top management salaries and the profit claims of financial wealth holders will allow for lower mark-ups on unit direct labour costs and thus higher labour income shares. Third, refocusing the management's orientation towards the long-run expansion of the firm will increase the bargaining power of workers and trade unions and therefore have a dampening effect on profit claims.

6.3.2 Reorientation of macroeconomic policies

The reorientation of macroeconomic policies – in particular, in current account surplus countries – should aim at improving domestic demand, employment and hence also imports into these countries. In Hein and Stockhammer (2010) a blueprint for a Post-Keynesian macroeconomic policy mix – as opposed to the New Consensus model focussing on labour market deregulation in order to reduce the NAIRU and on monetary policy for short-run real and long-run nominal stabilization[21] – has been developed which can be used as an orientation.

First, the interest rate policies of the central bank should abstain from attempting to fine-tune unemployment in the short run and inflation in the long run, as suggested by the New Consensus approach. Central banks should instead target low real interest rates in order to avoid unfavourable cost and distribution effects on firms and workers which favour rentiers. A slightly positive real rate of interest, below the rate of productivity growth, seems to be a reasonable target: Rentiers' real financial wealth will be protected against inflation, but overhead costs for firms will be reduced, allowing for a shift of income distribution in favour of labour with stimulating effects on aggregate demand. Further on, central banks must act as a lender of last resort in periods of liquidity crisis, and they should be involved in the regulation and the supervision of financial markets.

Second, fiscal policies should take responsibility for real stabilization, full employment and a more equal distribution of disposable income. Progressive income tax policies, relevant wealth, property and inheritance taxes, and redistributive social policies would improve the conditions for a (mass) income-led recovery. If required by surpluses in private sector financial balances, medium- to long-run government deficits should maintain aggregate demand at high levels, thereby allowing for high employment.[22] In particular, in current account surplus countries with private sector financial surpluses, governments will have to run budget deficits in order to stabilize aggregate demand at the national level, on the one hand, and in order to contribute to rebalancing the current accounts at the international level, on the other hand. Fiscal policies will therefore have a major role to play in rebalancing current accounts at the global and the regional levels. Unfavourable regressive distribution effects of public debt can be avoided by central bank policies targeting low interest rates and/or by appropriate taxation of capital income. Short-run aggregate demand shocks should be countered by automatic stabilizers and by discretionary counter-cyclical fiscal policies.

Third, wage policies should take over responsibility for nominal stabilization, that is, stabilizing inflation at some target rate which contributes to the maintenance of a balanced current account. If the distribution claims of firms, rentiers, government and the external sector are constant, nominal wages should rise according to the sum of long-run economy-wide growth of labour productivity plus the inflation target.[23] A reduction of the claims of the other actors, however, would allow for an increase of nominal wages exceeding this benchmark. In order to contribute to rebalancing the current accounts, nominal wage growth in the current account surplus countries will have to exceed the benchmark for an interim period, whereas nominal wage growth in the deficit countries will have to fall short of the benchmark during the adjustment process. In order to achieve the nominal wage growth targets, a high degree of wage bargaining co-ordination at the macroeconomic level, and organized labour markets with strong labour unions and employers' associations, and government involvement if required, seem to be a necessary condition. Legal minimum wage legislation should contain wage dispersion and thus contribute to a more equal distribution of income.

6.3.3 Reconstruction of international macroeconomic policy co-ordination and a new world financial order

On the international level, international policy co-ordination has to make sure that 'export-led mercantilist' strategies and the associated pressure on labour unions to moderate wage claims in favour of increasing international competitiveness no longer pay off. This implies that targets for current account balances have to be included into international policy co-ordination at both the regional and global levels.[24] At the global level the return to a cooperative world financial order and a system with fixed but adjustable exchange rates, symmetric adjustment obligations for current account deficit and surplus countries, and regulated international capital flows seems to be required in order to avoid the imbalances that have contributed to the present crisis and to preclude 'export-led mercantilist' policies by major economies. Keynes's (1942) proposal for an International Clearing Union is the obvious blueprint for this. As is well known, Keynes suggested an International Clearing Union in a fixed but adjustable exchange rate system, with the 'bancor' as international money for clearing operations between central banks, the Clearing Union as an international central bank financing temporary current account deficits, and selective controls on speculative capital movements between currency areas. What is most important for the present situation is that, according to Keynes (1942), whereas permanent current account deficit countries would be penalized in order to contract domestic demand (or to depreciate their currencies), also permanent current account surplus countries should be induced to expand domestic demand and thus to increase imports (or to appreciate their currencies), so that the whole burden of adjustment does not have to be carried by the deficit countries. This should give an overall impetus to world aggregate demand which will be needed in the future, not only in the short run but also in the long run.[25]

6.4 Summary and conclusions

In this chapter we have argued that the severity of the present crisis cannot be understood without examining the medium- to long-run developments in the world economy which has been dominated by financialization since the early 1980s: inefficient regulation of financial markets, increasing inequality in the distribution of income and rising imbalances at the global level. Our focus has been on the effects of the changes in distribution, triggered by finance-dominated capitalism embedded in a neo-liberal policy stance since the early 1980s, on aggregate demand and growth and on the global imbalances underlying the present financial and economic crisis, and, finally, on the requirements for distribution policies in an expansionary post-crisis economic policy regime.

Apart from redistribution, financialization has also had directly negative effects on capital accumulation in the business sector and positive effects on consumption of the private household sector. The latter may compensate for the partially negative demand effects of financialization through the decrease in the labour income share and the fall in real investment. The conditions for this are considerable wealth effects on consumption and an increase in financial and/or housing wealth. If these conditions are met, liberalization of financial markets, financial innovation and deterioration of creditworthiness standards may generate 'debt-led consumption booms', which, however, suffer from internal contradictions with regard to sustainability, if such a boom is founded on increasing debt–income ratios in the private household sector.

Based on these findings in the literature, we have examined the relationship between the redistribution, associated with financialization and neoliberalism, and the escalating global current account imbalances in the early 2000s, as one of the sources of the severity of the crisis which started in 2007. We have shown that during the trade cycle of the early 2000s two extreme 'types of capitalism under financialization' have developed, the 'debt-led consumption boom' and the 'strongly export-led mercantilist' type. Furthermore, two intermediate types have been found, the 'domestic demand-led' type and the 'weakly export-led' type. In particular, the 'debt-led consumption boom' countries, but also the 'domestic demand-led' economies, have acted as the world demand engines during the trade cycle of the early 2000s and have generated considerable current accounts deficits. In particular the 'strongly export-led mercantilist' economies, but also the 'weakly export-led' countries, managed to 'free ride' on the demand generated by the two other types. Therefore, in particular the two extreme types were complementary and have generated a highly fragile constellation on national and global levels which caused the severity of the financial and economic crisis.

The economic policy conclusion from our analysis is that a sustainable recovery strategy from the crisis can neither follow the 'debt-led consumption boom' nor the 'strongly export-led mercantilist' type, but has to be (mass) income- or wage-led. We have argued that a wage-led recovery strategy has to address the main causes for the falling labour income share in the period of neoliberalism and financialization: First, the bargaining power of trade unions has to be stabilized and enhanced; secondly, overhead costs of firms, in particular top management salaries and interest payments, and profit claims of financial wealth holders have to be reduced; and thirdly, the sectoral composition of the economy has to be shifted away from the high profit share financial corporations towards the non-financial corporate sector and the public sector. Furthermore, the tendencies towards increasing wage dispersion have to be contained and, in particular, progressive tax policies and social policies need to be applied in order to reduce inequality in the distribution of disposable income. We have claimed that a wage-led recovery strategy is at the core of and has to be embedded in a 'Global Keynesian New Deal' which, more broadly, will have to address the three main causes for the severity of the crisis: the inefficient regulation of financial markets; the increasing inequality in the distribution of income; and the rising imbalances at the global (and at regional) levels. The three main pillars of the policy package of a 'Global Keynesian New Deal' have been finally outlined: first, the re-regulation of the financial sector in order to prevent future financial excesses and financial crises; second, the reorientation of macroeconomic policies towards stimulating and stabilizing domestic demand, in particular, in the current account surplus countries; and third the reconstruction of international macroeconomic policy co-ordination and a new world financial order. We have shown that each of these pillars is intimately linked with a (mass) income- or wage-led recovery strategy.

Notes

1. On global imbalances and unequal distribution as causes for the present crisis, on top of widely accepted inefficient regulation of the financial sector, see, with different emphasis, Bibow (2008), Hein and Truger (2010, 2011), Horn et al. (2009), Fitoussi and Stiglitz (2009), Sapir (2009), Stockhammer (2010a, 2010b), UNCTAD (2009) and Wade (2009). In particular, see the early pre-crisis analysis by van Treeck, Hein and Dünhaupt (2007) focussing on the effects of financialization on distribution, aggregate demand, global imbalances and the resulting potential for instability. For a review of the changes in worldwide financial markets and related imbalances which fed the financial crisis see Guttmann (2009).
2. See Stockhammer (2010a, 2010b) for a similar distinction and Palma (2009) for a more extensive discussion of the relationship between neoliberalism and the present crisis.
3. See Hein (2012, chapter 6) for a similar study focusing on a set of European countries plus China, Japan and the United States.
4. See also Hein and Mundt (2012) for a review of income distribution, its determinants and the effects on aggregate demand and growth for the G20 countries through the lenses of 'financialization'.
5. See Crotty (1990) and Lazonick and O'Sullivan (2000) for theoretical assessments and Stockhammer (2004), van Treeck (2008), Orhangazi (2008) and Onaran, Stockhammer and Grafl (2011) for econometric studies.
6. See Barba and Pivetti (2009), Cynamon and Fazzari (2008), Guttmann and Plihon (2010), van Treeck, Hein and Dünhaupt (2007), and van Treeck (2009) for analyses on the United States, and Ludvigson and Steindel (1999), Mehra (2001), Onaran, Stockhammer and Grafl (2011), Boone and Girouard (2002), Dreger and Slacalek (2007) for estimations of wealth effects on consumption.
7. See Palley (1994), Bhaduri, Laski and Riese (2006), Dutt (2005, 2006a) and Bhaduri (2011a, 2011b) for theoretical models.
8. For similar analysis see van Treeck, Hein and Dünhaupt (2007), Bibow (2008), Fitoussi and Stiglitz (2009), Horn et al. (2009), Sapir (2009), UNCTAD (2009), van Treeck (2009), Wade (2009), Hein and Truger (2010, 2011), and Stockhammer (2010a, 2010b).
9. A similar development took place at regional level, in particular in the euro area. See Hein (2012, chapter 8), Hein and Truger (2011) and Hein, Truger and van Treeck (2012) for detailed analysis.
10. This may be an indication that changes in the balances of goods of services, and also in the current accounts, are dominated by relative dynamics of domestic demand and not so much by inflation differentials and changes in the real exchange rate.
11. Note that for Germany this finding is well in line with recent studies on the German demand regime which find re-distribution at the expense of the labour

income share to positively affect net exports, but this effect to be too small to over-compensate the negative impact of re-distribution on domestic demand, so that the overall demand regime in Germany remains wage-led, even under the conditions of increasing globalization (Stockhammer, Hein and Grafl 2011).

12. For 'debt-led consumption boom' economies, in 2009 real GDP growth rates in per cent were as follows: Australia: 1.2; Mexico: - 6.5; United Kingdom: -4.9, US: -2.6 (IMF 2011).

13. For 'strongly export-led mercantilist' economies, in 2009 real GDP growth rates in per cent were as follows: China: 9.1; Germany: -4.7; Indonesia: 4.5; Japan: -5.2; Republic of Korea: 0.2 (IMF 2011).

14. For 'weakly export-led' economies, in 2009 real GDP growth rates in per cent were as follows: Argentina: 0.9; Brazil: -0.2; Canada: -2.5; Russian Federation: -7.9; Saudi Arabia: 0.6 (IMF 2011).

15. For 'domestic demand-led' economies, in 2009 real GDP growth rates in per cent were as follows: France: -2.5; India: 5.7; Italy: -5.0: South Africa: -1.8; Turkey: -4.7 (IMF 2011).

16. For a critique of export-led strategies see also UNCTAD (2010: 77–97).

17. Since deficits or surpluses in the balance of goods and services are mainly affected by growth differentials it may be too restrictive to require balanced current accounts from developing countries in a productivity catch-up process. However, the risks of indebtedness in foreign currency with persistent deficits in the current accounts have to be considered as well.

18. See Bhaduri (2006), Cassetti (2003), Dutt (2006b), Hein and Tarassow (2010), Marquetti (2004), Naastepad (2006), Vergeer and Kleinknecht (2007), and the contribution by Naastepad and Storm in this book.

19. With the focus on functional income distribution and distribution policies our suggestions are perhaps closer to Kalecki (1944, 1971: 156–64) than to Keynes (1936, 1943). We have chosen the term 'Global Keynesian New Deal' nonetheless.

20. For detailed lists of required regulation see, for example, Ash et al. (2009), Fitoussi and Stiglitz (2009), Herr (2011) and Wade (2009).

21. For the New Consensus model see for example Goodfriend/King (1997) and Clarida, Gali and Gertler (1999).

22. On the 'functional finance' view proposed here, see Lerner (1943), Kalecki (1944), and Arestis and Sawyer (2004).

23. Trade unions would have to acknowledge that there are other ways to redistribute income apart from wage bargaining: 'The classical day-by-day bargaining for wages is not the only way of influencing the distribution of national income to the advantage of the workers' (Kalecki 1971: 164).'

24. For a more detailed discussion of required economic policy reforms in the EU and the euro area see Hein and Truger (2011) and Hein, Truger and van Treeck (2012).

25. See also Davidson (2009: 134–142), Guttmann (2009), Kregel (2009), UNCTAD (2009), and Wade (2009).

References

Arestis, P. and Sawyer, M. 2004. 'On fiscal policy and budget deficits', *Intervention. Journal of Economics*, vol. 1(2), pp. 61–74.

Ash, M. Balakrishnan, R., Campbell, A., Crotty, J., Dickens, E., Epstein, G., Ferguson, T., Ghilarducci, T., Greisgraber, J.M., Griffith-Jones, S., Guttmann, R., Jayadev, A., Kapadia, A., Kotz, D., Meerepol, M., Milberg, W., Modeley, F., Ocampo, J.A., Pollin, R., Sawyer, M. and Wolfson, M. 2009. *A Progressive Program for Economic Recovery and Financial Reconstruction* (New York and Amherst, MA: Schwartz Center for Economic Policy Analysis (SCEPA) and Political Economy Research Institute (PERI)).

Barba, A. and Pivetti, M. 2009. 'Rising household debt: its causes and macroeconomic implications – a long-period analysis', *Cambridge Journal of Economics*, vol. 33, pp. 113–37.

Bhaduri, A. 2006. 'Endogenous economic growth: a new approach', *Cambridge Journal of Economics*, vol. 30, pp. 69–83.

Bhaduri, A. 2011a. 'Financialisation in the light of Keynesian theory', *PSL Quarterly Review*, vol. 64(256), pp. 7–21.

Bhaduri, A. 2011b. 'A contribution to the theory of financial fragility and crisis', *Cambridge Journal of Economics*, vol. 35, pp. 995–1014.

Bhaduri, A., Laski, K. and Riese, M. 2006. 'A model of interaction between the virtual and the real economy', *Metroeconomica*, vol. 57, pp. 412–27.

Bibow, J. 2008. 'The international monetary (non-)order and the "global capital flows paradox"', in E. Hein, T. Niechoj, P. Spahn and A. Truger (eds), *Finance-led Capitalism? Macroeconomic Effects of Changes in the Financial Sector* (Marburg: Metropolis).

Boone, L. and Girouard, N. 2002. 'The stock market, the housing market and consumer behavior', *OECD Economic Studies*, no. 35, pp. 17–200.

Cassetti, M. 2003. 'Bargaining power, effective demand and technical progress: a Kaleckian model of growth', *Cambridge Journal of Economics*, vol. 27, pp. 449–64.

Clarida, R., Gali, J. and Gertler, M. 1999. 'The science of monetary policy: a New Keynesian perspective', *Journal of Economic Literature*, vol. 37, pp. 1661–707.

Crotty, J. 1990. 'Owner–management conflict and financial theories of investment instability: a critical assessment of Keynes, Tobin, and Minsky', *Journal of Post Keynesian Economics*, vol. 12, pp. 519–42.

Cynamon, B. and Fazzari, S. 2008. 'Household debt in the consumer age: source of growth – risk of collapse', *Capitalism and Society*, vol. 3(2), pp. 1–30.

Davidson, P. 2009. *The Keynes Solution: The Path to Global Economic Prosperity* (Basingstoke: Palgrave Macmillan).

Dreger, C. and Slacalek, J. 2007. 'Finanzmarktentwicklung, Immobilienpreise und Konsum', *DIW Wochenbericht*, vol. 74, pp. 533–6.

Dutt, A.K. 2005. 'Conspicuous consumption, consumer debt and economic growth', in M. Setterfield (ed.), *Interactions in Analytical Political Economy. Theory, Policy and Applications* (Armonk, NY: M.E. Sharpe).

Dutt, A.K. 2006a. 'Maturity, stagnation and consumer debt: a Steindlian approach', *Metroeconomica*, vol. 57, pp. 339–64.

Dutt, A.K. 2006b. 'Aggregate demand, aggregate supply and economic growth', *International Review of Applied Economics*, vol. 20, pp. 319–36.

Epstein, G.A. (ed.). 2005. *Financialization and the World Economy* (Cheltenham: Edward Elgar).

Fitoussi, J.-P. and Stiglitz, J. 2009. 'The ways out of the crisis and the building of a more cohesive world', *OFCE Document de Travail*, no. 2009-17 (Paris: OFCE).

Girouard, N., Kennedy, M. and Andre, C. 2007. 'Has the rise in debt made house-holds more vulnerable?', OECD Economics Working Paper, No. 535 8 ECO/WKP(2006)63.

Goodfriend, M. and King, R.G. 1997. 'The New Neoclassical Synthesis and the role of monetary policy', in B.S. Bernanke and J.J. Rottemberg (eds), *NBER Macroeconomics Annual: 1997* (Cambridge, MA: MIT Press).

Guttmann, R. 2009. 'Asset bubbles, debt deflation, and global imbalances', *International Journal of Political Economy*, vol. 38(2), pp. 46–69.

Gutttmann, R. and Plihon, D. 2010. 'Consumer debt and financial fragility', *International Review of Applied Economics*, vol. 24, pp. 269–83.

Hein, E. 2012. *The Macroeconomics of Finance-dominated Capitalism – and its Crisis* (Cheltenham: Edward Elgar).

Hein, E. and Mundt, M. 2012. 'Financialisation and the requirements and potentials for wage-led recovery – a review focussing on the G20', Conditions of Work and Employment Series No. 37 (Geneva: ILO).

Hein, E. and Stockhammer, E. 2010. 'Macroeconomic policy mix, employment and inflation in a Post-Keynesian alternative to the New Consensus model', *Review of Political Economy*, vol. 22, pp. 317–54.

Hein, E. and Tarassow, A. 2010. 'Distribution, aggregate demand and productivity growth – theory and empirical results for six OECD countries based on a Post-Kaleckian model', *Cambridge Journal of Economics*, vol. 34, pp. 727–54.

Hein, E. and Truger, A. 2010. 'Financial crisis, global recession and macroeconomic policy reactions – the case of Germany', in S. Dullien, E. Hein, A. Truger and T. van Treeck (eds), *The World Economy in Crisis – The Return of Keynesianism?* (Marburg: Metropolis).

Hein, E. and Truger, A. 2011. 'Finance-dominated capitalism in crisis – the case for a Keynesian New Deal at the European and the global level', in P. Arestis and M. Sawyer (eds), *New Economics as Mainstream Economics*, International Papers in Political Economy series (Basingstoke: Palgrave Macmillan).

Hein, E., Truger, A. and van Treeck, T. 2012. 'The European financial and economic crisis: Alternative solutions from a (Post-)Keynesian perspective', in P. Arestis and M. Sawyer (eds), *The Euro Crisis*, International Papers in Political Economy series (Basingstoke: Palgrave Macmillan).

Hein, E. and van Treeck, T. 2010. '"Financialisation" in Post-Keynesian models of distribution and growth – a systematic review', in M. Setterfield (ed.), *Handbook of Alternative Theories of Economic Growth* (Cheltenham: Edward Elgar).

Herr, H. 2011. 'Making an unstable financial system work. reform options', *International Journal of Labour Research*, vol. 3, pp. 133–55.

Horn, G., Dröge, K., Sturn, S., van Treeck, T. and Zwiener, R. 2009. 'From the financial crisis to the world economic crisis: The role of inequality', IMK Policy Brief, October. Dusseldorf: Macroeconomic Policy Institute (IMK) at Hans Boeckler Foundation.

Kalecki, M. 1944. 'Three ways to full employment', in Oxford University Institute of Statistics (ed.), *The Economics of Full Employment* (Oxford: Basil Blackwell).

Kalecki, M. 1971. *Selected Essays on the Dynamics of Capitalist Economy, 1933–1970* (Cambridge: Cambridge University Press).

Keynes, J.M. 1936. *The General Theory of Employment, Interest, and Money* (London: Macmillan)

Keynes, J.M. 1942. 'Proposal for an International Clearing Union', in *The Collected Writings of J.M. Keynes*, Vol. 25 (London: Macmillan, 1980).

Keynes, J.M. 1943. 'The long-term problem of full employment', in *The Collected Writings of J.M. Keynes*, Vol. 27 (London: Macmillan, 1980).

Kregel, J. 2009. 'Some simple observations on the reform of the international monetary system', Policy Note, 2009/8. Annandale-on-Hudson, NY: The Levy Economics Institute of Bard College.

Lazonick, W. and O'Sullivan, M. 2000. 'Maximizing shareholder value: a new ideology for corporate governance', *Economy and Society*, vol. 29(1), pp. 13–35.

Lerner, A. 1943. 'Functional finance and federal debt', *Social Research*, vol. 10, pp. 38–51.

Ludvigson, S. and Steindel, C. 1999. 'How important is the stock market effect on consumption?', *Federal Reserve Bank of New York Economic Policy Review*, July, pp. 29–51.

Marquetti, A. 2004. 'Do rising real wages increase the rate of labor-saving technical change? Some econometric evidence', *Metroeconomica*, vol. 55, pp. 432–41.

Mehra, Y.P. 2001. 'The wealth effect in empirical life-cycle aggregate consumption equations', *Federal Reserve Bank of Richmond Economic Quarterly*, vol. 87(2), pp. 45–68.

Naastepad, C.W.M. 2006. 'Technology, demand and distribution: a cumulative growth model with an application to the Dutch productivity growth slowdown', *Cambridge Journal of Economics*, vol. 30, pp. 403–34.

Onaran, Ö., Stockhammer, E. and Grafl, L. 2011. 'Financialisation, income distribution and aggregate demand in the USA', *Cambridge Journal of Economics*, vol. 35, pp. 637–61.

Orhangazi, Ö. 2008. 'Financialisation and capital accumulation in the nonfinancial corporate sector: a theoretical and empirical investigation on the US economy, 1973–2003', *Cambridge Journal of Economics*, vol. 32, pp. 863–86.

Palley, T. 1994. 'Debt, aggregate demand, and the business cycle: An analysis in the spirit of Kaldor and Minsky', *Journal of Post Keynesian Economics*, vol. 16, pp. 371–90.

Palma, J.C. 2009. 'The revenge of the market on the rentiers. Why neo-liberal reports of the end of history turned out to be premature', *Cambridge Journal of Economics*, vol. 33, pp. 829–69.

Sapir, J. 2009. 'From financial crisis to turning point. How the US "subprime crisis" turned into a world-wide one and will change the global economy', *Internationale Politik und Gesellschaft*, vol. 1/2009, pp. 27–44.

Stockhammer, E. 2004. '"Financialisation" and the slowdown of accumulation', *Cambridge Journal of Economics*, vol. 28, pp. 719–41.

Stockhammer, E. 2010a. 'Income distribution, the finance-dominated accumulation regime, and the present crisis', in S. Dullien, E. Hein, A. Truger and T. van Treeck (eds), *The World Economy in Crisis – the Return of Keynesianism?* (Marburg: Metropolis).

Stockhammer, E. 2010b. 'Neoliberalism, income distribution and the causes of the crisis', Research on Money and Finance, Discussion Paper No. 19, Department of Economics, SOAS.

United Nations Conference on Trade and Development (UNCTAD). 2009. *The Global Economic Crisis: Systemic Failures and Multilateral Remedies* (New York and Geneva: UNCTAD).

United Nations Conference on Trade and Development (UNCTAD). 2010. *Trade and Development Report 2010* (New York: United Nations).

Van Treeck, T. 2008. 'Reconsidering the investment–profit nexus in finance-led economies: an ARDL-based approach', *Metroeconomica*, vol. 59, pp. 371–404.

Van Treeck, T. 2009. 'The political economy debate on "financialisation" – a macroeconomic perspective', *Review of International Political Economy*, vol. 16, pp. 907–44.

Van Treeck, T., Hein, E. and Dünhaupt, P. 2007. 'Finanzsystem und wirtschaftliche Entwicklung: neuere Tendenzen in den USA und in Deutschland', IMK Studies 5/2007.

Vergeer, R. and Kleinknecht, A. 2007. 'Jobs versus productivity? The causal link from wages to labour productivity growth', TU Delft Innovation Systems Discussion Papers, IS 2007–01.

Wade, R. 2009. 'From global imbalances to global reorganisations', *Cambridge Journal of Economics*, vol. 33, pp. 539–62.

Data sources

Bank for International Settlements (BIS). Bank for International Settlements, Property Price Statistics, http://www.bis.org/statistics/pp.htm (accessed 20 May 2011).

International Labour Office and International Institute of Labour Studies (ILO/IILS). 2011. ILO data on wage shares.

European Commission. 2011. AMECO Database, http://ec.europa.eu/economy_finance/db_indicators/ameco/index_en.htm (accessed 21 May 2011).

International Monetary Fund (IMF). 2011. Word Economic Outlook Database, http://www.imf.org/external/pubs/ft/weo/2011/01/weodata/index.aspx (accessed 21 May 2011).

World Bank. 2011. World Development Indicators and Global Development Finance Database, http://databank.worldbank.org/ddp/home.do?Step=1&id=4 (accessed 21 May 2011).

Index

Printed and bound by CPI Group (UK) Ltd, Croydon, CR0 4YY